# Understanding
# ISLAM &
# CHRISTIANITY

# Understanding
# ISLAM &
# CHRISTIANITY

## JOSH MCDOWELL
## JIM WALKER

**HARVEST HOUSE PUBLISHERS**
EUGENE, OREGON

*Cover by Koechel Peterson & Associates, Inc., Minneapolis, Minnesota*

**UNDERSTANDING ISLAM AND CHRISTIANITY**
Copyright © 2013 by Josh McDowell Ministry and James Walker
Published by Harvest House Publishers
Eugene, Oregon 97402
www.harvesthousepublishers.com

Library of Congress Cataloging-in-Publication Data
McDowell, Josh.
Understanding Islam and Christianity / Josh McDowell and Jim Walker.
    pages cm
Includes bibliographical references.
ISBN 978-0-7369-4990-3 (pbk.)
ISBN 978-0-7369-4991-0 (eBook)
1. Christianity and other religions—Islam. 2. Islam—Relations—Christianity. 3. Apologetics. I. Walker, Jim, 1956- II. Title.
BP172.M393 2013
261.2'7—dc23

                                                                    2013002418

*To my wife, God's greatest gift to me.*
*Thank you for being who you are*
*and loving me through all these years.*

*—Jim Walker*

I want to thank Scott, Haythem, and Diane, who helped make this book possible. I also want to thank Jonathan Kendall for his New Testament support and input.

—Jim Walker

# CONTENTS

Christianity and Islam ........................................................ 9

1 Who Is Jesus? Similarities Between
  the Quran and the Bible ................................................. 15

2 The Messiah, the Son of Man, the Son of God ..................... 35

3 The Father, His Son, and Their Relationship ...................... 57

4 The Trinity: Development of the Doctrine ......................... 77

5 The Trinity: Foundation from the Bible ............................. 91

6 The Gospel and the Atonement ....................................... 109

7 Jesus' Crucifixion ........................................................ 125

8 Muhammad and the Bible:
  Is He the "Counselor" Foretold by Jesus? ........................ 147

9 Muhammad and the Bible:
  Is He the "Prophet" Foretold by Moses? ......................... 163

10 The Reliability of the New Testament (Part 1) ................... 183

11 The Reliability of the New Testament (Part 2) ................... 207

12 An Evaluation of the Quran ........................................... 231

13 The Quran Confirms the Christian Scriptures ................... 255

14 A Christian Evaluation of Muhammad ............................ 269

A Prayer for Salvation ..................................................... 281

Glossary ...................................................................... 283

Notes .......................................................................... 285

Bibliography ................................................................. 295

# Christianity and Islam

Islam and Christianity interact considerably today. Millions of Muslims have immigrated to the West in search of a better life and many evangelize for Islam. They have found converts, built mosques, and established communities. Many have become good citizens, performed beneficial duties, and served well in the armed forces. Likewise Christianity's efforts in the Islamic world have borne fruit, and meetings of Muslims and Muslim converts to Christianity occur in every Muslim country.

Usually their interactions are pleasant and enjoyable but at times they can be confrontational as one challenges the other's faith. Many Christians know their faith but know little about Islam. On the other hand, Muslims have many misconceptions about Christianity. The aims of this book are to provide answers for the body of Christ in their interactions with their Muslim friends and provide thought-provoking material for interested Muslims as they examine and evaluate the Christian faith.

## A Crucial Question: Who Is Jesus?

Muslim and Christian dialogue often delves into Jesus' identity. Was He just a great prophet? Was He the Messiah, the Son of God? Certainly He was a great man, but He claimed to be more. During His life on earth others realized that indeed He was more.

"Who is Jesus?" This same question was asked during Jesus' life.

> [Jesus] asked His disciples, "Who do people say the Son of Man is?"

9

They replied, "Some say John the Baptist; others say Elijah; and still others, Jeremiah or one of the prophets."

"But what about you, who do you say I am?"

Simon Peter answered, "You are the Messiah, the Son of the living God."

Jesus replied, "Blessed are you, Simon son of Jonah, for this was not revealed to you by flesh and blood, but by my Father in heaven…

From that time on Jesus began to explain to his disciples that he must go to Jerusalem and suffer many things at the hands of the elders, chief priests and teachers of the law, and that he must be killed and on the third day be raised to life (Matthew 16:13-21).

"Who is Jesus?"

Later in Jesus' life a similar but more intense question-and-answer exchange occurred. Jesus was on trial before the Jewish leaders, the Sanhedrin. Jesus was being examined and His life was in the balance. Caiaphas, the Jewish high priest, led the interrogation and those that sat in judgment were predisposed to put Jesus to death. They were striving to find some excuse, some justification, to pronounce a death sentence upon Him. They hated Him. Why did they hate Him?

The interrogation wore on but it was not going well for Caiaphas. Trite accusations yielded paltry results. Caiaphas became frustrated and his anger grew. Jesus was outwitting them at their game and Caiaphas's fury rose. Finally, when he could contain himself no longer his heart cried out and his voice exclaimed the point that enraged him most: "I charge you under oath by the living God: Tell us if you are the Christ, the Son of God!"

Again the question is asked: Who is Jesus? Was He the Son of God?

With that question, Caiaphas challenged Jesus to reveal His true identity. "Who are You, Jesus? Do You claim to be the Messiah, the Son of God?" That is why they hated Him. Jesus' answer was the most crucial answer of that day. Pain, suffering, and death awaited one answer. Behind this farce of a trial the fundamental question, "Who is Jesus?" was thrown down as a gauntlet and Jesus was challenged to answer.

And answer He did!

"I am," said Jesus. "You will see the Son of Man sitting at the right hand of the Mighty One and coming on the clouds of heaven."

The Sanhedrin reacted violently! "The high priest tore his clothes. 'Why do we need any more witnesses?' he asked. 'You have heard the blasphemy. What do you think?' They all condemned him as worthy of death. Some began to spit at him; they blindfolded him, struck him with their fists, and said, 'Prophesy!'"

Jesus had answered them boldly and truthfully! He was indeed the Messiah, the Son of God, and the Jews howled in anger. But Jesus went further! He told them that He was the one foretold by the prophet Daniel: "And you will see the Son of Man sitting at the right hand of the Mighty One and coming on the clouds of heaven." Jesus told them that it was He who would fulfill that messianic prophecy!

Jesus proclaimed that He was more than a prophet. He proclaimed Himself as the Messiah, the Son of God, as foretold by the prophets.

## Answering the Question

This question, "Who is Jesus?" has been asked throughout history and is still asked today. It is one of the most important questions of all time. Billions of people have asked and answered it and their answer affected their lives, their cultures, and their history.

The subject of Jesus' identity is a challenging one. According to Jesus it is also a spiritual one. Jesus told Peter that His true identity was revealed to him by God. This was not a lucky guess, this was not deductive reasoning, this was not the teaching of men, but rather Jesus' true identity was revealed to Peter by God:

"Blessed are you, Simon son of Jonah, for this was not revealed to you by flesh and blood, but by my Father in heaven."

"Who is Jesus?"

Islam answers exactly like many of the Jews of Jesus' time, "Some say John the Baptist; others say Elijah; and still others, Jeremiah or one of the prophets." While Islam answers that Jesus was a mighty prophet, Christianity answers that He was far more.

We will examine Jesus' identity and determine an answer by focusing on Jesus' core-nature, illustrated and demonstrated by His deeds, teachings, and self-description. There is a rich depth in the New Testament, and close examination yields facts about Jesus' identity that are often missed in a casual reading.

Further, we will investigate many of the topics that Christians and Muslims discuss. Many Christians will be surprised to learn that there is substantial agreement between Islam and Christianity about Jesus. His name is mentioned over 20 times in the Quran and there are more than 90 Quranic verses that refer to Him either directly or indirectly and many of these verses agree with the Bible's statements.

## Toward a Clear Understanding

When I (Jim Walker) began my study of Islam, years before the advent of the Internet, there were few books available in English. I began with books written by Christians and atheists and fortunately their scholarship was excellent. Over time I found books written by Muslims which gave me deeper insight into Islam. Now I have a substantial collection of Islamic literature written by dedicated Muslims.

However during the last few years we've seen books written by Christians, atheists, or members of other faiths who either consciously or unintentionally distort the true teachings of Islam. Their audience may not know much about Islam so they may believe whatever people publish.

Unfortunately, the same things happen in the Islamic world. Various Muslim writers have intentionally or unintentionally distorted the true teachings of Christianity, and many Muslims, who trust their religious leaders, have accepted those distortions and falsehoods. As an unfortunate result many Muslims have not learned Christianity from Christian sources but rather from Muslim teachers who propagate error.

So I'm asking the reader to bear this in mind because we will expose misconceptions that have been promoted in both the Christian and Islamic world. Let the Quran and the Bible speak for themselves and try your best to understand their meaning. Make an effort to evaluate honestly what the Scriptures say about Jesus and what He says about Himself.

Christian and Muslim dialogues and debates most frequently focus on several primary topics:

• Jesus' identity, was He the divine Son of God?

• Was Jesus crucified?

• Is the New Testament reliable as the Word of God?

• Is Muhammad's prophethood predicted by the Bible?

• Was Muhammad a real prophet of God?

• Is today's Quran the literal and reliable Word of God?

We wish to address these topics and more in the hope of opening the eyes, minds, and hearts of both Christians and Muslims to the teachings found in the Bible and the Quran. We will show evidence that Jesus claimed to be more than a prophet. We will address misconceptions about Jesus and the New Testament. We will also show that the Quran and the Bible agree about many things theological. It is not always an "either-or" proposition. Of course their theologies disagree about prominent points as well and some of those will also be discussed.

We pray that God will use this book to reveal to its readers what God revealed to Peter: Jesus is the Messiah, the Son of God.

## A Note About Quotations from the Quran in This Book

All quotations from the Quran in this book are from Muhammad Pickthall's translation, unless otherwise noted.* Pickthall's translation is accurate and widely accepted by Muslims. N.J. Dawood's translation of the Quran is also used in some places, as it is the easiest to read.†

---

* Muhammad M. Pickthall, *The Meaning of the Glorious Koran* (New York: Mentor, 1953).

† N.J. Dawood, *The Koran* (London: Penguin, 1995).

In some cases we will reference a passage but only quote a key portion of it. We encourage you to use a Bible and Quran and to read and evaluate all of the referenced passages in full. Don't rush through the read. Taking the time to examine the referenced passages completely will enable you to understand the details fully. At times we will bold or underline key phrases for emphasis.

# Who Is Jesus? Similarities Between the Quran and the Bible

I t might be considered odd to start an apologetic book by presenting similarities between the Bible and Quran on what is taught about Jesus. This is being done to show that although there is substantial disagreement between the two faiths there is also substantial agreement. Before we delve into the differences, we want to present areas of theological agreement between Christianity and Islam. Knowing and understanding the areas of agreement will aid the dialogue between Christian and Muslim. It is not necessary to approach the other with a preconceived, "180 degree out" attitude. When Christians understand that Muslims have similar theological beliefs then the approach can be more gracious for we share similar beliefs.

## Jesus' Birth

There are various aspects of the birth of Christ on which both Muslims and Christians agree. His birth is an excellent starting point because Christians and Muslims believe that Jesus' birth was a miracle. The Gospel of Matthew's account is found at Matthew 1:18-25. The Quran's account is found at 3:45-47. If you read and compare the two you'll see many similarities.

Both faiths agree that Jesus' birth was a miracle! Both agree that Mary was a virgin when she gave birth to Jesus. Both agree that an angel provided His name (the name Jesus is the transliterated Hebrew name "Yeshua" and means "the Lord saves" or "God is our salvation"). We have a common starting ground: God was involved with Jesus' miraculous birth. Nobody else was born this way. Adam was created by God from the dust of earth because there were no parents to give him birth, but no one, no person or prophet, was ever born in the miraculous way Jesus was.

(*Note*: The Muslim/Arabic name for Jesus is "Isa" but the angel would have given Him an actual Hebrew name. Yeshua is a historical Hebrew name. Some Muslim writers claim that Isa = Esau but it is unlikely that the angel would have named Jesus after a person who was considered to be profane in Jewish history. The name "Esau" means "hairy.")

## Jesus Was Sinless

Both Islam and Christianity agree that Jesus was sinless. Both agree that Jesus lived a perfect life of obedience to God. Jesus stated in John 8:45-47 that He was sinless, while the Quran describes Jesus as being sinless and perfect (faultless) in 19:17-22.

Some Muslims believe that all of the prophets were sinless. Others believe that some of the prophets did sin. However, there are verses in the Quran in which various prophets ask for forgiveness or are told by God to pray for forgiveness for their own sins, such as sura 11:47, 21:87, and 28:16. Consequently, when both texts are examined Jesus is the only one presented in Scripture as without sin.

Jesus' sinless life shows us His character. As a man He was subjected to many temptations, but He chose to walk in faith and in obedience to God. He was disciplined and self-controlled. He resisted the temptations and overcame sin. He did that His entire life. Think about that for a minute. All of us know how often we sin and know that it is difficult to even go an entire day without some evil emotion of hatred, jealousy, lust, or envy springing up out of our heart. We know how hard it is to refrain from saying the wrong thing. Jesus faced the same challenges we face and some of them were far more stressful than any of us will face. Yet each time He chose to follow and obey God. He lived a sinless life and we should strive to live a sinless life as well. Whether or not we believe He was the only sinless man, or one of a few sinless men, we can all agree that in this He was exceptional.

## Jesus Was a Prophet

Both Muslims and Christians agree that Jesus was a prophet. He had a unique and divine calling and ministry. He brought God's message to the people. In various places through the New Testament (for example, Matthew 13:53-57), Jesus describes Himself as a prophet. Likewise in the Quran (19:30) Jesus describes Himself as a prophet.

This is an important area of agreement between Muslims and Christians because this brings Jesus' ministry into our view: He had a special prophetic ministry given to Him. This ministry was important because it would bring God's word of love and truth to the people. Jesus' ministry is lightly mentioned in the Quran but it is the focus of the Gospels and described completely in the New Testament. When you read all four Gospels, you can sum up the primary message as:

> God so loved the world that he gave his one and only Son, that whoever believes in him shall not perish but have eternal life. For God did not send his Son into the world to condemn the world, but to save the world through him. Whoever believes in him is not condemned, but whoever does not believe stands condemned already because he has not believed in the name of God's one and only Son (John 3:16-18).

Yes, this is an often quoted verse. But there is a reason for that: It is the heart of Jesus' message. We know that Muslims do not believe that God has a Son, but here it must be said that, whether you agree with it or disagree with it, this is what the Bible teaches. We'll discuss this more in a later chapter.

Both faiths agree that Jesus was a prophet and He brought God's message. But let's define the ministry of "prophet" and the type of message a prophet is to bring. What exactly are prophets supposed to do and say?

Both the Bible and the Quran teach that a prophet's mission was both grave and powerful. Prophets were authoritative, speaking God's word to the people. Prophets were given demanding tasks that they were to fulfill in service to God and in ministry to the people. The overall aim of the prophet's ministry was to cause the people to repent, heed God's word, and live in faith and obedience. This often brought the prophets into conflict with people who rejected God's message.

Prophets' lives were not easy. They suffered at the hands of sinful men. Both the Quran and the Bible say that prophets were often killed by the people to whom they ministered (Luke 11:47 and sura 2:91). On the other hand, a prophet would face severe consequences if he himself went astray. Even a proven prophet, one who had worked miracles, could sin and attempt to mislead the people. That prophet who was once true had become false and must be punished. Deuteronomy 13:1-5 mandates that the prophet be put to death!

Like a prophet Jesus came with a message given to Him by God and He proclaimed it to the people of Israel. Many of the Jews believed in Him but many rejected Him. Jesus was faithful to God and proclaimed the message in the face of much hostility.

There are a number of functions and characteristics of a prophet. You can find these actions being performed by many of the biblical Old Testament prophets.

1. Proclaim God's words, be they commands, laws, or special messages.

2. Encourage those who serve God.

3. Warn those who are in sin.

4. Rebuke men, groups, tribes, or races of people.

5. Foretell what is to happen in the future.

6. Most importantly, teach the people about God's nature, that is, His character and attributes.

How did Jesus' words compare to the above list of functions and characteristics of a prophet?

- Jesus proclaimed God's words in Luke 4:16-19.
- He encouraged those who serve God in John 16:33.
- He warned those in sin in Luke 13:1-5.
- He rebuked people in Matthew 23:33-35.

- He foretold what would happen in the future in Matthew 24.

- Jesus taught the people about God's nature in John 4:24 and Luke 11:11-13.

Jesus fulfilled the office of prophet completely. He took His mission seriously, faced strong opposition, but persisted and preached God's word in various ways and ministered to the people.

## Jesus Performed Miracles

Not all prophets were known to have performed miracles but both faiths agree that Jesus performed many miracles! His miracles were performed in the eyes of His followers and in the eyes of people who refused to believe in Him because their hearts were hard. Many Jews saw that God was with Jesus because He was able to perform miracles that had never been performed in Israel's history. Here are several of His miracles found in the Bible:

- healed a blind man in Mark 10:46-52

- fed 5000 people in Matthew 14:13-21

- resurrected a synagogue ruler's daughter in Mark 5:21-43

Of course there are many more of Jesus' miracles described in the Bible. The Quran also says that Jesus performed miracles:

> And will make him a messenger unto the children of Israel, (saying): Lo! I come unto you with a sign from your Lord. Lo! I fashion for you out of clay the likeness of a bird, and I breathe into it and it is a bird, by Allah's leave. I heal him who was born blind, and the leper, and I raise the dead, by Allah's leave. And I announce unto you what ye eat and what ye store up in your houses. Lo! herein verily is a portent for you, if ye are believers (3:49).*

This is another strong agreement between Islam and Christianity:

---

* Quranic references refer to *sura* (similar to a chapter) and verse. Thus "3:49" designates sura 3, verse 49.

Jesus indeed performed many unparalleled miracles in the eyes of the people. These miracles were a proof to them that God's power was with Jesus. It was also a sign to them that God had not forgotten them but that He was still anointing people to speak to them.

In summary then both the Quran and Bible agree that these miracles were proof, or a sign, that Jesus and His teachings were from God. None of the prophets before Him ever performed such great miracles! More importantly they demonstrated God's love and outreach for His people.

## Jesus Ministered the Gospel

This is another point of agreement between Islam and Christianity. Both faiths agree that Jesus was given the message of the Gospel. "Gospel" comes from the Greek word "euangelion" and means "good news." "Gospel" in Arabic is "Injil." The word "Injil" is used 12 times in the Quran.

Here is a verse from the Quran:

> And We caused Jesus, son of Mary, to follow in their footsteps, confirming that which was (revealed) before him, and We bestowed on him the Gospel [Injil] wherein is guidance and a light, confirming that which was (revealed) before it in the Torah a guidance and an admonition unto those who ward off (evil) (5:46).

And here is a verse from the Bible:

> One day as Jesus was teaching the people in the temple courts and proclaiming the good news, the chief priests and the teachers of the law, together with the elders, came up to him (Luke 20:1).

Note that both texts say that Jesus ministered the Gospel (or good news). In fact the Quran says that Jesus was given the Gospel directly from God without the use of an intermediary angel!

Although the importance of the Gospel is stressed throughout the

Quran, it does not identify what exactly constitutes the Gospel. But it does identify the Gospel as a message that could be accessed and that must be followed by the Christians in Muhammad's day. The Quran specifically says:

> Let the People of the Gospel judge by that which Allah hath revealed therein. Whoso judgeth not by that which Allah hath revealed: such are evil-livers (5:47).

Clearly, the Quran is telling Christians at that time to judge by what God revealed in the Gospel. They could only do that if it was given to them in some kind of written and codified form. In fact, the Quran actually states that the Gospel was available to those in Muhammad's time. In the very next verse, The Quran says:

> And unto thee have We revealed the Scripture with the truth, confirming whatever Scripture was before it (5:48; see also 3:3).

It is therefore obvious that in the light of the Quran and Bible the Gospel's message then is very important. So what exactly is the Gospel message? The Quran states that there is "guidance and light" in the Gospel Scripture but it does not define the Gospel. The Bible goes into more detail. The first verse in Mark's gospel in the New Testament tells us that the Gospel is about Jesus:

> The beginning of the good news about Jesus Messiah, the Son of God (Mark 1:1).

There is more to the message than a call to believe in God. There is a requirement that the people of God are to believe in Jesus also, that the good news is about Jesus! But what specifically is this good news about Jesus? What's "good news" about Him? We will go into more detail in a later chapter. The point here is to show that both Islam and Christianity agree that Jesus was given a unique and special message, the gospel, to proclaim to the people. Jesus did proclaim the Gospel and instructed His followers to continue to do so.

## Jesus Was the Messiah

Both faiths agree that Jesus was the Messiah. The word "Messiah" is a Hebrew word and means "anointed one." It is "Christos" in Greek, "Christ" in English, and the Quran uses "al-Masih" (most Anointed) in Arabic. In fact that title is used for Jesus 11 times in the Quran! Nobody else in the Quran is called "al-Masih." As we noted before, the Quran states the angels gave Jesus the special title, "al-Masih":

> (And remember) when the angels said: O Mary! Allah giveth thee glad tidings of a word from Him, whose name is the Messiah, Jesus, son of Mary, illustrious in the world and the Hereafter, and one of those brought near (unto Allah) (3:45).

Further, this title, "al-Masih" that the Quran gives Jesus, identifies something special about Him. Grammatically, the definite article "al" gives the title "Masih" a unique meaning. It sets Jesus apart from other messengers and prophets and characterizes this anointing as unique and unmatched.

Also, supporting the idea that being called "al-Masih" is a distinguished title, the *Encyclopedia of the Qur'an* states:

> ...it should be noted that those which seem to indicate qualities that Jesus shared with other prophets do not do justice to the fact that he alone is called al-Masih in the Qur'an. It seems likely that the first hearers of the revelations would have been aware that al-Masih was a dignified title which the Christians held was uniquely applicable to Jesus. [1]

Likewise the Jews understood that there were many "anointed" people in the Old Testament but that there would be a special and unique "Anointed One." This is shown in the conversations Jesus had with various people. They asked Jesus if He was the Messiah, the special one they were waiting for. In fact, Jesus told them that He was the Messiah but they rejected Him (John 10:22-28).

Both Islam and Christianity agree that Jesus is the Messiah but the Quran does not identify what is special about Jesus as the Messiah. It does not explain what that title means.

The Bible does tell us what is special about the Messiah. One of the most informative Scriptures is found in the book of Matthew 2:1-6:

> After Jesus was born in Bethlehem in Judea, during the time of King Herod, Magi from the east came to Jerusalem and asked, "Where is the one who has been born king of the Jews? We saw his star when it rose and have come to worship him."

> When King Herod heard this he was disturbed, and all Jerusalem with him. When he had called together all the people's chief priests and teachers of the law, he asked them where the Messiah was to be born. "In Bethlehem in Judea," they replied, "for this is what the prophet has written:

> "'But you, Bethlehem, in the land of Judah, are by no means least among the rulers of Judah; for out of you will come a ruler who will shepherd my people Israel.'"

The Magi were devout men who were watching for the birth of the Messiah and when a sign was given to them they proceeded to search it out. They were men of faith and obedience and were determined to stay true to what God had shown them. They identified the Messiah as "the king of the Jews." Likewise the chief priests, on their understanding of the Torah, also identified the Messiah as a ruler. They knew that the Messiah was predicted in the Old Testament Scriptures to be born in Bethlehem. Jesus fulfilled that prophecy when He was born in Bethlehem. He was the Messiah and was to rule and shepherd God's people.

We'll more fully review "the Messiah" in a later chapter.

## Jesus Received Worship

Now we will take a step back and take a closer look at the Magi who sought Jesus out in Matthew chapter 2.

> After Jesus was born in Bethlehem in Judea, during the time of King Herod, Magi from the east came to Jerusalem and asked, "Where is the one who has been born king of the Jews? We saw his star when it rose and have come to worship him."

> When King Herod heard this he was disturbed, and all Jeru-
> salem with him. When he had called together all the people's
> chief priests and teachers of the law, he asked them where the
> Messiah was to be born (Matthew 2:1-4).

What did the Magi wish to do? What was their purpose? They knew that the one prophesied as the "king of the Jews" had been born. The Magi wanted to worship Jesus! Isn't that a questionable choice for men who were devoted to God? Wouldn't that be idolatry? Yes, unless they understood that the Messiah was to be worshipped as God. This is exactly what they did:

> On coming to the house, they saw the child with his mother
> Mary, and they bowed down and worshiped him. Then they
> opened their treasures and presented him with gifts of gold,
> frankincense and myrrh (Matthew 2:11).

These wise men were not the only ones who worshipped Jesus. When Jesus performed the miracle of walking on water (Matthew 14:22-33) His disciples realized who He was.

> And when they climbed into the boat, the wind died down.
> Then those who were in the boat worshiped him, saying,
> "Truly you are the Son of God."

Jesus did not rebuke the disciples for calling Him the Son of God or for worshipping Him!

After Jesus performed the miracle of healing a man who had been born blind, Jesus again was worshipped. Jesus spoke with the man after the Jewish clergy interrogated him:

> Jesus heard that they had thrown him out, and when he
> found him, he said, "Do you believe in the Son of Man?"
> "Who is he, sir?" the man asked. "Tell me so that I may believe
> in him." Jesus said, "You have now seen him; in fact, he is the
> one speaking with you." Then the man said, "Lord, I believe,"
> and he worshiped him (John 9:35-38).

F.F. Bruce, in his commentary on John writes:

> Naturally, the man does not know who the Son of man is, but
> he is very willing to learn, so he asks. Jesus replies in terms
> similar to those which he used when the Samaritan woman
> spoke of the coming Messiah: "It is I, the person talking to
> you" (John 4:26). The man has no further hesitation. On
> whom would he more readily believe than on the man who
> had restored his sight? He had already called him a prophet;
> now he confesses him as more than a prophet. If the vocative
> kyrie in verse 36 has the courtesy sense of "sir," in verse 38 it
> is more than a courtesy title; it implies that Jesus is a fit per-
> son to receive worship: "Lord, I believe," he said, and bowed
> low in reverence before him. So quickly has an honest and
> good heart progressed from recognizing the benefactor as
> "the man called Jesus" (verse 11) to confessing him as Lord. [2]

Jesus asked the man to believe in "the Son of Man." The man knew
that Jesus was from God, but he didn't know who the Son of Man was.
But he had faith in and love for Jesus and was willing to obey Him.
Jesus told him that He was the Son of Man. The man said, "Lord, I
believe." Then he worshipped Him.

This is the key…Jesus does not say to him, "Worship only God."
Instead Jesus receives his worship. But Jesus was not ignorant of the
Law of God! When Jesus was challenged by Satan, Jesus rebuked him
for asking for worship…

> Again, the devil took him to a very high mountain and
> showed him all the kingdoms of the world and their splen-
> dor. "All this I will give you," he said, "if you will bow down
> and worship me." Jesus said to him, "Away from me, Satan!
> For it is written: 'Worship the Lord your God, and serve him
> only'" (Matthew 4:8-10).

Glenn Miller sums up the perspective on worshipping other than
God:

...this point ALONE would eliminate all "Jesus is—in His nature—an angel." The worship of angels is forbidden by the above scriptural teachings, and explicitly in Col 2.18, and is contrasted with Jesus in Hebrews 1.2. This means—since worship is encouraged/afforded to Jesus in the NT—that Jesus CANNOT be an angel in nature, but only in function (as a prophet was also a "messenger"), and only then occasionally (in some cases, e.g., As messenger of the Covenant [Malachi] and Head of the Army in the OT/Tanaach). This is a strong argument against the belief of some groups that Jesus was an angel, or an archangel. His rebuke of the Angel of Light with "only God shall ye worship" is proof positive of this fact.

SUMMARY: The data in the NT is surprisingly uniform— "worship" is for GOD ALONE! *

Jesus was sinless, and He would not allow or receive the sin of idolatry or the worship of the wrong person! He knew the Law, He knew the punishment for worship of other than God. Yet He allowed others to call Him the Lord and the Son of God and He received their worship. No holy, devout man would allow this, no prophet of God would tolerate this, no great teacher would sanction this, unless it was acceptable and proper to do.

## Jesus Was a Great Teacher

So far we've examined several areas of agreement and common ground between Islam and Christianity. In this section we have another area of agreement: Jesus was a wise and gifted teacher. The Quran, in 5:110 notes how Jesus was gifted to minister to the people and John 3:2 shows how people acknowledged Jesus as a teacher from God. However here we want to delve into the substance of what He taught. Jesus, the gifted teacher, taught truths about Himself that had never been claimed by other prophets. Jesus understood the significance of His teachings and comprehended the ramifications of what He taught.

Although both Muslims and Christians agree that Jesus was a wise and gifted teacher, the Quran says very little about what exactly Jesus

---

* http://www.christian-thinktank.com/trin03g.html

taught. Commenting on the lack of material about Jesus in the Quran, the Muslim writer Neal Robinson wrote:

> Little is said about Jesus' teaching although at the annunciation Mary was told that he was destined to speak to mankind in the cradle and also when of mature age (3:46). To perform his task he was strengthened by the Holy Spirit and given signs (5:110, 2:87) and God taught him the Scripture and Wisdom and the Torah and the Gospel (3:48, 5:110). Jesus attested the truth of what was in the Torah (3:50, 5:46, 61:6). He made lawful some of the things that were forbidden to the Children of Israel in his day (3:50 cf. 3:93). He came to them with wisdom and made plain to them some of the things about which they were in disagreement (43:63). [3]

Therefore, as the Quran instructed Muhammad and his followers, we can find out more about what Jesus taught from the book of the "People of the Book" (that is, the Bible).

> And if thou (Muhammad) art in doubt concerning that which We reveal unto thee, then question those who read the Scripture (that was) before thee. Verily the Truth from thy Lord hath come unto thee. So be not thou of the waverers (10:94).

When you begin to read the New Testament you learn very quickly that Jesus frequently taught by using parables. This was a very effective teaching technique because parables, when used correctly, cause the hearers to listen, evaluate, and continue to ponder their meaning.

Parables convey aspects of a story with which the hearers are familiar. Farmers understand when you talk about tilling the ground or growing crops, fishermen understand about using nets and catching fish. But then the parable is meant to convey a much deeper moral lesson or spiritual truth. The parable is meant to have a profound dimension or meaning. Many physical aspects of the parable have counterparts in the moral lesson of the story. We are going to examine some of Jesus' teachings and focus on key points that are often overlooked.

### Jesus, Lord of the World: The Parable of the Wheat and the Tares

Jesus taught the parable of the wheat and the tares in Matthew 13:24-30. Thereafter He explained its meaning in verses 36-43. Take a couple minutes and read those passages.

Not only was Jesus teaching people about the last judgment, He was making strong claims about Himself and His rulership. *The Expositor's Bible Commentary* highlights this:

> The identification of the actors is over, and the description of the action begins. As the weeds are "pulled up" (verse 40; same verb as "collect" in verse 30b) and burned, so it is at the end. The kingdom we have known as the kingdom of heaven or the kingdom of God is also seen as the kingdom of the Son of Man, Jesus' kingdom (cf. 20:21; 25:31; cf. Dan 2:35; Rev 11:15). [4]

There are many things that can be highlighted, but here are the key points:

1. Jesus identified Himself as the sower: "The Son of Man." Jesus used this term most often to describe Himself.

2. Both the good seed and the bad seed are allowed to grow side by side until the time of judgment.

3. The harvesters are the angels who cast evil people into hell.

4. Who owns the field? The sower owns the field. It is his field—it is Jesus' world. Jesus is claiming ownership. Note Jesus says, "The Son of Man will send out 'his angels.'" Angels are meant to obey God; Jesus is saying that His angels are obeying Him and doing His bidding.

### Jesus, the Son of God: The Parable of the Wicked Tenants

This parable is found in Matthew 21:33-45. Take a couple minutes and read it. Note how this parable corresponds with both the Bible's and Quran's statements that the messengers that God sent were killed by the unbelievers. They fit together.

Are you able to correlate the parable's physical points with its spiritual truths? Who does the landowner represent? Who do the farmers represent? Who do the servants represent? (Hint: Cross-reference sura 2:91.) Who does the son represent?

Albert Barnes notes the Gospel message here:

> This beautifully and most tenderly exhibits the love of God, in sending his only Son, Jesus Christ, into the world to die for men. Long had he sent the prophets, and they had been persecuted and slain. There was no use in sending any more prophets to the people. They had done all they could do. God had one only-begotten and well-beloved Son, whom he might send into the world, and whom the world ought to reverence, even as they should the Father...Matthew 21:37. [5]

### Jesus, Judge of the World: The Parable of the Sheep and the Goats

The parable of the sheep and the goats is found in Matthew 25:31-46. Take a few minutes and read the parable. The primary lesson of the parable is that "followers of Jesus" are required to meet the needs of all fellow "followers of Jesus," and not just special or favorite ones. When a follower of Jesus helps a fellow follower, even one who is poor and of no account, he is doing that deed unto Jesus.

But note who is doing the judging. Jesus! He is claiming for Himself the right to judge the world. And where is Jesus going to sit? Take a look at the first two sentences and read them again.

The introductory comment to this passage in *The New International Commentary on the New Testament* (NICNT) ties this passage to Daniel's vision:

> Since 24:36 the theme of being ready to face the Son of Man at his parousia has dominated the latter part of the discourse. Now that theme comes to its majestic climax in a vision of the judgment that will then take place, when in fulfillment of the vision of Dan 7:13-14 the Son of Man is enthroned as judge over all the nations, and the great division will take place between those who are ready and those who are not

ready. In the preceding parables, we have seen indication of what "readiness" may be understood to mean, in terms of the lifestyle which the master will commend at his coming. Now we find a more explicit statement of the criterion of judgment, in the way people have treated "one of these my smallest brothers and sisters." [6]

Jesus would later tell the chief priests that He was the Messiah, the Son of God, and that He would "come with the clouds" as prophetically foretold by Daniel. This parable, the "sheep and the goats," presents a broader description of that event.

### Jesus, Lord of the Sabbath

Now, Jesus did more than teach in parables. Sometimes He was very straightforward. At other times He spoke in metaphors. We're going to take a look at one of His most bold statements about Himself.

> One Sabbath Jesus was going through the grainfields, and his disciples began to pick some heads of grain, rub them in their hands and eat the kernels. Some of the Pharisees asked, "Why are you doing what is unlawful on the Sabbath?"
>
> Jesus answered them, "Have you never read what David did when he and his companions were hungry? He entered the house of God, and taking the consecrated bread, he ate what is lawful only for priests to eat. And he also gave some to his companions." Then Jesus said to them, "The Son of Man is Lord of the Sabbath" (Luke 6:1-5).

Here the Pharisees accused Jesus' disciples of breaking the Law. Jesus answered them "The Son of Man is Lord of the Sabbath." Jesus was claiming to be Lord over the special day set aside to be lived in faith and obedience to God! The *NICNT* explains,

> Thus, he concludes by implication, the disciples have not violated the Sabbath, as they have been accused; rather, the Son of Man, who has authority over the Sabbath, has permitted them to pluck and eat on the Sabbath. This is not a rejection

of the Sabbath or of Sabbath observance in general, but it does undercut the utility of Sabbath observance as a boundary-keeping mechanism (that is, as a sign of faithfulness to God), and it designates Jesus as God's authorized agent to determine what was appropriate on the Sabbath. [7]

Jesus had the boldness, had the audacity, to declare Himself "Lord of the Sabbath"! Who did Jesus think He was!? *Jesus, the great teacher, not only identifies Himself as the Son of Man, but also as the Lord.* No prophet ever claimed that for Himself. Either Jesus was truly the Lord, or He was a false prophet who deserved punishment for breaking God's Law and blasphemy.

## Jesus Spoke in His Own Name

Jewish scholar Jacob Neusner understands exactly what Jesus was doing. He understood the deeper meaning and implication of Jesus' ministry. After a detailed explanation, Neusner presents a hypothetical question he would challenge Jesus with:

> I am troubled not so much by the message, though I might take exception to this or that, as I am by the messenger. The reason is that, in form these statements are jarring. Standing on the mountain, Jesus' use of language, "You have heard that it was said…but I say to you…" contrasts strikingly with Moses' language at Mount Sinai. Sages, we saw, say things in their own names, but without claiming to improve upon the Torah. The prophet, Moses, speaks not in his own name but in God's name, saying what God has told him to say. Jesus speaks not as a sage nor as a prophet…
>
> …At many points in this protracted account of Jesus' specific teachings, we now recognize that at issue is the figure of Jesus, not the teachings at all.
>
> …But what troubles me is simple, and if I could have walked up the mountain and addressed the master and disciples that day, I would have said: "Sir, how come you speak on your own say-so, and not out of the teachings of the Torah given

by God to Moses at Sinai? It looks as though you see yourself
as Moses, or as more than Moses…" [8]

Neusner's challenge is on target. He recognized that Jesus was claiming to be more than a prophet. Neusner is saying, "Who the heck are
you, Jesus, to speak and command in your name! Who do you think
you are to supersede Moses! Do you think you're greater than Moses?"
But then Neusner goes on to make a stunning error! He writes:

> But the Torah of Moses does not tell me that God is going to
> give instruction—*torah*—through someone besides Moses
> or the other prophets; or that there is going to be another
> Torah. [9]

How could Neusner have missed God's prediction in Deuteronomy 18:15-19?

> The Lord your God will raise up for you a prophet like me
> from among your own brothers. You must listen to him. This
> is what you requested from the Lord your God at Horeb
> on the day of the assembly when you said, "Let us not con-
> tinue to hear the voice of the Lord our God or see this great
> fire any longer, so that we will not die!" Then the Lord said
> to me, "They have spoken well. I will raise up for them a
> prophet like you from among their brothers. I will put My
> words in his mouth, and he will tell them everything I com-
> mand him. I will hold accountable whoever does not listen
> to My words that he speaks in My name" (HCSB).

Moses did foretell that another prophet like him would be raised
up by God. The prophets did foretell that a new covenant would be
established (Jeremiah 31:31-34). Perhaps Neusner's difficulty in taking
into account these Scriptures is similar to the difficulty that many Jews
had with Jesus: Jesus was bringing change, change to the old, established ways, change that cut across the grain of what the Jewish teachers
taught, change that threatened their status. He repeatedly made auda-
cious, unheard-of claims about Himself! This upset the Jews of Jesus'

time just as it troubles Neusner. Jesus, the great teacher, made many uncomfortable and angry with both His words and His actions. There was a choice to make: Accept Jesus as He said He was, or reject Him as a liar, false prophet, or demon-possessed madman. The Jews of Jesus' time made a choice, either for or against.

### Jesus, the Unique Prophet

Christian scholar Dr. Raymond Brown emphasizes the uniqueness of Jesus compared to *all* other prophets:

> But no prophet broke with the hallowed past in so radical a way and with so much assurance as did Jesus. Moreover, the certainty with which Jesus spoke and acted implies a consciousness of a unique relationship to God. The Gospel traditions agree in depicting him as a man who thinks he can act and speak for God. The superior authority and power manifested by Jesus and acknowledged by many who encountered him supposed more than that he was the final prophet of the last times through whom God's salvation breaks through. His implied relationship to God was more than that of an agent; God was acting not only through him, but in him. [10]

Over and over, the statements made about Jesus before He was born, the depth of His parables, and His straightforward statements and actions demonstrate that He was more than another prophet. He was the Messiah, the Son of Man, the Son of God.

Both Islam and Christianity agree on much concerning Jesus. He was born of a virgin, He performed great miracles, He was a prophet, the Messiah, and a great teacher. But when we look deeper into His teachings we find that Jesus said things that went beyond the claims of a prophet. He said He was the Son of Man, the Son of God. He said that He was Lord of the Sabbath. He said that He would judge the world, that He would give His followers eternal life. He received the worship of men. In short, Jesus made statements and performed actions that no prophet would dare to claim or attempt. Jesus went way beyond all other prophets. Jesus knew where He had come from; He knew who He truly was. And that is why He was able to make those statements and perform those actions with powerful confidence.

**2**

# The Messiah, the Son of Man, the Son of God

Muslims' question:
*"We agree that Jesus was a man, a prophet, and the Messiah,
but that doesn't mean he was God's Son."*

Jesus is described by many titles in the Quran, such as "the Word of
God," "a spirit from God," "a sign," "Son of Mary," and "the Messiah." Similarly, Jesus is described by many titles in the New Testament. We're going to look at three of the latter: 1) the Messiah, 2) the
Son of Man, and 3) the Son of God.

We will examine these titles in some depth and come to an understanding of what those titles meant to the people of Jesus' time, how
Jesus characterized them, and how those titles are linked together.
Those titles found fulfillment in Jesus and it is important to understand their characteristics both from Jesus' teachings and from the
viewpoints of those who ascribed them to Him. The Jews of Jesus'
time were taught by the Pharisees, scribes, teachers of the Law, and so
on. Additionally there were extra-biblical or extra–Old Testament writings, some more widespread and known than others, that used terms
and titles that were used by Jesus. Therefore it is critical that we understand how Jesus' audiences understood these terms.

Instead of starting with standard theological definitions, we believe
that it will be more beneficial to examine the understanding of those
terms from the perspective of the people who used them. "People" here
includes the Jewish priests and teachers. They loved and labored over
the study of their Scriptures. "People" also includes the laymen and
the common people found within Judea at that time. They too were

aware of at least two of these three titles and understood them. It is safe to assume that the Jews used these titles in their everyday religious conversations.

The people of Jesus' time were familiar with the titles "the Messiah," and "the Son of God." They used the titles frequently and understood their meaning and substance when they applied them to Jesus. Those who used them had distinct ideas about what they meant and signified. It is noteworthy that they often tied the titles "the Messiah" and "the Son of God" together.

## Jesus the Messiah

Muslims and Christians agree that Jesus was the Messiah. But although Muslims agree that Jesus is the Messiah they are not able to explain what the title "al-Masih" signifies because the Quran and Hadith do not define or explain its meaning or significance. Consequently, Muslim theologians do not address that question in any depth beyond a few general comments such as "Jesus was anointed" or that "he healed people by anointing them," or that "Messiah" was little more than a nickname. Since their source materials provide very little about "the Messiah," Muslim scholars truly have little to say. However the Bible does say a great deal about the Messiah, both in the Old Testament and in the New Testament.

What did the title "Messiah" mean to the Jews of Jesus' time?

Examination of the Gospels' "Messiah" references shows that many (but not all) of the verses can be classified under three themes:

1. Verses in which people *confess* that Jesus is the Messiah

2. Verses that describe *supernatural aspects* about the Messiah

3. Verses that portray the Messiah *majestically*

### Confessions

There are several confession verses related to the Messiah. Below we discuss several of them.

**1. Matthew 16:13-17.** Peter's confession that Jesus is the Messiah and the Son of the living God.

> When Jesus came to the region of Caesarea Philippi, he asked his disciples, "Who do people say the Son of Man is?" They replied, "Some say John the Baptist; others say Elijah; and still others, Jeremiah or one of the prophets." "But what about you?" he asked. "Who do you say I am?" Simon Peter answered, "You are the Messiah, the Son of the living God." Jesus replied, "Blessed are you, Simon son of Jonah, for this was not revealed to you by flesh and blood, but by my Father in heaven."

The Matthew 16 passage presents a striking revelation. Jesus asks His disciples who the people say He is. They tell Him that the people think He is another great prophet or man of God. To be considered a prophet is a great honor, but then Jesus asks Peter what he thinks and Peter replies, "The Messiah, the Son of God!"

Peter understood what he was saying and the distinction that Peter credited to Jesus as the Messiah went well beyond the honor paid to a prophet. When he said, "The Messiah," he tied "the Son of God" to that title. Jesus' disciples understood that the Messiah was the Son of God. Is there any homage, reverence, or admiration greater than to be identified as the Messiah, the Son of God? Jesus acknowledges that Peter got it right, Jesus indeed was the Messiah, the Son of God, and that was a truth revealed by God!

**2.** Earlier we noted that in **Matthew 26:57-65** Jesus was challenged if He was the Messiah, the Son of God. Jesus replied in the affirmative and declared that He is the Messiah, the Son of God! This passage tells us the same thing but from a different perspective. Instead of the words coming out of unlearned people, the words are now coming out of the mouth of the Jewish high priest. The man was a scholar, knowledgeable of Jewish Scriptures and theology. He was no theological novice. Caiaphas understood the words, and the problem that came with them (just as Jacob Neusner understood).

Jesus' identity was the bone of contention that caused the hatred and hostility. Caiaphas and the other Jewish leaders knew that the Messiah was indeed the Son of God. Jesus' disciples saw that Jesus was the Son of God close up and personal. But Caiaphas and the Jewish scholars knew by definition that the Messiah was the Son of God. Consequently they were outraged. Who did this Jesus think He was! Was He arrogant and vain enough to think that He was the Messiah, the Son of God?

"Yes!" Jesus replied. There was no lying, no backing down, no vague answer. Jesus met Caiaphas's challenge head-on, answered firmly, and went straight to the heart of the matter. Not only did He say He is the Messiah, the Son of God, He told them that He would be seated at God's right hand and return in the future!

**3. John 20:30-31.** The apostle John's confession of faith that Jesus is the Messiah, the Son of God.

> Jesus performed many other signs in the presence of his disciples, which are not recorded in this book. But these are written that you may believe that Jesus is the Messiah, the Son of God, and that by believing you may have life in his name.

We quote John 20 here because it establishes the importance of believing that Jesus is the Son of God. We are not going to gloss over this requirement or pretend it doesn't exist. John was very close with Jesus and understood His teachings. John knew that true faith rested upon a solid conviction in the One on whom people were to believe. "Jesus the Messiah, the Son of God" is part of the Gospel (Mark 1:1). If you remove Jesus from being the Son of God then you reduce Him to being only a prophet or a teacher. While that is a great calling in and of itself, it is a steep depreciation from being the Son of God. As a result, the real Gospel, the real work of Jesus, becomes valueless. John is saying that if a person is unwilling to acknowledge Jesus as the Son of God then he might as well put his faith in Confucius, Gandhi, or their favorite politician, as the Messiah.

### Supernatural Aspects of the Messiah

Earlier we showed that both the Quran and the Bible present Jesus as being a miracle worker. Now we are going to look at the Gospels to see what the people expected from the one known as "the Messiah" in terms of miracles or supernatural power. We want to understand what they believed and understood about the Messiah's power.

The Messiah was expected to be more than just a prophet. Not all prophets performed miracles. But the Messiah was expected to have power and perform great miracles. Here are several references to the Messiah as a miracle worker.

- John 7:31. The people knew that the Messiah would be able to work miracles.

- John 10:24-26. Jesus said that His miracles proclaim that He is the Messiah.

- John 12:30-34. The people knew that the Messiah was to reign forever (but they didn't know who the Son of Man was).

- Mark 15:31-32. The priests and teachers knew that the Messiah would be able to "come off the cross," that is, possess supernatural power to remove himself.

All of these passages show that the people of Jesus' time believed that the Messiah would be able to work miracles. Both the common people, and the Jewish leaders who rejected Jesus, admitted that He performed miracles (see John 11:47). They expected it of the Messiah. And when Jesus was crucified the Jews mocked Him because to them He was proven false! They knew that the Messiah was to be supernatural and powerful. Their mockery makes sense; if He was the Messiah, surely now He would come down off the cross, defeat the Romans, and establish His kingdom. Instead, they saw Him die. Here is the paradox: Jesus as the Messiah performed great miracles, more than other prophets, but in their eyes, Jesus as the Messiah was also far too human, far too weak, to fulfill the crowd's expectations for the Messiah. Today, many Muslims use this same argument against Jesus' divinity. We'll review that in more detail later.

### Majestic Verses

A number of Gospel verses provide additional details about the Messiah's identity. Not only was the Messiah to be God's unique, "Anointed One," the Messiah was to be given great authority and governance. This makes sense because the Jews believed that the Messiah would not only set up an earthly kingdom, but also rule it.

- Matthew 2:1-6 shows that prophecy establishes, and the wise men know, the Messiah is to be a "king."

- In Matthew 22:41-46 Jesus confronted the Pharisees about who He is declares He is the "Lord" and not just merely the son of David.

- In Luke 24:25-27 following His resurrection Jesus confronts the disciples about prophecy and His historical identity and the "Messiah."

All of these references establish that the Messiah was going to be a supreme ruler. The wise men recognized it because they knew the Messiah, the King of the Jews, would be worthy of worship. When the angel announced Jesus' birth (Luke 2:8-11), he stated, "He is the Messiah, the Lord." Jesus also said that the Psalms declared that the Messiah would be "the Lord," and asked the Jews rhetorically if they understood what that meant. Finally, the Luke 24 passage gives us additional insights into God's plan for the Messiah. Jesus explained the Scriptures that pointed to Him and showed that the Messiah was to suffer (just as the Quran states that other prophets suffered at the hands of the Jews), die, and then ascend into His glory.

What does "His glory" actually mean? Jesus refers to it in John 17:1-5.

> After Jesus said this, he looked toward heaven and prayed:
> "Father, the time has come. Glorify your Son, that your Son

may glorify you. For you granted him authority over all people that he might give eternal life to all those you have given him. Now this is eternal life: that they may know you, the only true God, and Jesus Christ, whom you have sent. I have brought you glory on earth by completing the work you gave me to do. And now, Father, glorify me in your presence with the glory I had with you before the world began."

The glory that Jesus claimed was majestic, royal, and eternal. The following from Leon Morris in *The New International Commentary on the New Testament* (NICNT) is an excellent explanation of what Jesus meant:

> Now Jesus prays to God to glorify him. He looks for glory in the last place that people would look for it, namely in the cross. And he sees this glory for which he prays as linked with his pre-incarnate glory with the Father. There is a clear assertion of Christ's pre-existence here (we have already seen such a claim, 1:1, 8:58, 16:28). There is also the claim that he had enjoyed a unique glory with the Father in that preexistent state. And now, as evil men are about to do their worst to him, he looks for the Father to glorify him again in the same way. It is the Father who will glorify him with true glory in the cross and in what follows...In the passion and all that was associated with it Jesus would be glorified with the true glory, a glory continuous with, and indeed identical with, the glory he had "before the world began." [1]

We've seen a number of historical references that deal with the nature and character of the Messiah and see that He has differing aspects. Some of these fit in nicely with what the Jews were expecting: a powerful miracle worker, a political leader who would rule, a heavenly figure. On the other hand, even though the Old Testament denotes a suffering servant, the Jews had a hard time grasping that the Messiah was one and the same and was going to suffer and die. To them the two concepts did not go hand in hand; rather, it had to be one or the other:

Be the ruler or be ruled. The Messiah cannot be both. Yet Jesus taught that He, as the Messiah, was both.

Scholars' studies on the Messiah in both the Old Testament and extra-canonical books (such as the Books of Enoch), pre–New Testament times, show that the revelations behind the theology and understanding of the Messiah developed and broadened over time. In other words, the revelations from God concerning the Messiah were progressive.

Dr. Raymond Brown explains the theological definition of the "Messiah" and ties it into the concept of progressive revelation:

> The English word "messiah" is from Aramaic mesiha, related to Hebrew masiah, "anointed"; the Greek word is christos, whence "Christ."…But the capitalized term "Messiah" is best confined to a precisely delineated concept, viz., the anointed king of the Davidic dynasty who would establish in the world the definitive kingdom intended by God for Israel. That God had sent leaders and prophets to deliver the chosen people (Moses, the Judges, Nehemiah, Ezra) is commonplace in Israel's theological understanding of its history. But messianism, as we shall discuss it, is involved with deliverance supplied in the framework of an institution, the monarchy. Such a notion of the Messiah is the product of a long development traceable in three stages. [2]

The Jews both before and during Jesus' time continued this vein of progressive revelation and believed that the Messiah was also the Son of God. This was illustrated by comments from Peter, Martha, the Jewish high priest, and more. The title "the Messiah" is linked to the unique title "Son of God." Whether you agree that Jesus is the Son of God or not you can see that the Scriptures unequivocally tie the Messiah and the Son of God together. They are one and the same person.

## The Son of Man

Muslims' question:
*"Jesus called Himself the 'Son of Man.'*
*Doesn't that prove He wasn't the 'Son of God'?"*

Usually when a person reads the Gospels for the first time he wonders, "What did Jesus mean when He called Himself the Son of Man?" "Did He mean that He was just a mere human and not a divine person?" "Is the Son of Man the same person as the Son of God?" and so on. Those are fair questions and they need to be answered.

The Quran gives Jesus a number of titles, but "the Son of Man" is not one of them. However, Muslims and Christians agree that Jesus called Himself "the Son of Man," and a number of Muslims I've dialogued with have no problem using that title because they believe it illustrates Jesus' humanity, something Muslims are keen to do. Jesus' humanity is a good starting point. After all, He was human and His references to the Son of Man reveal just how human He was! Unfortunately that is where some people stop thinking and cease to evaluate Jesus' statements about the "Son of Man." Just as His statements about the Messiah, which included both divine power and human suffering, seemed self-contradictory, Jesus' statements about the Son of Man reveal a person who is both human and divine.

The phrase "Son of Man" occurs over 80 times in the New Testament and most often Jesus is referring to Himself. Unlike the previous section where we were able to learn much from the people's usage of the term "Messiah," we will not learn much, if anything at all, from their use of the term "Son of Man" because they used it rarely. Therefore we must analyze Jesus' statements pertaining to the "Son of Man."

Jesus' use of the title "Son of Man" perplexed people. The title "son of man" is used in the Old Testament, extensively in the book of Ezekiel (appearing some 85 times), but not as a religious title of significance. There the title denotes a human, or a man addressed as a human, by God. However that is not the way Jesus applied the word to Himself. He frequently ascribed great powers and authority to "the Son of Man."

Obviously Jesus had more than either a simple human, or a super-Messiah, in mind when He called Himself the Son of Man. When viewed comprehensively the "Son of Man" possessed both mortal and divine qualities. But this was not altogether clear to the people who heard Him. Case in point: the crowd's question in John 12:34: The crowd spoke up, "We have heard from the Law that the Messiah will remain forever, so how can you say, 'The Son of Man must be lifted up'? Who is this 'Son of Man'?" Here we see the tension between Jesus the Messiah, a supernatural figure, tied to Jesus the Son of Man, a mortal who was going to be killed. They knew He was using that title to mean something more than a mere man but they were uncertain about what He meant.

Since there are two sides to the Son of Man, human and supernatural, we will examine a series of Gospel Scriptures that portray both. We'll start first with the human side.

### The Earthly Side of the Son of Man

In John 3:9-15 Jesus speaks with Nicodemus and tells him that the Son of Man is going to be killed. Jesus taught Nicodemus and stated that He was from heaven but He also was going to suffer and die according to God's plan! I'm sure Nicodemus listened and wondered, "What is Jesus telling me? He is a man from God, teaching powerfully and performing mighty miracles, but now He's telling me that He's got to die! The Messiah isn't supposed to die, but rule! How can this be?"

Similarly in Mark 8:27-32 Peter confessed Christ as the Messiah. Then Jesus foretells His death and His resurrection. Below are verses 31 and 32:

> He then began to teach them that the Son of Man must suffer many things and be rejected by the elders, the chief priests and the teachers of the law, and that he must be killed and after three days rise again. He spoke plainly about this, and Peter took him aside and began to rebuke him.

Here Jesus teaches His own death and resurrection. During this discussion Peter had proclaimed that Jesus was the Messiah! Jesus' disciples were full of faith and confidence in Him. But what did Jesus tell them next? Was it a "now we're ready, let's go get them!" type of speech? No, just the opposite! He told them, "I'm going to be killed and rise from the dead three days later!" Now, how did that fit together with what the disciples thought of Jesus? Jesus was not speaking figuratively or in parables about this topic; rather, He spoke plainly to them. Peter would not accept that Jesus, the Messiah, the Son of God was going to die. Peter was not going to let Jesus walk into His death: "You aren't going to die! You're the Messiah, the man we love, and I'm *not* going to let it happen!"

Likewise in Matthew 17:1-9, following Jesus' transfiguration on the mountain, He foretells not only His death, but also His resurrection!

> As they were coming down the mountain, Jesus instructed them, "Don't tell anyone what you have seen, until the Son of Man has been raised from the dead."

Here, Jesus was transfigured before James, Peter, and John, Moses and Elijah appeared with Him, and God announced that Jesus is His beloved Son, and instructed them to listen to Jesus! What more powerful experience could those disciples have had? What more proof was needed for them to be convinced fully about God's full support of Jesus? This was a moment of power if ever there was one! Now these disciples were ready for any command to action. They were ready to listen as they have never listened before.

But what does Jesus teach them next? He does not say, "Now I will establish my kingdom on earth! We'll defeat the Romans and restore the kingdom to the people!" Rather He predicts again His death and resurrection! Can you imagine what James, Peter, and John were thinking? "What! What do You mean You're going to die and rise from the dead? That makes no sense at all! We just heard God say You were His Son! How is it possible for a man as powerful as You to die? Surely something is wrong with what You are saying. If You are the Son of God, how can that be part of God's plan?"

Again we have a fusion of the two perspectives: human and divine. Here, in the midst of a mind-shattering experience with God, Jesus identifies Himself to His disciples as a mortal, the Son of Man, one who would be betrayed and suffer punishment and death. You can do a New Testament search and find many other similar examples.

### The Supernatural Side of the Son of Man

Now we'll take a look at the Son of Man in a supernatural light.

- In Matthew 12:1-8 Jesus says that the Son of Man is called the "Lord of the Sabbath"!

- In Matthew 12:39-42 Jesus identifies Himself as the Son of Man and states that He is greater than Jonah and Solomon! (Also see Luke 9:22.)

- In Matthew 16:24-28 and John 5:24-27 Jesus declares He is the Son of Man, will be the Judge, and those that wish eternal life must follow Him.

- In Matthew 24:15-31 Jesus states that false prophets shall arise and deceive many, but at the end of times, He, the Son of Man, shall return for His own.

**Four key truths about the "Son of Man":**

1. *The Son of Man is Lord of the Sabbath.* What did Jesus mean by saying that "the Son of Man is Lord of the Sabbath"? We mentioned this in the previous chapter simply to illustrate Jesus' claim as being greater than a mere prophet's claim. But what did He mean by "Lord of the Sabbath"?

   Jesus meant that as Lord of the Sabbath He allowed His disciples to pick grain. Jesus was exercising His authority over the Sabbath as the Son of Man! Further, as He said in Mark 2:27-28, "The Sabbath was made for man, not man for the Sabbath." And later, "How much more valuable is a person than a sheep! Therefore it is lawful to do good on the Sabbath." He was making the point that the Pharisees were interpreting and applying the Scriptures incorrectly. The Pharisees had missed God's intention that the Sabbath was to be a benefit for man, not a yoke of misery or drudgery. Dr. Ben Witherington adds:

> In terms of the Christological implications of this material, we have seen indirect evidence that Jesus viewed himself as more than just a prophet or teacher…He believes that he is implementing God's true intentions for humanity in institutions such as the Sabbath, even though the way he acts is at variance with the usual understanding in early Judaism of the Old Testament Sabbath texts. [3]

2. *The Son of Man will be three days and three nights in the heart of the earth.* In the Matthew 12:39-42 passage Jesus again foretells His death and states that He, the Son of Man, would spend three days and nights in the earth. Yet He also says He is greater than Jonah and Solomon!

3. *God gave the Son of Man authority to judge mankind and reward each person according to what he has done.* This type of judgment is reserved for God and God alone but He gave that authority to the Son of Man! Jesus is saying that the Son of Man possessed divine abilities.

4. *During the last days the Son of Man will return to earth in power and glory.* The Matthew 24:30-31 passage provides us the most powerful clue about why Jesus used the term "Son of Man." (As mentioned earlier, Jesus made a similar statement to the high priest in Matthew 26:62-64.) Jesus, the Son of Man, referenced Daniel 7:12-14,27, and He will return to earth coming with the clouds.

Ben Witherington explains Jesus' use of the Daniel 7 reference of "bar enasha" (Son of Man), and other Old Testament verses:

> There are certain Old Testament texts to which Jesus did seem to turn to express or serve as a commentary on his

self-understanding, for example, Dan. 7:13-14 (which seems to explain his use of bar enasha), the Daniel text combined with Ps. 110:1, or Ps. 110:1 by itself. Various texts in Zechariah about the shepherd or Coming One seem crucial to Jesus' sense of identity or, at least, to his means of expressing who he thought he was.[4]

Jesus taught His disciples about the last days in Matthew 24 and identified Himself as the Son of Man, but they may not have understood that He was referring to Daniel 7. But when Jesus made that statement to the Jewish high priest Caiaphas, He received an instant reaction! Caiaphas knew exactly what Jesus was saying, and for that He was sentenced to death!

### The Aramaic Phrase Bar'Ěnoš ("Son of Man")

Many Jewish scholars consider Daniel 7:13-14 to be a passage that predicts the Messiah. Here is an example.

> The Aramaic phrase Bar 'ěnoš "son of man" is a Semitic expression denoting a single member of humanity, a certain human being, hence "someone." This Aramaic phrase used by Daniel 7:13-14 to describe a quasidivine figure riding with the clouds of the sky has become an important element of the eschatological-apocalyptic decorum in both Jewish and Christian texts; an eclectic decorum made of various elements such as, the Davidic king, the chosen servant of Deutero-Isaiah, and the "son of man" of Daniel.
>
> That Dan 7:13-14 was read as a messianic prophecy in the Jewish circles in the Talmudic period (beginning with third century) may be seen in the excellent comparison made by one Rabbi between two messianic texts, Daniel 7:13 and Zechariah 9:7: "Rabbi Alexandri said, 'Rabbi Joshua opposed two verses, It is written, "And behold, one like the Son of Man came with the clouds of heaven" [Dan 7:13]

while [elsewhere] it is written, "[Behold, your king comes to you...] lowly, and riding upon an ass!"' [Zech 9:7]—if they are meritorious, [Messiah will come] with the clouds of heaven; if not, lowly and riding upon an ass. King Shapur [I] said to Samuel, 'You maintain that the Messiah will come upon an ass: I will rather send him a white horse of mine.'" [5]

Why did Jesus use the title "Son of Man"? He applied this title to Himself as a link to the scripturally identified (and by other esteemed Jewish religious writings) "Messiah." Jesus was claiming that identity for Himself. "Did He mean that He was just a mere human and not a divine person?" No, Jesus meant He was both. He was saying that He was the Messiah, but that He was also human. Part of His divine work was atonement for humanity, something we will cover in a later chapter.

### Is the Son of Man the Same Person as the Son of God?

Both titles apply to Jesus. However, the two titles denote different aspects of Jesus. The Son of Man, as revealed in Daniel 7 and as taught by Jesus in the New Testament, possessed both human and divine characteristics, while the "Son of God" demonstrated His integral divine union with God (as taught by Jesus and understood by the Jews of His time).

F.F. Bruce summarizes the themes behind Jesus' use of the term "Son of Man":

> "The Son of Man" was not a current title for the Messiah or any other eschatological figure.
>
> Jesus' special use of the expression (as distinct from its general Aramaic use in the sense of "man," "the man," or a possible use to replace the pronoun "I") was derived from the "one like a son of man" who is divinely vested with authority in Daniel 7:13f. Because it was not a current title, it was not liable to be misunderstood, as current titles were, and Jesus was free to take up the expression and give it what meaning he chose.

Jesus enriched the expression by fusing with it the figure of a righteous sufferer, probably the Isaianic Servant, so that he could speak of the suffering of the Son of man as something that was "written" concerning him. By suffering and vindication Jesus, the Son of man, became his people's deliverer and advocate.

A "Son of man" theology could be nothing other than a theology based on what can be ascertained about Jesus' understanding of his identity and life-mission. [6]

## The Son of God

Muslims' question:
*"How can God have a Son?"*

One important comment on the title "Son of God" must be made. The title "Son of God" brings with it an entire set of complexities, but at a minimum, it establishes Jesus as having a divine nature. In and of itself it is the single theme of many books and we will touch upon aspects of the title's meaning in this chapter. We will examine how that title was applied to Jesus and by whom it was applied. Since Islam rejects Jesus as the Son of God, and Muslims are quick to claim (without any proof and contrary to what the Quran teaches) that this New Testament theme has been corrupted by men inserting titles like "the Son of God" into the texts, it bears some investigation to see how that title is actually applied and if their claim has substance.

"Jesus, the Son of God" is the most challenging of titles. What does that title actually mean? How is it defined in the New Testament? Those who have studied this theme know that the meaning of the title "Son of God" is multifaceted and nuanced and at times the New Testament does not explain it as thoroughly as many would like. Some Scriptures seem ambiguous. Volumes have been written to address and explain it from a variety of different perspectives.

Three key points concerning the Son of God:

1. The four Gospels—the Injil—present a systematic chronological portrayal of Jesus as the Son of God.

2. The Son of God shares the very same characteristics that the Messiah and the Son of Man possess.

3. Jesus declared Himself to be God's Son and mandated that belief in this concept was essential for salvation and to enter eternal life in Paradise.

## 1. The Gospels—the Injil—Systematically Portray Jesus as the Son of God

What follows is a series of chronological verses that present a unified theme on the nature of the Son of God.

- Mark 1:1—"The beginning of the good news about Jesus the Messiah, the Son of God."

- Luke 1:26-38—"…So the holy one to be born will be called the Son of God."

- Matthew 3:16-17—God Himself clearly proclaims that Jesus is His Son: "This is my Son, whom I love; with him I am well pleased."

- John 3:16-21—Jesus declares that He is "the Son of God": "God so loved the world that he gave his one and only Son, that whoever believes in him shall not perish but have eternal life."

- Matthew 17:1-8—Jesus is transfigured and again God reaffirms, "This is my Son, whom I love; with him I am well pleased. Listen to him!"

- John 17:1-5—Jesus prays to God His Father: "Father, the hour has come. Glorify your Son, that your Son may glorify you."

- Matthew 26:63-64—"The high priest said to him, 'I charge you under oath by the living God: Tell us if you

are the Messiah, the Son of God.' 'You have said so,' Jesus
replied."

- John 20:31—"These are written that you may believe that
  Jesus is the Messiah, the Son of God, and that by believing
  you may have life in his name."

These passages show that from before His birth it was stated that
He would be the Son of God. From the beginning of His life until the
end Jesus was identified clearly, without exception, as the Son of God.
Those who claim otherwise are not being honest with their readers.

Some Muslim critics charge that the New Testament was corrupted
and assert that they added all the references to Jesus as the Son of God.
The answer to that charge is that in light of the passages above, it is hard
to believe, rather it is inconceivable that anyone who wanted to corrupt
the Gospel, God's Word, would be capable of weaving into so many
various accounts, from so many different perspectives, a theme that is
presented so comprehensively as Jesus being the Son of God. The documented history of the New Testament and the existing manuscript
evidence does not allow for that level of wholesale corruption. This is
not a case where a mere word, phrase, or passage would have been tam-
pered with, but rather the evidence shows that Jesus as the Son of God
is woven completely through the Gospel message and is established
from beginning to end! The declaration that Jesus is the Son of God is
proclaimed by the disciples, by the angels, by God, by Satan, by Jesus,
by the Old Testament Scriptures, and by the Jewish high priest. If one
is honest and approaches the New Testament with integrity, you will
understand that the Gospels have, from beginning to the end, always
proclaimed that Jesus is "the Son of God." This is the only honest conclusion that can be drawn.

## 2. The Son of God Shares the Characteristics of the Messiah and the Son of Man

This point does not have to be elaborated upon because we've
already established that the Scriptures tie and associate the Messiah

and the Son of Man to the Son of God. People close to Jesus asserted His identity as the Messiah, the Son of Man and Son of God:

1. Matthew 16:13-17. Peter's statement about Jesus.

2. John 11:17-27. Martha's confession.

3. Matthew 26:57-65. Jesus before the Jewish leaders (see also Mark 14, Luke 22).

Similarly, the Son of God shares the same abilities as the Messiah and Son of Man:

1. Son of God casting out demons (Matthew 8:32)

2. Son of God performing miracles (John 20:30)

3. Son of God returning in power (Matthew 26:63-64)

4. Son of God resurrecting the dead (John 5:25)

### 3. Jesus Declared Himself to Be God's Son and Mandated That Belief in This Was Essential for Salvation and Entry to Eternal Life in Paradise

What was Jesus' rationale for proclaiming Himself as the Son of God? As Jesus began His ministry, He was baptized by John the Baptist (see Matthew 3:16-17). Ben Witherington makes the following comment about Jesus' experience:

> If Jesus had a visionary experience at his baptism in which he was convinced he was anointed with the Spirit and was called God's Son with allusion to Psalm 2, then it would be difficult for him not to conclude that he was God's Mashiach. If he did have such an experience and drew such conclusions, then a clear explanation can be given for the course that Jesus chose and for the reason that he acted as one with sovereign authority and power. [7]

This is a powerful moment; He was being baptized by the mighty preacher John the Baptist. As Jesus leaves the water, people see the Holy Spirit descend upon Jesus in the form of a dove! This is a heavenly sign! Then the people hear a powerful voice from heaven: "This is my Son, whom I love; with him I am well pleased." Surely, Jesus had every right and every expectation to proclaim Himself as the Son of God.

Following His baptism Jesus began to minister in earnest. He told people the truth about His identity and His mission. People saw the proof and power of His ministry and realized that God was with Him. Previously we mentioned Jesus' conversation with Nicodemus. During their meeting Jesus not only stated the Gospel, He declared Himself to be the Son of God (John 3:13-19). Following that passage, John the Baptist proclaimed that Jesus was the Son of God and source of eternal salvation (John 3:31-36).

As time went on, Jesus gained a larger following and created controversy as He spoke out against the hypocrisy of various Jewish leaders. He debated with them and told them that God gave Him, the Son, the right to give eternal life to anyone who believed, and to raise the dead. In John 5:20-30 Jesus went on to emphasize that those who do not honor Him as the Son of God, cannot honor the Father and that He will be the Judge of mankind.

Finally, let's look again at why John wrote his Gospel:

> Jesus performed many other signs in the presence of his disciples, which are not recorded in this book. But these are written that you may believe that Jesus is the Messiah, the Son of God, and that by believing you may have life in his name (John 20:30-31).

The Scriptures here are clear: Jesus was always identified as the Son of God. God Himself proclaimed it, John the Baptist proclaimed it, and Jesus proclaimed it. Jesus said that it was necessary for His followers to believe that He was the Son of God. Of course we may not comprehend every meaning, every detail, and every nuance of the term "Son of God," but we should understand that Jesus is the Son of God and shares a union with God the Father.

## Conclusion

This chapter's goal was to show that three primary titles given to Jesus exhibit different facets of His identity, and that these titles are tied together and find their fulfillment in Jesus. He is the Messiah, the Son of Man, and the Son of God. The person behind each of these titles had the ability to perform miracles, was going to judge the world, and would suffer, die, and rise again.

The people of Jesus' time had identified the Messiah as being the Son of God. However, they did not understand that the Messiah would also suffer and die. Jesus' teachings and actions show that He knew He was more than a prophet. He came with a difficult mission that was given to Him by God. He knew He would fulfill that mission. As Witherington observes:

> Jesus neither was, nor considered himself to be, an ordinary person. He did not conceive of himself merely in terms of a prophet or teacher. Rather, he saw himself as God's Mashiach, and Shaliach, as the final Shepherd of God's people. It was this self-perception expressed in word, deed, and especially symbolic action during the last week of his life, that led to Jesus' death as "King of the Jews." [8]

The great challenge that confronts truth seekers today is accepting Jesus as the Son of God. Yet Jesus taught that this is one of the most important elements of faith and a requirement for eternal life. As John later said, "Whoever has the Son has life; whoever does not have the Son of God does not have life."

3

# The Father, His Son, and Their Relationship

Muslims' question:
*"How can the Father be God and Jesus be God?"*

reviously we asked a question that has not been answered: What does "Jesus, the Son of God" actually mean? This is a complex and multifaceted title and an entire branch of theological study. "Christology" exists to examine the intricate traits of Jesus' identity, character, and attributes. There is even an "Islamic Christology"! Thousands of books have been written and continue to be written on this topic. Consequently, this chapter is not intended to be a complete analysis of Jesus' divinity. However, we are going to investigate a primary aspect of Jesus' deity by examining the term "Son of God." We will discuss its meaning and present aspects of Jesus' relationship with God the Father as the Word of God incarnate, that is, as a human.

## What Did Jesus Mean?

When Jesus identified Himself as the Son of God and said that God was His Father, just what did He have in mind? If we hear the phrase "father and son" we usually think that the father "fathered" his son, that is, that he had sex with the son's mother, she became pregnant, and nine months later the son was born. In that light it is understandable for a person who hears the terms "God the Father" and "Jesus, God's Son" to think that somehow God took some type of fleshly form, had physical relations with Mary, and impregnated her. In fact this is what Muhammad believed and what the Quran teaches. We'll deal with that in more depth later.

### The Jewish Understanding of Jesus' Claim

But this is not what the Bible teaches and this is not what the Jews of Jesus' time understood when Jesus identified Himself as the Son of God. They understood that Jesus was speaking analogically. That is why none of them ever challenged Him with a question such as, "What! Are You saying that our God had sex with Your mother!?" They understood that Jesus was laying claim to divine nature and they never made those mistaken accusations.

Why did Jesus use the "Father and Son" terminology? He used those terms because they best illustrate His relationship with God. Humans are able to understand its relational aspects and this terminology gives us the closest analogy to their relationship for it portrays their unity and their intimate relationship. Just as a son possesses many of the same traits of his father, so too Jesus possessed the same essence, the same character, the same traits and abilities as God. Just as father and son love each other deeply, so too do Jesus as the Son, and God as the Father love each other deeply. And just as a son is submitted and obedient to his father, so too Jesus is submitted and obedient to God the Father. In human terms the son shares his father's nature but is submitted and obedient to the father. Likewise, Jesus shared a divine nature but was submitted and obedient to God. Since He possessed a divine nature He was able to perform the greatest miracles. Jesus said He did what the Father did, that is, that His actions were done in obedience to God. Jesus, the Word of God, shared divinity and existed eternally with God. They are indeed different but they both share the same essence.

The Jews also understood Jesus' claim of equality of substance, of divinity, of nature, and they objected strongly! John 5:16-23 shows this. They objected to Jesus' calling God His Father. They understood that it meant that Jesus was claiming to have a divine nature. They were not worried or concerned about God having sexual relations with a woman because they knew that it was not necessary for Jesus to be the awaited Messiah, the Son of God.

Examine Jesus' reply to their challenge. He says that He can do what God does. Just as God can raise the dead and give life, so too He can give life. He states that God gave Him authority to judge and that those who do not honor Him do not honor God. In this reply Jesus establishes that He possesses the divine nature and accordingly He will carry out the functions that are understood to be reserved for God alone. Jesus as the Son of God is able to do what is reserved for and only capable of being done by God.

The Jews also understood that Jesus was not claiming to be a "son of God" like so many others are called "sons of God" in the Bible. For example Adam is called the son of God and the tribe of Ephraim is also called God's son. The Jews understood Jesus' meaning clearly: Jesus clearly defined and identified Himself as the unique, special, one-of-a-kind, "only begotten" Son of God.

John 19:6-7 further illustrates this point. The Jewish scholars knew their theology and understood that point as well. They knew that other people in the Torah had been called "sons of God." However, they understood exactly what Jesus meant: He was the unique Son of God and possessed divinity. He claimed to be greater than Moses, He exercised authority over their Scriptures, He ruled over their religious tenets by saying He was Lord over the Sabbath. Yes, the Jews got it right, Jesus was claiming to be something far greater than a mere human creation "son," greater than a mere prophet. Rather, He claimed that He was the fleshly embodiment of the divine nature.

### The Christian Position

John Gilchrist sums up the Christian position:

> We believe that the eternal Son of God, one with the Father from all eternity, united to him in one Spirit, "became flesh and dwelt among us" (John 1:14), and took "the form of a servant, being born in the likeness of men" (Philippians 2:7). We do not believe that God took to himself offspring and that he sired a son, another god, when Jesus was born. We believe in the incarnation of the Son of God, we do not believe in adoptionism, a one-time Christian heresy which is, in fact what the Qur'an is actually opposing.[1]

Gilchrist later explains the term "Son of God":

> The expression "Son of God" is principally analogical. It indi-
> cates the relationship between the first two persons of the Tri-
> une God. They are equal in essence, indeed of one essence,
> yet one is subject to the other's authority. The human anal-
> ogy goes no further than this—an earthly father and his son
> are both human to the full, yet the second must bow to the
> authority of the first. Muhammad erred when he supposed
> the likeness to extend to such issues as the taking of offspring,
> a consort, etc., but we too will err if we do not make it very
> clear that no matter what we believe about Jesus, he is sub-
> ject to the Father's authority. When he came to this earth he
> came as the Father's ambassador to redeem men from sin
> and, being found in human form, took his subjection to the
> Father's authority to the point of a servant-to-Master rela-
> tionship. [2]

People often overlook the relational aspect of Jesus to His Father
when discussing what Jesus meant by "the Son of God," and the details
of this relationship get lost in the analysis of whether or not Jesus is
divine. Often when Christians and Muslims discuss this topic they
tend to focus solely on a set of verses that support their arguments
and fail to investigate this relationship as a means to understanding
Christ's divinity. But the foundational scriptural viewpoint is one of
God the Father being in relation to His Son. This is an important part
of the equation that must be taken into account along with the other
Scriptures.

When Jesus spoke of Himself as the Son, He most often also
referred to God as His Father. This fundamental relationship between
Jesus and His Father must be grasped to some degree because it reveals
both Christ's divinity and the hierarchy between Jesus and God. When
you pause and examine what Jesus actually said, you realize that He was
not flying solo, He was not doing His own thing; rather, He was working in conjunction with the Father. Thus when Jesus called Himself the
"Son of God" He was illustrating both His divine character and His

submission to God. This is what Jesus proclaimed and required, this is what the early church taught, and this is what the Scriptures teach.

### Key Scriptures About the Relationship

Here are several passages that present facets of Jesus' relationship with His Father.

- *Matthew 11:22-27.* "All things have been committed to me by my Father. No one knows the Son except the Father, and no one knows the Father except the Son and those to whom the Son chooses to reveal him" (verse 27).

- *John 5:16-27.* "The Father judges no one, but has entrusted all judgment to the Son, that all may honor the Son just as they honor the Father. Whoever does not honor the Son does not honor the Father, who sent him" (verses 22-23).

- *John 6:35-40.* "All those the Father gives me will come to me, and whoever comes to me I will never drive away" (verse 37).

- *Matthew 25:31-36.* "Then the King will say to those on his right, 'Come, you who are blessed by my Father; take your inheritance, the kingdom prepared for you since the creation of the world'" (verse 34).

- *John 17:1-8.* "Father, the hour has come. Glorify your Son, that your Son may glorify you. For you granted him authority over all people that he might give eternal life to all those you have given him" (verses 1-2).

Each of these passages illustrate different facets of Jesus' relationship with God, and they each illustrate aspects of Jesus' divine nature.

*The New International Commentary on the New Testament* (NICNT) on John 5:18 states:

> The Jews did not miss the significance of Jesus' words. He had called God "his own Father," and this meant that he was "making himself equal with God." "His own" interprets what

was said in the previous verse. Jesus was not teaching that God is the Father of all. The Jews would have accepted that. His claim meant that God was his Father in a special sense. He was claiming that he partook of the same nature as his Father.[3]

And on verses 22-23:

> The thought moves on to that of judgment. Arising out of the life-giving activities of the Son comes the thought that the Father does not judge people. This was something new to Jews. They held that the Father was the Judge of all people, and they expected to stand before him at the last day. Jesus tells them now that the Father will exercise his prerogative of judging for the express purpose of ensuring that people give the Son the same honor as they do to himself. This is very close to an assertion of deity. Those who fail to honor him fail to honor the Father who sent him.[4]

Finally, the John 17 passage illustrates another important facet of Jesus' relationship with His Father: the relationship they had together before the creation of the world (verse 24). Jesus was with His Father in relationship and in glory before the world began. And entering into relationship with Jesus constitutes eternal life. *The Expositor's Bible Commentary* states on verses 2 and 3:

> The two sentences following the petition are parenthetical and explanatory. The first (verse 2) indicates the scope of the authority Christ exercised in his incarnate state. He was empowered to impart eternal life to those who had been given to him. This Gospel is replete with assertions that life is in Christ: "In him was life, and that life was the light of men" (1:4). "The Son of Man must be lifted up, that everyone who believes in him may have eternal life" (3:15-16). "The water I give him will become in him [who drinks it] a spring of water welling up to eternal life" (4:14; see also 5:21,26; 6:33,54; 10:10; 11:25; 14:6). These words and others like them

emphatically express the central purpose of Jesus: to glorify the Father by imparting life to men.

The second sentence (verse 3) defines the nature of eternal life. It is not described in chronological terms but by a relationship. Life is active involvement with environment; death is the cessation of involvement with the environment, whether it be physical or personal. The highest kind of life is involvement with the highest kind of environment. A worm is content to live in soil; we need not only the wider environment of earth, sea, and sky but also contact with other human beings. For the complete fulfillment of our being, we must know God. This, said Jesus, constitutes eternal life. Not only is it endless, since the knowledge of God would require an eternity to develop fully, but qualitatively it must exist in an eternal dimension. As Jesus said farther on in this prayer, eternal life would ultimately bring his disciples to a lasting association with him in his divine glory (verse 24).[5]

Now we've only presented five passages out of many in which the relationship between Jesus and His Father is expressed. This relationship shows two entities, one certainly divine, the other possessing both human and divine characteristics, acting in perfect harmony, in an intimate and loving relationship, working together for mankind's good. If one examines their relationship one cannot help but realize Jesus' true nature: He certainly was one with the Father. Examining the details and reading in between the lines shows that Jesus did possess divine characteristics. We see Jesus seated upon a throne judging the world, Jesus with the Father in glory before the world began, Jesus the only source of eternal life, Jesus being honored, Jesus having all things given to Him by the Father. This parallels the Daniel chapter 7 passage and proclaims Jesus' divinity.

No man, no matter how mighty a prophet, would make the claims Jesus did. In fact, if only a great prophet would have made the claims that Jesus made, then he would have been guilty of blasphemy. The relationship Jesus had with the Father establishes His divine nature; He was in perfect union with God.

## Muslims and the Son of God

This topic is perhaps the greatest stumbling block for Muslims because Islam ties believing in Jesus as the Son of God to "shirk," worshipping or associating other than the one God with divinity. This is an unforgivable sin and therefore Islam rejects the sonship of Jesus. As a result there exists in the minds of Muslims a large, daunting bridge, over a dark and deep chasm. Crossing that bridge is going beyond the point of no return and entering a foreign, unknown, and fearful country. They count the cost. Choosing Jesus over Islam often involves family rejection, persecution, torture, and even death. It is a higher cost than many Westerners would pay.

A key verse on this is from the Quran's chapter "Repentance," 9:30:

> And the Jews say: Ezra is the son of Allah, and the Christians say: The Messiah is the son of Allah. That is their saying with their mouths. They imitate the saying of those who disbelieved of old. Allah (himself) fighteth against them. How perverse are they!

Similarly, there are several other Quranic verses that reject Jesus as the Son of God every bit as strongly. Note here however that the Quran calls a curse upon the Christians and prays for God to harm them: "God confound them!" Other translations of that phrase read, "Allah curse them!" "Allah fight them!" "Allah destroy them!" Muhammad, in the Quran, then calls the Christians "perverse" for believing that Jesus is the Son of God. This is not a mild denouncement; this is an outright curse and condemnation! Also note here the error: The Quran says that the Christians are making up the belief that Jesus is the Son of God only verbally: "That is their saying with their mouths." Rather it is written in the Word of God, the New Testament, that Jesus is the Son of God.

Islam's rejection of Jesus as the Son of God is bold and powerful but it is doubtful that Muhammad understood the theology behind

Jesus' sonship. Subsequent Islamic writings (the Hadith, the Sira) fail to define the term adequately. As a result, many Muslims today do not understand the details behind the term. Both the Quran and Hadith fail to address the term "Son of God" in a Christian context and fail to acknowledge its Christian definition.

The belief of followers of Jesus that He claimed in the Bible to be God's Son is a often-visited topic of conversations between Muslims and Christians. Following Jesus' death and resurrection, Christians, those who believed that Jesus was the Son of God, were sometimes put to death. Today in Islamic countries Muslims who become Christians and believe Jesus is the Son of God also face punishment and death. This is a serious subject in Islam and consequences are heavy.

Consequently, our following comments are not meant to be critical, but rather an honest dialogue concerning Islam's and Christianity's different accounts of the sonship of Jesus. Obviously both the biblical and Quranic accounts of Jesus' sonship cannot be correct. One may be correct, but both cannot be, because they contradict each other. Read both the biblical and the Quranic accounts, evaluate their contexts, and decide for yourself on their reliability and accuracy. Since Christianity demands acceptance and belief in Jesus as the Son of God, and Islam decries that belief as an unforgivable sin, then accepting this element of faith has eternal, and painful, consequences. Their positions are opposed and cannot be reconciled. Consequently, it behooves the reader to examine this in depth.

### What Does the Quran Teach About the Claim That Jesus Is the Son of God?

The Quran and the Bible teachings concerning Jesus' sonship are significantly different. Are the Quran's statements accurate?

It is important to examine a number of Quranic verses in chronological order. The first verse is from sura "The Jinn," 72:3:

> And (we believe) that He—exalted be the glory of our Lord!— hath taken neither wife nor son.

This chapter was spoken by Muhammad about three years before he fled to Medina. By this time Muhammad was familiar with the general beliefs of the Christians and Jews (even one of his relatives was considered to be a Christian scholar), but it is apparent that he did not understand their doctrines properly. Allah did not marry, so he could not have had sexual relations with a woman to father children. Hence he had not "begotten any children."

The Muslim scholar Ibn Kathir (c. 1301–1373) states this when commenting on this verse:

> Allah says, "{He has taken neither a wife nor a son}" meaning, far exalted is He above taking a mate and having children. This means that when the Jinns accepted Islam and believed in the Qur'an they professed Allah's magnificence above having taken a spouse and a child (or a son)...Mujahid, Ikrimah, Qatadah and As-Suddi, all said, "{the foolish among us}." "They were referring to Iblis."...The foolish also carries the meaning of everyone in the category who claims that Allah has a spouse or a son. [6]

About two years later, while still in Mecca, Muhammad repeated this theme in 6:100-101:

> Yet they ascribe as partners unto Him the Jinn, although He did create them, and impute falsely, without knowledge, sons and daughters unto Him. Glorified be He and High Exalted above (all) that they ascribe (unto Him). The Originator of the heavens and the earth! How can He have a child, when there is for Him no consort, when He created all things and is Aware of all things?

Here Ibn Kathir is more explicit in his comments:

> ...Allah mentions the misguidance of those who were led astray and claimed a son or offspring for Him, as the Jews did with Uzayr, the Christians with Isa and the Arab pagans with the angels whom they claimed were Allah's daughters. Allah is far holier than what the unjust, polytheist people associated with Him. [7]

Ibn Kathir understood Muhammad's teachings. Muhammad taught that Christians held the doctrine that God took Mary as His wife or concubine, impregnated her, and as a result she later gave birth to Jesus. The Quran challenges, "Allah could not have had a son because he took no wife."

Later in Medina, Muhammad, still not understanding the Christian doctrine of Jesus' sonship, continued to speak out against the idea that God had fleshly relations with Mary:

> And they say: Allah hath taken unto Himself a Son. Be He glorified! Nay, but whatsoever is in the heaven and the earth, His. All are subservient unto Him. The Originator of the heavens and the earth! When He decreeth a thing, He saith unto it only: Be! and it is (2:116-117).

Again Ibn Kathir comments on the Quran's rejection of Jesus' sonship:

> This and the following Ayat refute the Christians, may Allah curse them, and their like among the Jews and the Arab idolators, who claimed that the angels are Allah's daughters. Allah refuted all of them in their claim that He had begotten a son...All creatures are Allah's servants and are owned by Him. Therefore, how could one of them be His son? The son of any being is born out of two comparable beings. Allah has no equal or rival sharing His grace and greatness, so how can He have a son when He has no wife? [8]

Ibn Kathir refers to a union of flesh to produce offspring. Since there was no woman comparable to Allah then Allah could not have taken a wife to have relations with.

Note here that in all of these verses a physical union (with Mary), is presented and rejected by the Quran. Muhammad countered that concept and said that Allah only needed to speak "Be" and in that fashion Mary conceived miraculously.

Muhammad did not understand the very essence of Christianity. His knowledge of Christianity seems to be flawed and inaccurate, that is, that a follower of Jesus believes that God had sex with Mary! This is contrary to what the Bible teaches. We believe that Jesus, in eternal relationship with God, took upon Himself human form.

Christians believe (and the Bible clearly teaches) that Mary was impregnated by the Holy Spirit, that is, that she conceived miraculously. The Christian Scriptures teach that the phrase "Jesus the Son of God" means that Jesus, as the Word of God, took on a human form from conception to His death.

The Jews of Jesus' time understood Jesus' claim. Jesus claimed to be the Son of God, yet the Jews who opposed Him strongly never accused Jesus of saying that God had sex with His mother! As mentioned previously, these knowledgeable Jews understood Jesus' claim as the Son of God clearly and they rejected it, not because they thought Jesus was implying that God had sex with Mary, but rather that Jesus was claiming divinity. However, unlike the Jews, Muslims often fail to understand the meaning and theology behind the phrase "Son of God" and thus reject it strongly.

Our appeal to our Muslim readers is to now reconsider the biblical evidence concerning Jesus' sonship. The Bible does not teach that God had sex with Mary.

John Gilchrist summarizes this argument:

> Muhammad's misconception of the true Christian and biblical doctrine of Jesus as the Son of God argues strongly against his claim that the Qur'an was being revealed to him. Once again the book shows itself to be a victim of the limited knowledge of its prophet. If God was the author of the Qur'an he would have known what the universal belief of the Christians really was and would not have taken a heresy (adoptionism) as the belief of the whole Church (which is in the incarnation of the Son in human form). Muhammad was obviously ignorant of the true Christian doctrine and, seeing only the pagan Arab belief in the generation of daughters of Allah before him, mistook the Christian belief to be one and the same thing. [9]

In this light, our challenge to the Muslim reader is to understand what Caiaphas, the disciples, and the Samaritan woman understood: The Messiah was the Son of God. Jesus' claim infuriated Caiaphas, but Caiaphas knew that Jesus was not claiming that God had sex with His mother, but rather that Jesus claimed divinity.

## The Father-and-Son Relationship and the Incarnation

Thus far we've presented the relationship between God and Jesus as father and son. We've addressed and corrected the error that God took Mary as His wife and impregnated her. Now we'll focus on another aspect of Jesus' relationship with God: the incarnation.

The *Baker Encyclopedia of the Bible* defines "incarnation" as

> Literally, "in flesh"; theologically, the doctrine that in Jesus of Nazareth God took on human flesh and became the divine God-man. [10]

Let's first review Scriptures related to the incarnation and note their main points. I'll quote key excerpts from each passage but please read the entire passage for background and context.

John 1:1-18 (the Prologue, the Word became flesh).

> In the beginning was the Word, and the Word was with God, and the Word was God. He was with God in the beginning. Through him all things were made; without him nothing was made that has been made. In him was life, and that life was the light of men. The light shines in the darkness, but the darkness has not understood it.

This prologue, dedicated to identifying and describing Jesus as the Word of God, states that He was with God and was God, that He was Creator, that He was the Light, that He became flesh, and that He provided man with the opportunity to know the Father.

John 8:48-59 (Jesus debating the Jews about His identity).

> "You are not yet fifty years old," they said to him, "and you have seen Abraham!" "Very truly I tell you," Jesus answered, "before Abraham was born, I am!" At this, they picked up

stones to stone him, but Jesus hid himself, slipping away from the temple grounds.

Here Jesus declared that faith in Him would bring eternal life. The Jews rejected His claim and challenged Him, just as Muslims today challenge, "Do you think You are greater than the prophets?" Jesus answered in the affirmative but did so with an even more bold and powerful declaration: "Abraham saw Me!" and ended by saying He preceded Abraham!

The third passage, John 3:31-36, is also from John, but it contains details not only about the incarnation, it also reveals the relationship between the Father and the Son, and provides the message of the Messiah: the Gospel. John declares Jesus pre-existed and then states the Gospel: Faith in Jesus is required for eternal life.

### Discussion of the Three Key Passages

There are a number of things to note about these passages but all of them state that Jesus existed prior to His birth with God in heaven, and each presents the relationship of Jesus to God in a Father-to-Son relationship.

Here are several scholars' writings about the incarnation and each presents an important aspect:

> To say that this being became flesh is the problematic statement, since John does not give us any immediate, nearer description of what he means. We have to consider the clause in the context of the Gospel as a whole. John does not mean that the Word turned into flesh or that it merely assumed a fleshly clothing like a Greek god who could instantly transform himself into a human bodily form and move about among men, his real nature and identity being hidden from them except, perhaps, when he demonstrated supernatural powers. It would be truer to say that John opposes such views. Rather, the Word took on a fleshly form of existence. He was, therefore, still the Word. [11]

Against this background the absolute use of "I AM" by the Johannine Jesus becomes quite intelligible; he is speaking in the same manner in which Yahweh speaks in Deutero-Isaiah. For instance, in John 8:28 Jesus promises that when the Son of Man is lifted up (in return to the Father), "then you will know ego eimi"; in Isa 43:10 Yahweh has chosen Israel, "that you many know and believe me and understand ego eimi." The absolute Johannine use of "I AM" has the effect of portraying Jesus as divine with (pre) existence as his identity, even as the Greek OT understood the God of Israel. [12]

These quotes from Marshall and Brown make the point that Jesus, in pre-existence as the divine Son, the "I AM," chose to become man not in a fanciful fleeting garb, but as fully human, experiencing life as a man so that we may be reconciled with God. If we look at the root of this relationship between Jesus, the Word of God, and God, we find the strongest statement about Jesus possible: "The Word was God."

The NICNT on John 1:1-2 states:

> The high point is reached in the third affirmation: "the Word was God." Nothing higher could be said: all that may be said about God may fitly be said about the Word. This statement should not be watered down... John is not merely saying that there is something divine about Jesus. He is affirming that he is God, and doing so emphatically as we see from the word order in the Greek...

> He says "the Word was God," not, "God was the Word." The latter would have meant that God and the Word were the same; it would have pointed to an identity. But John is leaving open the possibility that there may be more to "God" than the "Word" (clearly he thought of the Father as God, and his later references indicate a similar status for the Spirit). But he lays it down unequivocally that nothing less than "God" will do for our understanding of the Word. [13]

We have used the Scriptures to present Jesus' relationship to God in the analogy of a father-and-son relationship. At the same time the Scriptures present Jesus as being divine. They show us that as a man He was certainly limited but as "the Word made flesh and dwelling among us" He wielded divine power. Before coming to earth, Jesus pre-existed as deity; "the Word was God." Jesus was not God the Father, but He is God the Son.

John's Gospel, chapter 1, moves from Christ's pre-existent identity to the incarnation in verses 9 through 14. The NICNT states on verse 14:

> Now comes the most concise statement of the incarnation. "The Word" refers to him who is nothing less than God. "Became" is in the aorist tense, and indicates action at a point of time. "Flesh" is a strong, almost crude way of referring to human nature...Notices that this is the first time that John indicates that the Word and Jesus are to be taken as the same. Up to this point it would have been quite possible for the reader to take "the Word" to refer to some supreme cosmic principle or the like. But in one short, shattering expression John unveils the great idea at the heart of Christianity—that the very Word of God took flesh for our salvation." [14]

And on verse 18 the NICNT comments:

> But in reality it forms the climax to the entire Prologue, stressing as it does that Christ is in the closest possible relationship to the Father. There is also the thought that, though Moses was highly esteemed by all Jews, yet in the system he inaugurated nobody could "see" God. By contrast, Jesus Christ has revealed him...
>
> This final expression brings out the closeness of the Father and the Son. It also carries overtones of affection... [15]

We have moved from describing Jesus' relationship with God, one that illustrated both His unity and obedience to the Father, to substantiating His claim of divinity, to Jesus as the Word, "the Word was with God and the Word was God," to His incarnation and subsequent ministry. But in this we have not examined one of Christianity's greatest and primary tenets, one that stumbles Muslims greatly: the Trinity. We will discuss the Trinity in more detail in the next chapter.

## Conclusion

This chapter focused on Jesus as the Son of God and it covers a great deal of theological ground. We have addressed several critical theological themes:

1. Explain the meaning of the term "Son of God" and the "Father and Son" relationship of Jesus to God.

2. Characterize Islam's incorrect definition of the Christian theology behind Jesus as the Son of God and challenge Muslims to reconsider the biblical evidence.

3. Present Jesus as the Word of God and describe aspects of His incarnation.

In addressing these themes, we have looked to the scriptural data that describes the incarnation for a very good reason: Many Muslims have the misunderstanding that Christians believe that Jesus was only divine. So when a Muslim reads New Testament passages that describe Jesus' humanity, he thinks that such passages disproves the Christian's belief in Jesus' divinity. But Christians believe that Jesus was both human and divine, based on biblical passages that teach both. In being fair to the text of the New Testament we have to look at all the passages that describe Jesus—those that describe His humanity and those that describe His divinity. We ask ourselves what the Bible is communicating to us, and we've seen that the Bible describes Jesus as having a human nature and a divine nature.

So the question really isn't, "Does the Bible teach Jesus' divinity and humanity?" because it clearly does. The questions we have to ask ourselves are, "Does it make sense that Jesus could be both human and divine? Does it make sense that God could incarnate Himself in the person of Jesus of Nazareth?" Careful thought about these questions reveals that the answer to both of them is yes.

The Bible teaches us that Jesus was a person with two natures, one divine and the other human. There is nothing contradictory about this because the ideas of "person" and "nature" are mutually exclusive. Something's "nature" is what it is. Something's "person" is who it is.

The Muslim may offer another objection: "If Jesus is God incarnate, and He died, then didn't God also die and therefore cease to be? But God cannot die or cease to be, so this idea of incarnation does not make sense." This is not a difficult objection to answer. Spiritual entities are not limited to the physical. Rather, they are transcendent.

For example, Muslims and Christians recognize that every person has an immaterial soul. That soul is not destroyed upon the person's physical death. Rather, the soul persists. If that is true of normal humans, why would it be impossible for Jesus' divine nature to persist beyond His death? Consider this as well: Muslims believe that the Quran is the transcendent Word of God. But copies of the Quran, in paper, ink, and glue, sit on the shelves of millions of Muslim homes. If any copy of the Quran (or even all of them) were to be destroyed in a fire would the Quran cease to exist? No Muslim would believe that, because they believe that the Quran is transcendent and not limited to ink, paper, and glue. In the same way, the death of Jesus' physical body didn't result in the destruction of His transcendent, divine nature.

The theme of Jesus' sonship and divinity is complex and challenging. Perhaps its complexity reveals more about an infinite God than it does about us. The early church also wrestled with this theme and determined that this is what Jesus taught.

To sum up this chapter, we quote Ben Witherington, who in turn quotes Ray Brown:

> Yet, as Raymond Brown points out, if the question, "Are you God?" had been asked of Jesus during his lifetime, the question would have meant "Are you the Father in heaven?" not "Are you the second person of the Trinity?" Later Trinitarian

thinking cannot be read back into early Judaism. Put in those terms, Jesus' answer to the question would have been no... One must then ask questions like, What did Jesus imply when he left the suggestion that he should be seen as David's Lord? I think he implied that he should be seen not merely as a greater king than David but in a higher and more transcendent category...

Jesus knew his own identity which involved a unique relationship to God that we call the divinity of the Son. Christians of a later period were able to formulate Jesus' identity as "true God and true man," a formulation better than any other that had been attempted but certainly not exhaustive of the mystery...The idea that he was divine I find on most Gospel pages. An attempt to lessen the self-evaluation of Jesus to something like "he thought only that he was a prophet" would, in my judgment, involve proving the Gospels misunderstood Jesus. No Old Testament prophet acted in such independence of the Mosaic Law; and it is remarkable that one never finds in reference to Jesus a prophet formula such as, "The word of God came to Jesus of Nazareth."...Jesus' intuitive knowledge of his self-identity would have been a knowledge of what we call in faith being God and being man, and certainly such self-knowledge can have been no less difficult to express than our knowledge of being human. [16]

## 4

# The Trinity: Development of the Doctrine

Muslims' question:
*"I believe in only one God, not in three gods.*
*Christians seem to believe in three gods.*
*What do you mean when you say that the Father, the Son*
*(Jesus), and the Holy Spirit are one God?"*

The Christian teaching that there is one God who exists in three persons, known as "the Trinity," is one of the fundamental doctrines of the Christian faith. The doctrine of the Trinity is puzzling and difficult to understand and is often described as a "mystery." It has been analyzed, discussed, and debated for centuries. It is understandable for someone unfamiliar with Christianity to have sincere questions regarding this doctrine.

Since early Islam, Muslims have doubted and challenged the Trinity and it continues to be a contentious point in the ongoing faith-discussions between Muslims and Christians. Undergirding this problem is that Muhammad did not understand the definition of the Trinity. Muhammad seemed to believe, as the Quran states, that Christians believed in a Trinity that included Jesus, Mary, and the Father (5:119). No wonder so many Muslims consider the Trinity false! Christians just as heartily reject that view of the character of God.

Unfortunately, many Muslim writers have refused to take into account and address the actual Christian definition of Trinity. Instead they choose to attack the incorrect doctrine and declare it polytheism. Some have claimed that the original Christians believed that Jesus was only a special messenger of God and that the apostle Paul invented a falsehood that Jesus was God thereby corrupting the Christian faith. Others claim that early Christianity was led astray by Greek philosophy, and others claim that the doctrine of the Trinity was invented at the Council of Nicaea. All of those claims are incorrect and that will be proved from the historical Christian records that we will review.

Muslims and Christians agree that there is only one God and that the worship of other gods is a great sin. But coming to an understanding of Christianity's Trinity is a fearful intellectual chasm for a Muslim to cross. I (Jim Walker) have found that in most of my dialogues Muslims find it safer to deal with the incorrect definition of the Trinity than to come to grasps with understanding it to some degree.

This chapter's goal is to provide a bridge for that chasm and a basis for those who do not understand the Trinity but wish to. While it may be impossible to fully comprehend and understand God as revealed in the Bible we will see that belief in the Trinity is faithful to the Scriptures and is not illogical or unreasonable. We seek to provide sincere Muslims a basis for understanding that Christianity teaches that there is only one God and He alone deserves our worship. We intend to examine the Scriptures, show how they fit together consistently, and provide the foundation for the doctrine of the Trinity. With that goal in mind we will investigate the Trinity's historical, biblical, theological, and analogical frameworks.

Please note that many books and studies have been written by Christian scholars on the Trinity and one or two chapters here cannot do full justice to its study. However we do provide references for further study and encourage those who wish to examine this topic in more depth to do so.

## Definitions of the Trinity

The Old Testament states emphatically that there is one God (Deuteronomy 6:4). Likewise the New Testament teaches there is one God. It also makes these three points:

1. There is only one God (Mark 12:29; Romans 3:30).

2. The Father, Son, and Holy Spirit are each divine
   (1 Corinthians 8:6; Philippians 2:5-11; Acts 5:3-9).

3. The Father, Son, and Holy Spirit are distinct persons.

Integrating these points yields: *There is one God in three distinct persons, the Father, the Son, and the Holy Spirit.* The challenge is to describe and understand how these three "persons" can be of one and the same divine essence, God. Many scholars and councils have defined the Trinity in similar ways and here is one.

The *Evangelical Dictionary of Theology* defines the Trinity simply:

> Trinity. The term designating one God in three persons. Although not itself a biblical term, "the trinity" has been found a convenient designation for the one God self-revealed in Scripture as Father, Son, and Holy Spirit. It signifies that within the one essence of the Godhead we have to distinguish three "persons" who are neither three gods on the one side, not three parts or modes of God on the other, but coequally and coeternally God.[1]

We'll start with a historical review of the development of the Trinity. A review of the Scriptures that undergird the Trinity will follow. We believe it is beneficial to start with the doctrine's history because it is based upon the earliest Church Fathers' study of the Scriptures and the teachings of the apostles. This history lays the context of why and how the doctrine of the Trinity came to be established.

## Historical Development of the Doctrine of the Trinity

The development of the doctrine of the Trinity occurred over a long period of time. Christianity did not spread by the power of the sword; instead the early Christians were persecuted and oppressed, tortured and killed. It took many years for the scattered churches to determine and define the New Testament canon and develop key doctrines. During this time of oppression they continued to study what they held as Scripture and adhered to the teachings of the apostles. Church Fathers continued to develop these core doctrines, often as rebuttals to non-Christian beliefs or philosophies, as the faith matured. Early Christians did not "create" the doctrine of the Trinity. Rather, it was developed to clarify and express what the Scriptures have always taught.

First, we'll examine some of the earliest writings on the subject of the deity of Jesus which show that the early church believed in Christ's deity. As the church grew and matured she began to articulate the details of God in three persons, God the Father, God the Son, and God the Holy Spirit; one God, existing in three persons. These early Christian teachings and proclamations laid the basis for the culmination of the official doctrine of the Trinity at Nicaea in AD 325.

### The Earliest Writings

Long before the term "Trinity" came into use the earliest Christian writings show that the early Christians believed in the deity of Christ. The most ancient testimony comes from the epistles of St. Paul; *not Paul's words*, but rather the creeds, poems, or hymns he quotes. Chronologically, these precede both Paul's letters and the codification and compilation of the New Testament canon. These statements of faith often read clumsily in Greek but instead read as rhythmic poetry when back-translated into ancient Aramaic, which was the language peculiar to the original Jewish community of converts from Pentecost. Coupled with the fact that Paul quotes these to his audiences (already existing as organized churches), indicates that they were known and established in the days following Peter's first sermon. Below are two of these:

**Philippians 2:5-11:**

> In your relationships with one another, have the same mind-set as Christ Jesus:
>
> Who, being in very nature God,
>> did not consider equality with God something
>>> to be used to his own advantage;
> rather, he made himself nothing
>> by taking the very nature of a servant,
>> being made in human likeness.
> And being found in appearance as a man,
>> he humbled himself
>> by becoming obedient to death—
>>> even death on a cross!

Therefore God exalted him to the highest place
　and gave him the name that is above every name,
that at the name of Jesus every knee should bow,
　in heaven and on earth and under the earth,
and every tongue acknowledge that Jesus Christ is Lord,
　to the glory of God the Father.

The *Orthodox Study Bible* comments:

This passage is a hymn already in use in the Church, quoted here by St. Paul because it calls us to ponder the humility of Christ, a truth necessary for suffering Christians to understand and live out. The passage has been incorporated into many hymns of the Orthodox Church. Christ is He who, being in *the form of God*, is also in *the form of a bondservant*. [2]

## Colossians 1:15-20:

The Son is the image of the invisible God, the firstborn over all creation. For in him all things were created: things in heaven and on earth, visible and invisible, whether thrones or powers or rulers or authorities; all things have been created through him and for him. He is before all things, and in him all things hold together. And he is the head of the body, the church; he is the beginning and the firstborn from among the dead, so that in everything he might have the supremacy. For God was pleased to have all his fullness dwell in him, and through him to reconcile to himself all things, whether things on earth or things in heaven, by making peace through his blood, shed on the cross.

F.F. Bruce in *The New International Commentary on the New Testament* (NICNT) remarks on this passage:

These six verses are cast in a form of rhythmical prose which is found in much early Christian hymnody. The repetition of key words or phrases indicates the strophic arrangement...

To say that Christ is the image of God is to say that in him
the nature and being of God have been perfectly revealed—
that in him the invisible has become visible. "No one has ever
seen God," says the Fourth Evangelist; "the only-begotten
one, himself God, who has his being in the Father's bosom,
it is he who has declared him" (John 1:18). Later, the same
evangelist reports Christ himself as saying, "He who has seen
me has seen the Father" (John 14:9). [3]

These passages establish that the original Christians believed in the
deity of Christ long before the term "Trinity" came into use. Subsequent writings of the early Church Fathers repeat and authenticate
what these earliest of Christians believed: Jesus was God revealed in
the flesh.

Also, these passages contain a response for Muslims who decry that
the Christian God had to eat, sleep, grew tired, etc. and say, "Allah
does not need to eat and sleep," that is, Christianity's God was a weak
human. For some reason many Muslims I've dialogued with refuse
to or fail to understand the plain statements found in these passages:
Jesus, in the form of God, emptied Himself, took on a human nature,
lived as a man in that human nature, and died a man's death. This is
stated clearly throughout the Gospels and declared plainly in Philippians 2:6-11 and in 1 Timothy 3:16. If you are sincere and wish to understand the Christian doctrine of the Trinity then grasp this significant
point: *Jesus existed as God but at one point emptied Himself and lived as
a man with two natures.*

### The Writings of the Apostolic and Ante-Nicene Church Fathers

We move to the writings of the early Church Fathers. They based
their writings on what they had learned from the apostles, disciples of
the apostles, or earlier church leaders, and on what later became the
New Testament.

Even though the official doctrine of the Trinity was to come many
years later, their writings show that they believed in the deity of Christ
and of the Holy Spirit. Of that, there is no doubt. And they believed

that Jesus, the Holy Spirit, and the Father were distinct persons. During this pre-Nicaea period these writings laid a solid foundation for the development of the doctrine of the Trinity.

Kelly states that the foundation for the Trinity was being established prior to the definition of the New Testament canon:

> Before considering formal writers, the reader should notice how deeply the conception of a plurality of divine Persons was imprinted on the apostolic tradition and the popular faith. Though as yet un-canonized, the New Testament was already exerting a powerful influence; it is a commonplace that the outlines of a dyadic and a triadic pattern are clearly visible in its pages. It is even more marked in such glimpses as are obtainable of the Church's liturgy and day-to-day catechetical practice. [4]

During this time there were many theological controversies and challenges from within and without. Meeting these challenges, correcting false teachings, refuting paganism and Gnosticism, and establishing the church were the primary focal points of the church leaders. Kelly states:

> The third century saw the emergence of conflicting tendencies in Trinitarian thought which were to provide the material for later controversies. Hitherto the overriding preoccupation of Christian theism had been with the unity of God; the struggle with paganism and Gnosticism thrust this article well into the foreground. As a result, while theologians were obscurely aware of distinctions within the one indivisible Godhead…they showed little disposition to explore the eternal relations of the Three, much less to construct a conceptual and linguistic apparatus capable of expressing them. [5]

Roger Olson writes in "The Trinity":

> The early church fathers of the second through the fourth centuries realized this gradually as they encountered opponents

of Christianity such as the anti-Christian orator Celsus. They found it necessary to invent terms such as trinitas (trinity) and homoousios (of the same substances) to describe the relationship between the father and his son—the Logos (Word) when confronted with heretics who denied the deity of Jesus Christ and the personhood of the Holy Spirit. Heresy is the mother of orthodoxy. The doctrine of the trinity developed gradually after the completion of the New Testament in the heat of controversy, but the church fathers who developed it believed that they were simply exegeting divine revelation and not at all speculating or inventing new ideas. [6]

The early Church Fathers studied the Scriptures and based their work upon what the Scriptures taught and from what they had learned from earlier Christians. Based upon that they declared Jesus to be divine, the Son of God, God revealed in the flesh.

One of the most comprehensive Protestant works on the Trinity is "The Holy Trinity" by Robert Letham. He comments on the second-century Christian scholars:

> In the second century, the apologists (Justin, Tatian, Athenagoras, Theophilus of Antioch) began to explore the relation of the pre-existent Christ to the Father...Two things were stressed—his eternal oneness with the Father, as the Word immanent in God, and also his appearance in human history, as the Word emitted or expressed... [7]

Over time they began to develop a theological response to how the Father, Son, and Holy Spirit could each be God as an individual person and yet constitute one God, not three distinct Gods. Approximately 100 years before the Council of Nicaea, Tertullian, an ante-Nicene (before the council of Nicaea) Church Father, is credited as the first to use the term "Trinity" in describing God. Below is a small selection of quotes and excerpts from their writings.

**Ignatius of Antioch (c. AD 50–117).** Ignatius was an apostolic Father. It is believed that he was appointed by the apostle Peter to be the bishop of Antioch, and that he, like Polycarp, was a disciple of the apostle John. In many of his letters he referred to Jesus as "God."

> To the Church at Ephesus in Asia…chosen through true suffering by the will of the Father in Jesus Christ our God (Letter to the Ephesians 1 [AD 110]). [8]

> For our God, Jesus Christ, was conceived by Mary in accord with God's plan: of the seed of David, it is true, but also of the Holy Spirit. [9]

In *Early Christian Doctrines*, J. Kelly comments on Ignatius's writings:

> Further, the triadic formula occurs thrice at least in his letters…Much more frequently, however, he speaks of God the Father and Jesus Christ, declaring that "there is one God, Who has revealed Himself through His Son Jesus Christ, Who is His Word emerging from silence."…Ignatius even declares that He is "our God," describing Him as "God incarnate" and "God made manifest as man." He was "in spirit united with the Father." In His preexistent being "ingenerate"—(the technical term reserved to distinguish the increate God from creatures), He was the timeless, invisible, impalpable, impassible one Who for our sakes entered time and became visible, palpable and passable. [10]

**Justin Martyr (c. AD 100–165).** Justin Martyr was a prominent teacher and apologist for the faith. He founded a school in Rome and challenged opponents of Christianity be they pagan or Jewish.

> We will prove that we worship him reasonably; for we have learned that he is the Son of the true God himself, that he holds a second place, and the Spirit of prophecy a third. For this they accuse us of madness, saying that we attribute to a crucified man a place second to the unchangeable and eternal God, the Creator of all things; but they are ignorant of the mystery which lies therein (First Apology 13:5-6 [AD 151]). [11]

Kelly quotes parts of Justin's work:

So the Logos, "having been put forth as an offspring from the Father, was with Him before all creatures, and the Father had converse with Him." And He is divine: "being Word and first-begotten of God, He is also God." "Thus, then, He is adorable, He is God."[12]

**Irenaeus (c. AD 115–202).** Irenaeus was an early Church Father and bishop of Lyons, France. It is believed that he sat under Polycarp. He wrote many documents establishing and defending the Christian faith.

For the Church, although dispersed throughout the whole world even to the ends of the earth, has received from the apostles and from their disciples the faith in one God, the Father Almighty...and in one Jesus Christ, the Son of God, who became flesh for our salvation; and in the Holy Spirit (Against Heresies 1:10:1 [AD 189]).[13]

Speaking of Irenaeus's writings Kelly quotes and comments:

Naturally the Son is fully divine; "the father is God, and the Son is God, for whatever is begotten of God is God." The Spirit, too, although Irenaeus nowhere expressly designates Him God, clearly ranked as divine in his eyes, for He was God's Spirit, ever welling up from His being. Thus we have Irenaeus' vision of the Godhead, the most complete, and also most explicitly Trinitarian, to be met with before Tertullian.[14]

**Tertullian (c. AD 160–220).** Tertullian was an early Church Father who is credited with using the term "Trinity" ("trinitas") when writing about the nature or character of God. He wrote an entire book, *Against Praxeas,* defending the theology of the Trinity.

Kelly writes of Tertullian:

Like Hippolytus, he argued that, though three, the Persons were severally manifestations of a single indivisible power, noting that on the analogy of the imperial government one and the same sovereignty could be exercised by coordinate agencies…His characteristic way of expressing this was to state that Father, Son and Spirit are one in "substance." Thus Father and Son are one identical substance which has been, not divided, but "extended" the Saviour's claim, "I and my Father are one" indicated the Three are "one reality," not "one Person," pointing as it does to identity of substance, not mere numerical unity.[15]

As a general summary, Kelly states the position of three of the ante-Nicene Fathers:

> Hippolytus and Tertullian were at one with Irenaeus in regarding the Three revealed in the economy as manifestations of the plurality which they apprehended, however obscurely, in the immanent life of the Godhead.[16]

The early church worshipped Jesus as God. That distinguished them. Paralleling Kelly's comment Letham comments:

> The early church was characterized by the way it regarded Jesus Christ. In the NT, he is given the devotional attention reserved in the OT for Yahweh alone. However, in no sense did the church see this as conflicting with OT worship. Nor was it thought of as in any sense polytheistic. The church understood its worship of Jesus as within the boundaries of OT monotheism. This worship began at a very early stage of the church's existence.[17]

The writings of the ante-Nicene Church Fathers show that they believed in the unity within the Godhead and the divinity of Christ and of the Holy Spirit. They continued to build upon what the earliest Christians believed. However, even though the early Church Fathers believed in the principles of the Trinity and the term "Trinity" came into use there was still no formal church-established doctrine of the Trinity.

## The Council of Nicaea

Through time, the early church dealt successively with various theological challenges. Eventually the doctrines defining the relationship between the Father, Son, and Holy Spirit came to the forefront. The theological differences within the church became more pronounced and caused division. Schaff states:

> The theology of the second and third centuries was mainly apologetic against the paganism of Greece and Rome, and polemic against the various forms of Gnostic heresy. In this conflict it brings out, with great force and freshness the principal arguments for the divine origin and character of the Christian religion and the outlines of the true doctrine of Christ and the holy trinity, as afterwards more fully developed in the Nicene and post-Nicene ages. [18]

By this time Christianity had spread widely and church problems began to become political problems. These harsh doctrinal divisions within the church began to affect the empire. They needed to be settled and an official position established. Unity needed to be restored. The Christian Roman emperor, Constantine, called an official church council, held in Nicaea, in Bithynia (now in modern-day Turkey). The "Council of Nicaea" was held to address the Trinity and other key topics of the day.

The *Orthodox Study Bible* summarizes the situation:

> Then, in the early fourth century, a heresy with potential for Church-wide disruption appeared, propagated by one Arius, a presbyter in Alexandria, Egypt. He denied the eternality of the Son of God, claiming contrary to the apostles' doctrine that the Son was a created being who came into existence at a point in time and thus was not truly God. This deadly error struck the Church like a cancer. Turmoil spread almost everywhere. The first Church-wide, or Ecumenical, Council met in Nicea in AD 325 to address this issue. Some 318 bishops, along with many priests, deacons and laymen rejected the

new teaching of Arius and his associates, upholding the apostles' doctrine of Christ, affirming the eternality of the Son and His consubstantiality with the Father. Their proclamation of the Apostolic teaching concerning Christ included a creed, which, with the additions concerning the Holy Spirit made in 381 at the Council of Constantinople, forms the document we today call the Nicene Creed. [19]

Although the Council of Nicaea established the doctrine of the Trinity for the church, the dispute, sometimes violent, about the nature of God continued for hundreds of years. Various Christian realms held to non-Trinitarian views for hundreds of years following Nicaea. However, the church did establish the doctrine of the Trinity, based upon Scripture and the writings of the early Church Fathers. This was one of the defining moments of Christianity. It was not easily achieved but it was built upon a solid foundation; it was built upon the only substantial evidence available. No other logical, comprehensive, or consistent conclusion could be drawn.

## Conclusion

We have reviewed the early history of the doctrine of the Trinity and have shown how the earliest Christians believed that Jesus was divine, how the ante-Nicene Church Fathers taught Jesus' deity, and how the Council of Nicaea established what the early church already believed: one God in three persons, the Father, the Son, and the Holy Spirit.

What we hope we have made clear is that the concept of three persons, yet one God, was basic to the earliest believers' faith. The early Christian disciples realized this after their experience with the life, death, and resurrection of Jesus. That they so quickly began to be persecuted and yet stood firmly in the faith can only persuade us that they embraced Jesus as God. Note that this is why the Jewish leadership wanted to kill Jesus (John 8:59; 10:31).

The disciples of Jesus, Jews fully devoted to "One God" theology, experienced in their relationship with Jesus a revelation of the "Emmanuel, God with us," as spoken in the Old Testament by the prophet Isaiah (7:14). This is why Letham states that the early Christians (many were Jewish converts) worshipped Jesus without any concern that they were committing idolatry or worshipping a false God: They knew that God had been, and still was, with them.

# The Trinity: Foundation from the Bible

There are many verses in the Bible that point to or declare the deity of Christ and of the Holy Spirit. There are many excellent books and Internet articles that detail and discuss these. We can only examine a limited number of these verses. When the many verses are taken as a whole and weighed together, they establish the deity of Christ and of the Holy Spirit. This is exactly what the early Church Fathers learned from the apostles and their study of sacred text and Scripture.

## New Testament Verses Supporting the Deity of Christ and the Trinity

Below is a selection of passages from the New Testament, along with scholarly analyses. At the end of this chapter will be a listing of additional "Trinity-verses" from both the New and Old Testaments. Please read the referenced verses (not quoted here) along with the commentary.

**John 1:1-3.** Morris, in *The New International Commentary on the New Testament* (NICNT) on John 1:1, writes:

> There never was a time when the Word was not. There never was a thing that did not depend on him for its existence… John is affirming that the Word existed before creation, which makes it clear that the Word was not created.
>
> …John thinks of the Word as coming to earth in the person of Jesus of Nazareth (v. 14). At the same time he partakes of the innermost being of God, for "the Word was God."

...Now he goes on to the Word's personal character in relation to the Father. Not only did the Word exist "in the beginning," but he existed in the closest possible connection with the Father. The expression does not differentiate between the two. Perhaps John is by implication refuting any idea that the Word is an emanation from God, quite distinct from the Godhead. The Word and God are not identical, but they are one.

The high point is reached in the third affirmation: "the Word was God." Nothing higher could be said: all that may be said about God may fitly be said about the Word...John is not merely saying that there is something divine about Jesus. He is affirming that he is God, and doing so emphatically as we see from the word order in the Greek.

We should perhaps notice that John refers to Jesus as God again in verse 18 and in 20:28. If the present passage refers to Jesus in his pre-incarnate state as God, verse 18 takes up the thought for the incarnate Word and 20:28 for the risen Christ. John thus asserts the deity of his Lord at three very important places in his narrative.[1]

**Philippians 2:5-8.** *The Expositor's Bible Commentary's* comments on 2:6 (CD-ROM):

> Christ's preincarnate status is then stated. Two assertions are made: He existed in the form of God and he did not regard his existing in a manner of equality with God as a prize to be grasped or held onto. "Being in very nature God" is, literally, "existing in the form of God." The term morphe denotes the outward manifestation that corresponds to the essence, in contrast to the noun schema (2:7), which refers to the outward appearance, which may be temporary.[2]

**Colossians 2:9.** *The Expositor's Bible Commentary's* comments on 2:9 (CD-ROM):

> Nearly every word in this statement is significant. "For," linking this and the following verses to v. 8, shows that the

warning there rests on what is said here about Christ and his fullness. The phrase "in Christ" (see comment at 1:2), by its position within the sentence, is emphatic, the thought being that in Christ alone the fullness of deity dwells. "Lives" (lit., "dwells") translates katoikei, a verb that suggests taking up permanent residence. The tense is present, stating a general truth and denoting continuous action. The full thought, then, is that in Christ the fullness of deity permanently resides, finding in him "a settled and congenial home" (H.C.G. Moule, p. 144). The context suggests that the primary reference is to Christ in his present glorified state. As Robertson puts it, "The fullness of the Godhead...dwells 'in the once mortal, now glorified body of Christ' (Ellicott), now 'the body of his glory' (Philippians 3:21)" (p. 81).

"Fullness" translates pleroma, a word used earlier in 1:19 (see comment there). Here it is defined by the addition of tes theotetos ("of the Deity"). The word theotetos is found only here in the NT, though a similar but weaker word (theiotes, denoting divine nature) is found in Romans 1:20. Theotetos is an abstract term, meaning not just divine qualities and attributes but the very essence of God—"the whole glorious total of what God is, the supreme Nature in its infinite entirety" (H.C.G. Moule, p. 144). [3]

**Hebrews 1:1-14.** F.F. Bruce comments on Hebrews 1:5-14:

In these ten verses our author adduces seven Old Testament passages to corroborate his argument that the Son of God is superior to the angels...

He is the very image of the essence of God—the impress of his being. Just as the image and superscription on a coin exactly correspond to the device on the die, so the Son of God "bears the very stamp of his nature" (RSV). The Greek word character, occurring here only in the New Testament, expresses this truth even more emphatically than eikon, which is used elsewhere to denote Christ as the "image" of God (2 Corinthians 4:4; Col. 1:15). Just as the glory is really in the effulgence, so the being (Gk. hypostasis) of God is really in Christ, who is its impress, its exact representation and embodiment. What God essentially is, is made manifest in Christ. To see Christ is to see what the Father is like...

And now at length the Messiah had appeared. In a fuller sense than was possible for David or any of his successors in the ancient days, this Messiah can be addressed not merely as God's Son (v. 5) but actually as God, for he is both the Messiah of David's line and also the effulgence of God's glory and the very image of his being. [4]

This is just a sampling of the many Scriptures that refer to Jesus' deity and at the end of this chapter we provide more. There are many books and websites that reference far more Scriptures, and go into far more detail than we can here. However, they establish that Jesus is the Son of God, God revealed in human form, the Word made flesh. He who has seen Jesus has seen the Father.

## Old Testament–New Testament Correlations

There are several examples of New Testament events which set forth Jesus' divinity by tying themselves to Old Testament statements and events. The Old Testament does not formally teach the Trinity but as we look back through the lens of the New Testament we see that the triune God was present all along. Here are two examples.

*Daniel 7:13,14,28 coupled with Matthew 26:62-66 and Revelation 1:7-8.* We mentioned this correlation earlier. Jesus identified the Daniel passage with Himself while He was on trial. Later John ties "He who comes with the clouds" as the "Alpha and Omega, the Lord God Almighty" (see 1:8; 21:6; 22:13; Revelation 3:11; 22:7,12,20).

*Isaiah 6:1-5 and Isaiah 42:8, coupled with John 12:41, John 17:5, and Revelation 4:2-3.* Isaiah writes in 6:1 that he saw the Lord Almighty on His throne in His glory. In Isaiah 42:8 Isaiah records the Lord God saying no one shares in His glory or praise. John states that Isaiah saw Jesus' glory and spoke about Him! Later John records Jesus' prayer in which Jesus states His glory with the Father before the world began!

This is summed up in John's vision in Revelation 4:2-11 of God on the throne in glory.

Who did Isaiah see in glory? Jesus. Who did John see in glory? Jesus. Jesus asked God to glorify Him, but God does not share His glory with a lesser being. Would Jesus pray an arrogant, idolatrous prayer? Would Jesus lie and claim God's glory for Himself if it were not His? Of course not. Jesus is the Lamb of God on the throne (Revelation 7:17; 22:3), the Son of God, the Almighty, the Creator.

There are more Old Testament–New Testament scriptural tie-ins in the Bible but these two suffice to show us Jesus' identity.

## The Names and Characteristics of Deity

There is another method that can be used to prove Christ's divinity. In the Old Testament, God is called or identified by a number of names that are usually only reserved for God. Many of us who have read and studied both the Old and New Testaments are aware of some instances where Jesus and the Holy Spirit are identified by those very names. As mentioned earlier, that is one fact that led Neusner to confront what Jesus had done. Jesus dared to accept praise and stature that was reserved for God alone!

Many people have passed off those shared names as simple titles of honor. Those that reject the Trinity deny that deity is behind those names. But when one makes a deeper, more thorough examination of those shared names, the evidence is overwhelming and the critic's casual throw-off remark does not bear this weight. We're going to take a look at the use and context of these shared names.

In his book *The Trinity*, Edward H. Bickersteth catalogues these uses of shared names. He lays down his first assertion and states five categories of proof:

> That Scripture, in the Old and the New Testament alike, proves the co-equal deity of Jesus Christ with that of the eternal Father.
>
> 1. by a comparison of the attributes, the majesty, and the claims of the Father and the Son;

2. by the appearances of God to the Old Testament saints;

3. by the direct and Divine worship paid to Christ;

4. by the conjunction of the Father and the Son in Divine offices:

5. by explicit assertions that Christ is Jehovah and God.

For just as in algebra, from the combination of two known quantities the unknown is found out; as in trigonometry, if out of the six parts of a triangle any three, one being a side, are given, the other are discoverable, from which simple law have resulted all the triumphs of astronomy; so, in searching the Scriptures, those humble students, who prayerfully compare and combine them, shall know "the things that are freely given to us of God." [5]

Bickersteth shows that Jesus and God share many divine titles and attributes such as being "everlasting," "the first and the last," "Almighty," "the Holy One," and being there and creating "in the beginning." Bickersteth concludes this section with several statements:

Here Scripture asserts, that the Father is eternal, and the Son eternal. Now One, who is from everlasting, must needs be God. But there are not two Gods. Therefore the Son is one with God, and is God.

In like manner Scripture asserts that the Son, equally with the Father, is the first and the last; is omnipresent, immutable, almighty; is incomprehensible, absolutely holy, indefectible; is the Creator, preserver, and Governor of all things in heaven and earth; is the Searcher of all hearts, the final Judge, and the Awarder of everlasting life and death. Now One, possessing such properties and fulfilling such offices, must needs be God. But there are not two Gods. Therefore the Son is one with God, and is God. [6]

Bickersteth proceeds through the cases to show how God in the

Old Testament and Jesus in the New are identified and treated in identical ways (such as both receiving worship).

Bickersteth goes into great detail and proves repeatedly that Jesus' disciples and many non-disciples, originally all Jews, gave Jesus the same titles they gave to Jehovah, YHWH of the Old Testament. They would not so easily taint and corrupt their faith in the all-powerful God by ascribing His name, His character, His being, with a mere man, a mere teacher, a mere prophet. No! They understood who God was and they understood what they were doing when they gave to Jesus God's names, titles, and character. They knew that Jesus was God revealed in the flesh, who existed with the Father and Holy Spirit, but emptied Himself and came as a man, but who now sits on the throne at the right hand of the Father.

## Verses Supporting the Deity of the Holy Spirit

Throughout the Bible, the Holy Spirit is identified as the Spirit of God, the Spirit, the Spirit of Jesus, the Spirit of Christ, the Spirit of Truth, the Counselor, and so on. The arguments made for Christ's divinity can also be made for the Holy Spirit. Throughout the Old and New Testaments the Holy Spirit is tied to God, associated with God, and named as God. In fact, Jesus was conceived by the Holy Spirit!

We will not delve deeply into this but the Scriptures ascribe to the Holy Spirit the same names and characteristics as God. For example, He is omnipresent, powerful, and eternal. The Holy Spirit speaks, comforts, and leads. He is holy, joins us to Christ, and gives us life. The Holy Spirit can be grieved, lied to, and blasphemed. The Holy Spirit can send people out, and keep people from going.

The Holy Spirit has all the attributes of an eternal "person," that is, God. The Holy Spirit is not a mystical force—He is the third person of the Trinity. Letham comments on the New Testament's portrayal of the Holy Spirit:

> Due to the invisibility and anonymity of the Spirit, his presence is not normally noted, even though it may be known that he is present. His presence is known by what he does…

The NT, while never explicitly calling the Holy Spirit "God," ascribes to him divine characteristics. Among other things, fellowship with one another, and with the Father and the Son, is by the Holy Spirit. The Spirit sanctifies, gives joy in sufferings, opens people's minds to believe, enables us to worship, and brings about union with Christ...

His divine status becomes clearer when we examine Jesus' teaching in John 14-16 on the coming of the Holy Spirit at Pentecost, where he links the Spirit expressly with the Father and the Son, entailing identity of status and consequently of being. Here he calls the Spirit "another paracletos" (John 14:16)—another like himself. [7]

For reference, two Scriptures that point to the deity of the Holy Spirit are Acts 16:6-7 and 1 Corinthians 2:10,11.

As a summary on the divinity of the Holy Spirit, Letham writes:

The Holy Spirit is prominent in John, and is clearly distinct from the Father and the Son, especially in the Paraclete saying in chapters 14-16. True worship is to be directed to the Father in Jesus, the truth, by the Spirit...

In summary, the Father loves the Son, sends the Son, and glorifies the Son. He also sends the Holy Spirit in Jesus' name, in response to his request, and is worshiped in the Son and in the Spirit...

The three work together in harmony. Through the Holy Spirit, they come together to the disciples, who as a consequence live in the Father and in the Son. [8]

## Discussion

We have reviewed the historical development of the Trinity and the scriptural base upon which it stands and shown that this doctrine's foundation is established firmly upon Scripture and the beliefs and teachings of the earliest Christians. Its development was not spurious, not random, not haphazard. Rather, it was coherent, methodical, and judicious. The doctrine of the Trinity is the only logical and consistent conclusion that could be drawn when the composite teaching of Scripture is analyzed. But proving that the Trinity is based upon a firm foundation is not the same thing as fully understanding it. The "three persons but one essence" is foreign to our thinking.

Let's now move into framing the Trinity in simple ways to help us understand it better. We don't think we will ever comprehend it completely, but we should be able to grasp some of the meaning behind the word "Trinity" and understand God better. As Francis Schaeffer said,

> We do not need to have exhaustive knowledge of a thing in order to know truly, as long as it is there, I am there, and we have sufficient correlation together. [9]

Let's begin with the Westminster Confession, which gives us a more modern definition of the Trinity:

> In the unity of the Godhead, there be three persons, of one substance, power, and eternity: God the Father, God the Son, and God the Holy Ghost: the Father is of none, neither begotten, nor proceeding; the Son is eternally begotten of the Father; the Holy Ghost eternally proceeding from the Father and the Son.

This is an excellent place to start when trying to grasp the concept of the Trinity. Each person of the Trinity is equal in essence, but different in function. The Father sent the Son to reconcile sinful man to a holy God. Scripture states that, "There is one God, and one mediator between God and mankind, the man Christ Jesus" (1 Timothy 2:5). Meanwhile, the Son has sent the Spirit to be the helper and counselor of those that have been reconciled to God. Jesus told the disciples, "When the Advocate comes, whom I will send to you from the Father—the Spirit of truth who goes out from the Father—he will testify about me" (John 15:26).

Another way to approach understanding the Trinity is to look at the law of noncontradiction. This law simply states that A cannot be both

A and not A at the same time in the same sense. As the Persian Muslim philosopher Avicenna (Ibn Sina) so eloquently and wittily put it, "Anyone who denies the law of non-contradiction should be beaten and burned until he admits that to be beaten is not the same as not to be beaten, and to be burned is not the same as not to be burned."

If we were to define the Trinity as "one God and three Gods" that would be a contradiction. Or if we were to define the Trinity as "one nature and three natures," that would also be a contradiction. We are not saying either of these things at all. There is one God in His nature and He exists as three persons. This is a totally different statement. Though it may be hard for the human mind to comprehend it is not a logical contradiction and cannot be discarded as such. For just as the Quran presents contrasting statements on specific topics, such as violence (10:99 vs. 9:5), the Bible presents contrasting statements about God. Contrasting does not mean contradictory.

Like the doctrine of the incarnation, the Trinity is quite difficult to understand. However, that does not make it false. After all, we are exploring the nature and characteristics of an infinite, transcendent God. It seems quite expected that such a God would be beyond our total comprehension yet be logically coherent. In fact, if God were easy to understand in His very being, if He were one in nature and one in person just like human beings are, we would rightly begin to suspect that maybe we conceived of God so that we can understand Him instead of taking Him as He revealed Himself.

The Bible presents two contrasting points about God: 1) There is only one God, one divine essence, and 2) there is a plurality of persons within this divine essence. (As a friend stated: "We can understand this as "what" God is, is singular, but "who" God is, is plural.") Our choice is to either take both of these truths and understand them in a valid, logically consistent way, or accept one truth and minimize and reject the other. In early Christian history those that accepted the Trinity accepted the full claim of both truths, while the "Modalists" and "Monarchianists" accepted only one truth at the expense of the other. More on them later.

## Analogies for the Trinity

Aside from the straightforward academic presentation of the Trinity we can use analogies because they depict truths or similarities from one topic and enable us to see them in our focus topic. But note that analogies have their limitations and cannot be 100 percent effective when trying to explain an attribute of an eternal, "three persons in one being" God. Each analogy can be used to illustrate a specific point perhaps, but it cannot account for every aspect of the Trinity. All analogies fall short in some way or another. As Berkhof states:

> Various analogies suggested to shed light on the subject. From the very earliest time of the Christian era attempts were made to shed light on the Trinitarian Being of God, on the trinity in unity and the unity in trinity, by analogies drawn from several sources. While these are all defective it cannot be denied that they were of some value in the Trinitarian discussion. [10]

Here are some useful analogies.

**Water, ice, steam.** Each of these consists of, and is fully, the same substance, $H_2O$, but each has individual characteristics. These exist as liquid, solid, and gas. A person who was unfamiliar with all three chemical states of $H_2O$ would probably not believe you if you told them "all of these are the same essence." He would probably believe you once you explained and demonstrated this to him. Likewise, each person of the Trinity is fully God, but each is a different person.

**Space-dimensional.** Another way to approach this understanding is to view it from the perspective of spatial dimensions. Space is referenced by the first dimension—simple distance. All of space is seen by mankind in the second dimension, as in the two-dimensional area of a photograph. Finally though, we each experience space in the third and final dimension. All dimensions exist simultaneously, each is real, each is distinct, each is part of a whole—dimension.

C.S. Lewis uses this analogy in *Mere Christianity*:

A world of one dimension would be a straight line. In a two-dimensional world, you still get straight lines, but many lines make one figure. In a three dimensional world, you still get figures but many figures make one solid body. In other words, as you advance to more real and more complicated levels, you do not leave behind you the thing you found on the simpler levels: you still have them, but combined in new ways—in ways you could not imagine if you knew only the simpler levels.

Now the Christian account of God involves just the same principle. The human level is a simple and rather empty level. On the human level one person is one being, and any two persons are two separate beings—just as, in two dimensions (say a flat sheet of paper) one square is one figure, and any two squares are two separate figures. On the Divine level you still find personalities; but up there you find them combined in new ways which we, who do not live on that level, cannot imagine. In God's dimension, so to speak, you find a being who is three Persons while remaining one Being, just as a cube is six squares while remaining one cube. Of course we cannot fully conceive a Being like that: just as, if we were so made that we perceived only two dimensions in space we could never properly imagine a cube. But we can get a sort of faint notion of it. And when we do, we are then, for the first time in our lives, getting some positive idea, however faint, of something super-personal—something more than a person. It is something we could never have guessed, and yet, once we have been told, one almost feels one ought to have been able to guess it because it fits in so well with all the things we know already. [11]

These analogies provide different ways to understand facets of the Trinity. Of course, no analogy can fully define the biblical Trinity. Each analogy has limitations but they can serve to open our mind to understanding from a different perspective.

## The Incomprehensible Nature of the Triune God

Everyone agrees that understanding the Trinity comprehensively is challenging. But being challenging does not make it untrue or illogical. Throughout history people have had, and still do have, trouble understanding the physics of the universe, the biology of life, and the complexity of the mind. Do we then claim to be able to comprehend an eternal God, creator of all of those things we cannot understand? Glenn Miller of www.christian-thinktank.com has this to say about the challenge of understanding the Trinity comprehensively:

> And, to be QUITE FRANK, I would expect a "God" to be a bit more complex than everything He created! I would expect SOME overlap, perhaps, say in the notion of "personality" but for me to say that God COULD NOT have three interior Persons would be VERY intellectually presumptuous (especially for a mortal creature of only 5'10"!). To say that a God who could speak a universe into existence HAS TO BE no more complex in His nature than humans are would be GROUNDLESS speculation of the most ludicrous sort! I think Feuerbach would call it "making God in OUR image"![12]

Only God can know Himself comprehensively. Further, John Gilchrist believes that the complexity of the Trinity is a positive aspect of the discussion and quotes a Muslim writer in support:

> Another favorite argument against the Trinity found in Muslim writings is that it appears ultimately to be incomprehensible and is therefore "opposed to reason" (Mohammed Sadiq, quoted in "A Moslem on the Trinity," *The Muslim World*, vol. 10, p. 410). The Christian defense that the doctrine is vested in a mystery appears to be a clear proof of its untenable nature.
>
> Not so at all. The doctrine is not contrary to reason, it is simply above the realms of finite human reasoning. A Muslim writer wisely says:

Almighty God is much dissimilar to His creatures, and
Deity is much more sublime than simple minds can imagine (Afif Tabbarah, *The Spirit of Islam*, p. 71).

If so, why should the incomprehensible nature and mystery
of the Triune God be seen as an argument against its reality? Once it is conceded that God's character and nature are
above human understanding, surely one should expect to
find that the full revelation of his being and personality will
baffle the power of the human intellect to comprehend him.
Islam's argument that its concept of God's unity must be pre-
ferred over ours because it is simpler and more amenable to
human understanding seems to us to be a very good reason
to reject it. The issue is not whether a doctrine can be reduced
to terms relative to human understanding before it can be
accepted, it is simply whether it is true or not. [13]

## Errors to the Left, Errors to the Right

Earlier we mentioned two common errors when thinking about
the triune God: modalism and monarchianism. These two doctrines
were argued and dealt with by the early church, yet they continue to
be argued today!

Modalism is the belief that there is one person—God, who repre-
sents Himself in three forms. This would be akin to one person who
performs three roles as husband, father, and teacher (remember, the
Trinitarian view is three persons who are each divine). In the pre-
Nicene period, a priest named Sabellius championed this belief, hence
modalism is also called "Sabellianism." God appears as the Father, or
as the Son, or as the Holy Spirit. There is no real personal distinction
between the Father, Son, or Holy Spirit; they are just manifestations,
or modes of one essence: God.

Monarchianism is the belief that only the Father is God, Jesus was
only a great man, and the Holy Spirit is not a "person" but only a force
or presence of God. An early champion of this doctrine was Paul of
Samosata, who was a bishop of Antioch (not to be confused with the
apostle Paul). He was removed from his official ministry in 269 by a

gathering of Antioch church leaders who rejected his teachings. Arius's doctrine, "Arianism," which precipitated the Council of Nicaea, is a variant of monarchianism. Today, Jehovah's Witnesses and Unitarians believe a form of monarchianism. Another variant within monarchianism is the "adoptionist" belief that after Jesus proved Himself He was granted supernatural powers.

The New Testament states clearly that belief in Jesus as the Son of God is a requirement. This means a belief that Jesus was with the Father in the beginning, was involved in creation, was before Abraham, was "I am," sits at the right hand of the Father, and will be the final judge of mankind. Any other "Jesus" is not Christianity's Jesus. But modalism and monarchianism do not allow this.

## Why Does It Matter Whether or Not I Believe in the Trinity?

The early church took doctrine seriously. These Christians were often paying for their faith with their own blood. They wanted to know God intimately and understand Him accurately. They studied the teachings of the early Church Fathers and Scriptures in earnest because they wanted to get it right. However, some people have asked questions like, "Does it really matter if I believe in the Trinity? It is very confusing and does not make sense. After all, that term isn't even in the Bible!"

What is at stake is remaining true to the idea that God is unchanging through eternity and that He has revealed the truth about Himself through His Son, Jesus, and through the Scriptures. The Christians who debated, argued, and fought for this definition of God understood that if worshipping a false God is a punishable sin then it behooved them to get it right. This had eternal consequences for all men. Of all things, they needed to understand and present God accurately. The early Christians worshipped Jesus as they worshipped God and the Scriptures define Jesus to be the Son of God. There could be no compromise about this truth. Either Jesus was who He claimed to be, or He was a great teacher, a great miracle worker, but also a liar and false prophet as well. No! The early Christians had to be accurate as they strove to know and understand God.

Fortunately today all of the major Christian denominations teach the Trinity as one of their basic doctrines. Why? Because they understand its importance. Even recent church leader Bert Waggoner, the current leader of the Vineyard church denomination, addresses the question.

> There has been a renewed focus on the trinity, and understanding it has great significance for what we do socially and in community. As evangelicals, we have come through a long period of "Christ-alone-ism," where everything was simply Christ. Then along came the charismatic renewal, with a pneumatic focus on the Holy Spirit. I believe that if we are going to be a mature movement, we need to be characterized by a whole expression of the trinity, working out the nuances of what that means for us as the people of God.[14]

Waggoner understands the importance of the Trinity in a Christian's life and theology. Accepting or rejecting the Trinity matters because we want to have correct doctrine, we want to walk in truth. It matters because if we are serious about our faith we need to understand what the Bible teaches. It matters because an aspect of the Trinity is related to our salvation.

## Conclusion

This chapter's goal was to provide a firm basis for believing in and understanding the Trinity. To that end we've presented a summary of the historical development of the doctrine of the Trinity and shown that this doctrine is rooted in Scripture, the beliefs of the earliest Christians, and the teachings of the early Church Fathers. We've provided the scriptural basis for this doctrine and shown that the doctrine of the Trinity is integral to the Scripture's teaching about God. We've discussed aspects of the Trinity and offered some analogies to help understand some intricate aspects.

We've seen that as the early Christians learned from the apostles and later studied the New Testament writings, they realized that Jesus was fully God but that He was not the Father. Likewise this study extended to the Holy Spirit. This belief was manifest in their writings and worship service. The Father is God, the Son is God, the Holy Spirit is God. The doctrine of the Trinity was formed upon revelation from God and it is a logical construct. The early church did not invent the doctrine of the Trinity, rather it took what the Scriptures taught and formulated the doctrine. The Council of Nicaea did not invent the doctrine, rather it established what the church leadership believed and taught. Just as Christians are "monotheists" (a word also not found in the Bible), so too they believe in the Godhead: the Trinity. The doctrine of the Trinity is hard to conceive of and understand but it is the only doctrine that can be derived logically and consistently from the Scriptures.

We end this chapter with a quote from Robert Letham:

> The mission of the church to spread the gospel also requires the practice of love, of self-effacement, of looking to the interests of others. Without it, our preaching will be undermined. With it, it is reinforced...Especially in the context of engagement with Muslims, the love paradigm of Richard of St. Victor is pertinent, provided it is biblically based, rather than forged out of Richard's rationalism...*Notwithstanding, it is precisely with the question of love that the Islamic doctrine of Allah founders, and, with it, the Islamic doctrine of humanity.*[15]

**For further study: verses that substantiate the Trinity**

Genesis 1:26; 11:7; 2 Samuel 23:2-3; Isaiah 9:6; 34:16; 48:12-13; 63:10; John 5:18; 8:58; 10:30; 14:16-17; Acts 5:3-4; 8:29; 13:1-3; 20:28; Romans 9:5; Colossians 1:15-20; Titus 2:13; Hebrews 9:14; 2 Peter 1:1; 1 John 5:20

# The Gospel and the Atonement

Muslims' question:
*"Why would God dishonor His Son and let Him die such a horrible, humiliating, unjust death for someone else's sins?"*

This question is answered by Isaiah 53:1-12, a prophecy about Jesus. He took our infirmities, was crucified, bore our iniquities and sins, and He would rise again and rule in eternal life. This is what the Gospel defines as the "good news." It is the essence of the Christian message.

Both Christianity and Islam agree that Jesus ministered the Gospel. As mentioned in an earlier chapter, the Quran 3:3-4, 3:48-51, and 5:46-47 state that the Gospel (Injil) was given to Jesus. These verses provide specific details of the Quranic view about Jesus and the Gospel:

1. The Gospel was revealed for the guidance of mankind.

2. Jesus' message provides new dietary laws.

3. Jesus confirmed the Torah that was in existence in the hands of the Jews He ministered to (the same one we have today).

4. Jesus commanded the Jews to fear God and obey Him.

5. The Christians of Muhammad's time are to judge according to the Gospel (the one that existed in Muhammad's time is essentially the same one that exists today).

These Quranic verses provide aspects about the Gospel message given to Jesus, but neither they, nor the other Quranic verses, actually define or explain the Gospel. Previously we quoted the Muslim writer, Neal Robinson, on this theme. He stated the same when he wrote concerning the Quran's details of Jesus and His teachings: "Little is said about Jesus' teachings…"[1]

These verses provide a general message of obedience to God. (Some of the additional details mentioned above, such as turning a clay bird into a living bird, come from New Testament Apocrypha sources—not the Bible—such as the Infancy Gospel of Thomas.) There is no reason to define Jesus' message with the unique title, "The Gospel," if it were only a general continuation of previous messages, with minor modifications. The Quran has various Old Testament prophets receiving revelations and preaching God's word, but Islam specifically recognizes the Torah and Psalms, while the other proclamations are not distinguished even though they brought new facets of God's word to the Israelites. Clearly, the Quran distinguishes the Gospel but fails to define it.

## The Gospel: One Message or Four Books?

Additionally there is confusion within Islamic theology with respect to defining the context of the word "Gospel." The New Testament contains four "Gospels" that were written by either Jesus' apostles (Matthew, John), or men associated with the apostles, (Mark—with Peter, Luke—with Paul). These are described in Christianity as the "four Gospels." However the Quran uses the singular word "Gospel" and implies it was written as a book. Therefore some Muslims have claimed that the "four Gospels" are corruptions of Jesus' original book.

However, that shows a lack of understanding of the use of the word "Gospel." It can mean either Jesus' message, and the subsequent message of His disciples, or one of the four, or all four of the New Testament books identified as Gospels. The context of how the word "Gospel" is used defines its meaning. For example, the "Gospel" message can be found in each of the four "Gospels," that is, Matthew, Mark, Luke, and John. The confusion arises in the Quran's use of the word "Gospel." Sidney Griffith addresses this, and makes several good points in the *Encyclopedia of the Qur'an*:

In a number of passages the Qur'an clearly presumes in its audience a prior knowledge of Gospel characters and narratives (q.v.). In some passages the Qur'an closely parallels narratives to be found in the canonical, Christian Gospel (cf. e.g. Q3:45-47); in others one finds some motifs familiar from the apocryphal Gospels of the Christians, or other sources of early Christian lore (cf. e.g. Q 5:110)...

Qur'anic uses of the term Injil, however, are all in the singular and betray no awareness of multiple Gospels...

There is some evidence that the term Gospel was also sometimes used in the early Islamic period to indicate the whole New Testament, in the same way that the name of the Torah was used not only for the Pentateuch, but for all the books of the Jewish scriptures. [2]

Griffith is saying that the Quran assumes its hearers, at least the Christian ones, had some knowledge of the existing Gospel, and that the Quran intermingles various Christian (and probably apocryphal) stories with New Testament stories. He allows that early Islam used the singular word "Gospel" to accommodate the four "Gospels" of the New Testament in the same manner as the word "Torah" was used to mean the entire Old Testament. As such the Quran may actually be referring to the entire New Testament and its message when the word "Gospel" is used. It's not certain that Muhammad understood the differences of how the word "Gospel" could be used within Christianity and that is why the Quran is unable to provide much definition or distinction.

Another key part of this topic is the historical record of Christianity in Arabia. The various branches of Christianity that spread to Arabia all used the four Gospels and taught them to their followers. The Christians of Muhammad's time, those that knew their Scriptures, knew and used the four Gospels. The major Christian influences upon the Arabian Peninsula, the Syrian, Palestine, Byzantine, and Ethiopian churches all used the New Testament that contained the four Gospels.

In fact, the earliest extant biography of Muhammad, Ibn Ishaq's

*Sirat Rasul Allah* (Guillaume's *The Life of Muhammad*),[3] records Muhammad meeting with and discussing theology with Christians from Najran who were affiliated with the Byzantine faith. The New Testament they used is essentially the same one we use today.

Therefore, when you read the Quran in that light, and realize that the singular word "Gospel" implies the four "Gospels," that is, those of Matthew, Mark, Luke, and John, it makes much more sense. It fits the known historical record and it corroborates the Quran's position on confirming the Scriptures that existed during Muhammad's lifetime. Those Scriptures were in the possession of the Christians that he addressed.

As mentioned earlier, the Christians whom Muhammad addressed had this Gospel with them and they were to judge according to it:

> Therefore let those who follow the Gospel judge according to what God revealed therein. Evil-doers are those that do not judge according to God's revelations (5:47).[4]

## What Is the Gospel?

The word "Gospel" means "good news" or "glad tidings." When Jesus preached the "Gospel" He was preaching the "good news" of God bringing salvation to His people. Remember, Jesus' name means "the Lord saves," or "the Lord is our salvation," and the Gospel message is tied to God bringing salvation to man.

Further, a similar good news or "glad tidings" theme is used throughout the Old Testament when God ministered to the Israelites. The *Baker Encyclopedia of the Bible* notes:

> Where the message is gospel for the Israelites (cf. 1 Samuel 31:9) and is based on fact (cf. 1 Kings 1:42-43), the news is in every case but one (Jeremiah 20:15) expressly related to God. Gospel owes its existence and bears its witness to action which he has taken, action moreover that is saving in character. In 2 Samuel 18, the good news is not merely that David

has been delivered from his enemies, but that the Lord has accomplished this…[5]

The encyclopedia goes on to detail the many aspects of God's salvation for the Israelites and shows that God has a plan of salvation for Israel that has been at work throughout their history.

Obviously, God's plan of salvation for the Israelites is a key theme found in the Old Testament. It was something God affected for the Israelites throughout their history and something He promised them in the future. When Jesus ministered the Gospel He was fulfilling God's promise of salvation to the Jews. But Jesus expanded the scope of God's promise to the Gentiles as well. In verses such as John 3:16, Matthew 28:19, and Luke 24:47 Jesus taught that this promise, this hope, was to be extended to the Gentiles as well as the Jews. Therefore, this Gospel, this message, did not appear out of a vacuum, instead it was always a part of God's plan for mankind. Jesus fulfilled God's plan and took it to its next stages.

## The Gospel Message: A Chronological Review

As mentioned above, God's plan of salvation was promised and prophesied long before Jesus was born. Let's examine the various biblical passages.

As detailed above, the *Baker Encyclopedia of the Bible* noted many instances of "glad tidings" and God's salvation for the Jews. Isaiah 53:1-12 is a key passage describing God's future plan. Isaiah contains many important predictions about Jesus' ministry. Below are verses 11 and 12:

> After he has suffered,
>    he will see the light of life and be satisfied;
> by his knowledge my righteous servant will justify many,
>    and he will bear their iniquities.
> Therefore I will give him a portion among the great,
>    and he will divide the spoils with the strong,
> because he poured out his life unto death,
>    and was numbered with the transgressors.

For he bore the sin of many,
   and made intercession for the transgressors.

The prophet Isaiah prophesied that a future righteous servant would bear the sins of many and after His suffering He would live again. This prediction was fulfilled by Jesus. Following this message chronologically, we find this theme repeated in the message that the angels give to Joseph about Mary's child:

> She will give birth to a son, and you are to give him the name Jesus, because he will save his people from their sins" (Matthew 1:21).

Isaiah prophesied that a man would bear the sins of many, and the angels told Joseph that Mary's son would save His people from their sins. Moving forward into Jesus' life we find Jesus beginning His ministry and teaching others about the Gospel. Jesus was sent by God to save the people from punishment for their sins. Jesus was the savior of the world. Putting true faith in Jesus is the requirement. Throughout His life Jesus confirmed that bearing others' sins and saving them from God's punishment was part of His ministry and He continued to preach the Gospel:

> Not so with you. Instead, whoever wants to become great among you must be your servant, and whoever wants to be first must be your slave—just as the Son of Man did not come to be served, but to serve, and to give his life as a ransom for many (Matthew 20:26-28).

Finally, during one of the most intimate and tender times Jesus spent with His disciples occurred the night before He was taken by the Roman soldiers. There He gave them the same Gospel message. It was full of love for those that followed Him:

> While they were eating, Jesus took bread, and when he had given thanks, he broke it and gave it to his disciples, saying, "Take and eat; this is my body." Then he took a cup, and

when he had given thanks, he gave it to them, saying, "Drink from it, all of you. This is my blood of the covenant, which is poured out for many for the forgiveness of sins. I tell you, I will not drink from this fruit of the vine from now on until that day when I drink it new with you in my Father's kingdom." When they had sung a hymn, they went out to the Mount of Olives (Matthew 26:26-30).

After His resurrection Jesus met several disciples while they traveled and again taught them the exact same message:

He said to them, "How foolish you are, and how slow to believe all that the prophets have spoken! Did not the Messiah have to suffer these things and then enter his glory?" And beginning with Moses and all the Prophets, he explained to them what was said in all the Scriptures concerning himself (Luke 24:25-27).

Long after Jesus rose from the dead and ascended to heaven, Jesus' disciples continued to preach that same message. Read the whole of Acts chapter 3. Here is an excerpt (verses 13-15) of Peter's words as he preaches the "Gospel" to the Jews:

The God of Abraham, Isaac and Jacob, the God of our fathers, has glorified his servant Jesus. You handed him over to be killed, and you disowned him before Pilate, though he had decided to let him go. You disowned the Holy and Righteous One and asked that a murderer be released to you. You killed the author of life, but God raised him from the dead. We are witnesses of this.

Notice that the Gospel message is unchanged from Isaiah, to the angel's words, to Jesus' teaching before and after His resurrection, to Peter and Paul's writings. Jesus came to save people from the punishment for their sins and to reestablish a loving personal relationship with God. True faith in Jesus is the requirement to obtain God's forgiveness of sins and salvation.

## Islam's Questions About the Gospel

Muslims' question:
*"If God is just, shouldn't I, not someone else,
be punished for my own sins?"*

This is a fair and reasonable question. Why should God allow an innocent and righteous man, Jesus, to bear others' sins, suffer a painful crucifixion and die, while forgiving the guilty of their sins?

### Salvation in Islam

Further, a Muslim could ask,
*"Why can't I believe in God and Muhammad's message, obey them, and do good works to earn my place in Paradise?"*

Before going into any answers let's lay some groundwork concerning salvation in Islam. Islamic and Christian theology are distinctive and when the same word "salvation" is used it is often defined differently. "Salvation" in Christianity is different than "salvation" in Islam.

Salvation in Islam requires faith in Allah, repentance from evil, acceptance of Muhammad's prophethood, and good works. With the exception of Allah's mercy, the good works must outweigh the bad works. Regarding the judgment and entering Paradise, the Quran states:

> Now there hath succeeded them a later generation whom have ruined worship and have followed lusts. But they will meet deception. Save him who shall repent and believe and do right. Such will enter the Garden, and they will not be wronged in aught (19:59-60).

and

> The weighing on that day is the true (weighing). As for those whose scale is heavy, they are the successful. And as for those whose scale is light: those are they who lose their souls because they used to wrong Our revelations (7:8-9).

The "Five Pillars" of Islam are tied into professions and acts of faith and doing good works. However, Muslims know that as they can repent from evil deeds, and they have put their true faith in Allah and in Muhammad as his messenger, they still face the question: "Do my good deeds outweigh my bad deeds?" Assurance of salvation is not usually assumed or given in Islam. (Muhammad promised a very select few that they would be granted entry into Paradise.) The final scales, or judgments, will determine who enters Paradise and who enters hellfire.

This is echoed in the *Reliance of the Traveller*, which is a "Classic Manual of Islamic Sacred Law." Here is a quote related to salvation in Islam with respect to believing in the last day:

> Believe means to be convinced that it will come to pass with all it implies, including the resurrection of the dead, their reckoning, the weighing of their good deeds against their bad ones, their passing over the high, narrow bridge that spans the hellfire (sirat), and that some will be put in hell out of justice, and some in paradise out of Allah's pure generosity. [6]

Further, the *Reliance of the Traveller* comments indirectly on the subject of Muslims being put in hell:

> So the meaning of these statements is to show the agreement between the Koran and sunna on this, for the early Muslims had great fear, and did not find in the Koran that true monotheists would leave hell, and were afraid of unending punishment. [7]

The great challenge for the Muslim is to ensure that one's good deeds outweigh their bad deeds. Even Muhammad found this to be a challenge. In fact Muhammad spent a great deal of time praying for forgiveness:

> Narrated Abu Huraira:
>
> I heard Allah's Apostle saying "By Allah! I ask for forgiveness from Allah and turn to Him in repentance more than seventy times a day." [8]

Certainly then we can conclude that salvation in Islam is very difficult to obtain. When you take into account a person's motives and thoughts, greed for money, lust for women, jealousy of others, hatred, selfishness, pride and arrogance, and so on, then indeed a man's heart is very wicked and sinful. How will a man perform enough good works to counterbalance the bad?

### More Important Differences

This brings us to another key difference between Islamic and Christian theology: man's nature. Islam teaches that men have a nature that can choose freely between good and bad deeds, thoughts, and motives, even if it is inclined to sin. Christianity teaches that men have a fallen nature, due to Adam's sin, and that men are predisposed to sin. Given the weight of the historical and sociological evidence about human nature, it appears that Christianity is closer to the truth. Mankind's history, like our own personal life in deed, word, and thought, is filled with sin.

Another similarity between Islam and Christianity is that both are commanded to do good works, but the difference centers on the motivation for the good works. Muslims need them to counterbalance their sinful deeds, whereas Christians are commanded to do them, based upon the changing of their nature, their character, and their soul. The motive for "works" for a Muslim is to gain salvation; for a Christian they are done because they have salvation.

Salvation in Christianity starts with a person putting his faith in Jesus. Jesus told Nicodemus, "You must be born again" (John 3:7). This new birth occurs within the heart or spirit of a person who receives Jesus as Lord. It is like a spiritual seed that is growing within that person, as part of that person's soul and as it matures, that person will do good deeds naturally. Of course that person will have sins to deal with but there is forgiveness for the sins of the person who has truly put his faith in Jesus. We are not talking about mere intellectual belief, but rather a true, sincere belief that causes a person to take action based upon that belief.

Another aspect of this key difference of salvation in Islam and Christianity is that Jesus taught that a new birth is required. This new birth, a spiritual birth, will change the heart of a Christian over time and propel him to good works. Jesus taught His disciples that they were branches on a vine (John 15). They are to "abide" in Him, and the good fruit, that is, good works, will come as a natural outworking of the change within. Good deeds are often called "good fruit" in the Bible. Just as a fruit tree bears fruit according to its nature, so too Christians are to change and perform good deeds that result from the change within, and become more Christlike.

Implicit in the Muslim question above is the supposition that if a man can live a pure and holy life, then it would be fair and just of God to allow him to enter Paradise.

The Christian answer to this is threefold:

1. Your nature itself is tainted and cannot be made pure enough and acceptable to God by your own efforts, thus God would not tolerate a sinful creature to enter heaven.

2. You cannot do enough good works to outweigh the sins of your actions, words, and thoughts to earn your salvation. Jesus, the great teacher, taught that even sins of the heart are enough to separate you from God (Matthew 5:27-28).

3. Even if your good works could outweigh your sins, God is obligated to punish you for your sins.

Look at it this way: Just as a human court must punish you for breaking the law, so it is with God's Law. You have broken God's Law and under that Law, the penalty must be paid. Even if you have done many good deeds, those good deeds do not absolve you of your sins, that is, your crimes against God. If God's Word is true, then He is obligated to punish the lawbreaker. If God were to simply say, "I've decided that I'll just forgive you for breaking my Law" without the debt paid, then He would be whimsical, not holding to His own rules and requirements.

### The Justice of God

This leads us back to the first question:

*"If God is just, shouldn't I, not someone else, be punished for my own sins?"*

Both Muslims and Christians believe that God is just. In our legal systems, if a person commits a crime he is punished for that crime, or is forced to make restitution for that crime. "Surely I deserve to be punished for my sins and crimes, correct?"

Yes, that is correct. But the answer to this question extends beyond the width of the logical response to the question. Christians also believe, as the Bible teachers, that "God is love," and it is in this love that God has chosen to make a way for an impure people to become forgiven, purified, and accepted and welcomed by Him. Since the answer to question #1 is that we can't earn our salvation by our good works, then we need God's help to have any possibility of success.

It is interesting that among all of Islam's names for God, "Father" is not one of them. In Christianity, the love of God is given as the love of a Father for His people. If mankind is unable to earn salvation due to the fallen nature, abundance of sin, or both, then the case is closed. However, God, out of His great love, similar to a love a father has for his children, took the next step to help them in a way children are often unable to help themselves. He made a sacrifice for mankind. Jesus said it this way:

> Not so with you. Instead, whoever wants to become great among you must be your servant, and whoever wants to be first must be your slave—just as the Son of Man did not come to be served, but to serve, and to give his life as a ransom for many (Matthew 20:26-28).

John the Baptist also understood about Jesus' mission and identified Jesus as "the Lamb of God, who takes away the sin of the world!... I have seen and I testify that this is God's Chosen One" (John 1:29-34).

John used the term "Lamb of God" because he knew that under the Old Testament Law, lambs were used as sacrifices for sin. He knew that

Jesus was our sacrifice for sin. Jesus said He was a ransom for us. This act of being a "ransom" or sacrifice for us is not something that appeared with Jesus. It is prefigured in the Torah, in the book of Leviticus:

> For the life of a creature is in the blood, and I have given it to you to make atonement for yourselves on the altar; it is the blood that makes atonement for one's life (Leviticus 17:11).

When God established His covenant with the Israelites He instituted the offering of sacrificial animals to atone for their sins. "Atone" means to make amends or reparations for one's sins or crimes, to the end of effecting reconciliation. The Israelites offered animal sacrifices and obtained atonement, reconciliation with God, and forgiveness of their sins. This was the primary way that forgiveness was effected. The cost of an animal was dear to the Israelites. It showed them that they deserved harsh punishment from God for their sins. It signified their payment to God for their transgressions. There are unique instances in the Old Testament where God forgave sins without requiring animal sacrifice, but they were very few and they were the exception, not the norm. The covenant that God established with the Israelites required animal sacrifice.

In staying within the framework of the Old Testament covenant, God sent Jesus to be our sacrifice because without God intervening on our behalf we would all be judged and punished as a sinful, tainted, impure people. Just as God allowed the sacrifice of animals to make atonement for the sins of the Israelites, so Jesus was the ultimate, perfect sacrifice. Because Jesus was sinless, He was acceptable as a holy sacrifice to be presented before God.

### The Work of God's Servant

We started this chapter with a quote from Isaiah chapter 53. What many fail to realize is that this theme actually starts with Isaiah 52:13-15. Take a few minutes and read Isaiah 52:13-15 and chapter 53.

J. Alan Groves, in "Atonement in Isaiah 53," has analyzed the language of Isaiah and notes the following about the "Servant":

Yahweh's own lips declared that the Servant was to be identified with Yahweh himself. The Servant had been accorded,
by honorific language spoken by the voice of Yahweh himself, a position belonging only to Yahweh. No one else in Isaiah is so honored or set apart…It should not be overlooked
that the one who has borne the sin of others (Isa. 53:12) will
be the one who is lifted up by Yahweh (Isa 52:13). The word-
play is not accidental.[9]

Groves's conclusion is strong for he declares confidently that Isaiah 53 demands purification and the Servant effected that through His
sacrifice:

> While the Torah spoke of atonement as the only means by
> which the wrath of Yahweh against sin and uncleanness
> could be stayed, the Torah knew no atonement that pro-
> duced the universal and permanent purification envisioned
> in Isaiah. Such extraordinary purification required an atone-
> ment of equally extraordinary and radical nature. Isaiah
> made clear that certain means would not secure this purifi-
> cation. It would not be by means of the traditional vehicle of
> atonement—e.g. Levitical sacrifice (Isa 1:11-15). Nor would
> it be by means of repentance (Isa 6:10) or Israel's suffering
> in the Babylonian exile. Rather, it would be accomplished
> by a new thing (Isa 48:7), something previously unknown
> and not derived from human experience or wisdom—the
> astounding suffering of one righteous Israelite (Isa 52:13–
> 53:12), who bore the sins of others. This alone would make
> an atonement sufficient to accomplish the global, permanent
> purification revealed in Isaiah's vision.

> Therefore, while in terms of the Torah, human suffering and
> death as the means of atonement is unexpected, startling,
> and even appalling, it is the means toward which the glori-
> ous purification envisioned in Isaiah pressed. Only an atone-
> ment based on the Servant's sacrifice could accomplish the
> purification that Isaiah envisioned.[10]

Groves's analysis of Isaiah leads him to conclude that the Servant in chapters 52 and 53 is suffering and dying with a divine purpose: He is making atonement for God's people and purifying them permanently. This is the exact same Gospel that Jesus preached. Jesus is the Messiah, the Suffering Servant of Isaiah.

## Conclusion

The key points of this chapter are as follows:

- Islamic and Christian theology agree that Jesus ministered and preached the Gospel but Islamic theology fails to define the Gospel.

- Gospel means "good news" or "glad tidings" and its theme is one of God bringing salvation to His people. Historically that theme is tied to God's efforts on behalf of His people.

- The Gospel message of salvation is unified and detailed chronologically in the Scriptures from the Old Testament times through the New Testament times.

- Man cannot possibly do enough good works to earn his salvation.

- God sent Jesus to be an atonement for our sins and to effect reconciliation between God and man.

- Repentance from our sin, true and sincere faith in Jesus' death for our sins, belief in His resurrection, and acceptance of and obedience to Jesus' Lordship over our lives are required to enter into God's salvation for us. We don't earn it, we receive it as a gift, thereafter we walk in obedience to our loving Father.

We'll close this chapter with a comprehensive review of the components that form the "Gospel" from *The New International Commentary on the New Testament* (NICNT) from Matthew 26:

The words by which Jesus explains this extraordinary idea combine three phrases which together draw out the redemptive significance of his death.

(a) "Blood of the covenant" directly echoes Exodus 24:8 (and cf. Exodus 24:6 for the "pouring out" of that blood) and so recalls the original basis of Israel's life as the special people of God; mention of "the covenant" also recalls Jeremiah's prophecy (Jeremiah 31:31-34) that at the heart of God's restoration of his people there would be a "new covenant," grounded in a new relationship of "knowing God" and in the forgiving and forgetting of their sins.

(b) "Poured out for many" recalls the "many" who are repeatedly referred to in Isa 53:11-12 as the beneficiaries of the suffering and death of the servant of God, an allusion already familiar to us from 20:28 where again it was specifically linked to the purpose of Jesus' death; here the Isa 53 allusion is further suggested by the verb "poured out," which is used in Isa 53:12 of the servant "pouring out his life to death."

(c) The final phrase, "for the forgiveness of sins," not only recalls the servant's death for the sins of his people (Isa 53:5-6,8,10,11,12) but also further reinforces the allusion to Jeremiah's new covenant prophecy, where the basis of this new relationship is that "I will forgive their wickedness, and will remember their sins no more"; it also recalls to the reader the original statement of Jesus' mission in 1:21, to "save his people from their sins." [11]

Muslims and Christians agree that "God is great" (Allahu Akbar) and that God is "full of loving-kindness" (al-Wadud). Jesus' incarnation, crucifixion, atonement, and reconciliation, show that God loves in the greatest way. Jesus made a way to restore our fellowship with God and that each one of us through faith in Jesus can be brought into God's family.

# 7

# Jesus' Crucifixion

Muslims' question:
*"The Quran says that Jesus was not crucified.
What evidence do you have that Jesus was crucified?"*

This chapter will examine the question of whether Jesus was crucified or not. The Bible and Quran present opposing statements and we'll survey the evidence behind His crucifixion. There is more to the crucifixion than just the physical act of nailing Jesus to the wood; there is a spiritual reason behind the crucifixion. For the crucifixion to have any value to us we must understand that spiritual reason. The physical crucifixion and the spiritual rationale are cemented together and both aspects must be understood together.

John 19:13-20 and Luke 23:26-46 describe the crucifixion event.

> When they came to the place called the Skull, they crucified him there, along with the criminals—one on his right, the other on his left. Jesus said, "Father, forgive them, for they do not know what they are doing." And they divided up his clothes by casting lots. The people stood watching, and the rulers even sneered at him. They said, "He saved others; let him save himself if he is God's Messiah, the Chosen One" (Luke 23:33-35).

However, opposing the New Testament's account, the Quran states:

> ...because of their saying: We slew the Messiah, Jesus son of Mary, Allah's messenger—they slew him not nor crucified him, but it appeared so unto them; and lo! those who

disagree concerning it are in doubt thereof; they have no knowledge thereof save pursuit of a conjecture; they slew him not for certain (4:157-158).

## Conflict Between the Accounts

The Bible says Jesus was crucified; the Quran says He was not. Therefore the question is "Was Jesus crucified?" The evidence is very strong and directs us to one logical and conclusive answer.

Crucifixion was used by various Mediterranean and Mideastern countries to put people to death hundreds of years before Jesus. This painful method of execution was used to intimidate criminals. There were various forms of crucifixion used depending on the time and place of the execution.*

There are several differing Islamic interpretations of the 4:157-158 passages in the Quran. Some Muslims accept Jesus' crucifixion but most do not. Most Muslim scholars believe that someone else, such as Judas Iscariot, or someone who looked like Jesus, or one of Jesus' disciples, or a Roman soldier, or Simon of Cyrene, and so on, was crucified in Jesus' place.

Related to the "but it appeared so unto them" portion of 4:157-158, here are additional translations that provide a more complete perspective:

- but so it was made to appear to them (Yusuf Ali's [1])
- but they thought they did (Dawood's [2])
- but it appeared to them so (like Isa) (Shakir's [3])

Islamic scholarship is divided over this passage's meaning and their various commentaries betray a lack of certainty. There are a number of excellent writings on this subject that delineate the differing Islamic positions, such as John Gilchrist's *The Crucifixion in Islam and Christianity*, and Glenn Miller's: http://christian-thinktank.com/qdeath1 .html and http://christian-thinktank.com/4157.html.

---

* For more details, see Josh McDowell and Sean McDowell, *Evidence for the Resurrection* (Ventura, CA: Regal, 1996), pp. 162-169.

Proceeding with the majority-accepted (and more Quranically sound) Muslim belief that "it appeared that Jesus was crucified, but he was not" is the understanding that those who carried out the act of crucifixion actually believed they crucified Jesus. Therefore, those that carried out the crucifixion and those that witnessed it truly believed that Jesus was crucified and consequently told others they crucified Him. The Jews who claimed Jesus was crucified were sincere. After all, they saw it with their own eyes. What more proof would they need? However, their belief was erroneous because it rests upon a mistaken observation: The person who the people saw crucified was not Jesus.

Did the witnesses get it right? Or could they have been mistaken because God made it appear that it was Jesus being crucified? On the other hand, how would that fit with the Christian accounts of the disciples conversing with Jesus after His death and resurrection?

It also must be highlighted that the Quran does not state what happened exactly. Was somebody else crucified in Jesus' place? The Quran does not say clearly. Did Allah cause everyone to experience a delusion and think that Jesus had been crucified?—the Quran does not say. Were nails driven through Jesus' hands, but someone replaced Him and He was miraculously taken off the cross? The Quran does not say. A gap exists in the Quran's account on Jesus' crucifixion and there is a mass of Islamic conjecture and guesswork that tries to fill the gap. However, since the majority of the world's Muslims believe that Jesus was not crucified and someone else was crucified in His place, we are going to proceed on that interpretation. In this case Christians and Muslims agree that someone was crucified but don't agree on who was crucified.

The question is "Was Jesus crucified?" and there are at least two ways to arrive at an answer.

One way is the way of *blind faith:* "The Quran says 'No!' and that is what I believe!" There is no thinking required, no investigation and examination of the evidence, no discussion needed. Instead it is a simple case of blind faith. Now blind faith is not necessarily always a bad thing and many religious people, including Christians, make statements such as, "God said it, I believe it, that settles it!" Frequently in some cases blind faith helps someone to obey God's commands in a confusing situation, and that is a good thing. But in other cases blind faith can have disastrous consequences. Many years ago people were starving during a great famine and they were told that a vein of nearby clay was given to them by a deity to eat in times of famine. The villagers ate it and died en masse. It would have been better for them to have investigated the belief before eating the clay.

In the same way our question of whether or not Jesus was crucified holds heavy consequences. Since we are talking about issues related to heaven and hell, eternal life or eternal punishment, we think a wise man or woman would want to investigate the belief and consider all of the evidence.

Therefore, the other way to approach this is to *examine all of the available evidence*. This approach takes into account eyewitness testimony, testimony of people involved, post-event testimony, theological testimony and support, and medical evidence. A logical person would examine all of the data before arriving at a conclusion.

## Resolving the Conflict: Method 1—The "Blind Faith" Approach

We'll start with the "blind faith" approach. It is based upon sura 4:157-158 and takes it at face value: Jesus was not crucified but it appeared that He was. Therefore, even if there are many testimonies, or many types of evidence, that state Jesus was crucified, it does not mean that the crucifixion of Jesus took place because God made someone look like Jesus to be crucified. This could be called "the Muslim substitution theory."

Muslim apologist Ahmed Deedat proclaimed the blind-faith approach when he debated me (Josh McDowell). He stated:

> The Muslim believes this authoritative statement as the veritable Word of God. And as such, he asks no questions, and he demands no proof. He says, "There are the words of my lord: I believe, and I affirm." [4]

Here is additional background for this approach—an excerpt from Ibn Kathir's commentary on the crucifixion is below. Similar versions of this story were also presented by the great Muslim scholar Muhammad ibn Jarir al-Tabari, and Muhammad's cousin, Ibn Abbas.

The Jews also said,

*"We killed Al-Masih, `Isa, son of Maryam, the Messenger of Allah,"*

meaning, we killed the person who claimed to be the Messenger of Allah. The Jews only uttered these words in jest and mockery,

When Allah sent `Isa with proofs and guidance, the Jews, may Allah's curses, anger, torment and punishment be upon them, envied him because of his prophethood and obvious miracles; curing the blind and leprous and bringing the dead back to life, by Allah's leave... `Isa performed other miracles that Allah honored him with, yet the Jews defied and belied him and tried their best to harm him. Allah's Prophet `Isa could not live in any one city for long and he had to travel often with his mother, peace be upon them.

Even so, the Jews were not satisfied, and they went to the king of Damascus at that time, a Greek polytheist who worshipped the stars. They told him that there was a man in Bayt Al-Maqdis misguiding and dividing the people in Jerusalem and stirring unrest among the king's subjects. The king became angry and wrote to his deputy in Jerusalem to arrest the rebel leader, stop him from causing unrest, crucify him and make him wear a crown of thorns. When the king's deputy in Jerusalem received these orders, he went with some Jews to the house that `Isa was residing in, and he was then with twelve, thirteen or seventeen of his companions. That day was a Friday, in the evening.

They surrounded `Isa in the house, and when he felt that they would soon enter the house or that he would sooner or later have to leave it, he said to his companions, "Who volunteers to be made to look like me, for which he will be my companion in Paradise." A young man volunteered, but `Isa thought that he was too young. He asked the question a second and third time, each time the young man volunteering, prompting `Isa to say, "Well then, you will be that man."

Allah made the young man look exactly like `Isa, while a hole opened in the roof of the house, and `Isa was made to sleep and ascended to heaven while asleep...

*And (remember) when Allah said: "O `Isa! I will take you and raise you to Myself."*

When `Isa ascended, those who were in the house came out. When those surrounding the house saw the man who looked like `Isa, they thought that he was `Isa. So they took him at night, crucified him and placed a crown of thorns on his head. The Jews then boasted that they killed `Isa and some Christians accepted their false claim, due to their ignorance and lack of reason. As for those who were in the house with `Isa, they witnessed his ascension to heaven, while the rest thought that the Jews killed `Isa by crucifixion. They even said that Maryam sat under the corpse of the crucified man and cried, and they say that the dead man spoke to her. All this was a test from Allah for His servants out of His wisdom.[5]

Ibn Kathir's incredible tale creates more questions and problems than it answers. Jesus ascends to heaven out of the roof of the house but the deputies don't see Him ascend or question it. Allah allows an innocent man to die in Jesus' place. With so many miracles happening around them, couldn't Allah simply have taken Jesus up to heaven? Why would the young man have to suffer and die in the first place? Further, no amateur historian would have a difficult time deconstructing Ibn Kathir's tale for it contains historical-political errors as well. If a Muslim accepts Ibn Kathir's account he'll have to choose blind faith over reason and common sense as well as over historical facts.

Glenn Miller chronicles a major investment from Muslim scholars in developing a comprehensive story concerning the crucifixion of Jesus.* The 4:157-158 Quranic passages are the heart of their theories and they develop elaborate explanations to justify their various interpretations. We've not seen any develop an argument built upon historical evidence. Rather they build upon the statements in the Quran and Hadith and then expand it with their imagination.

---

* See http://christian-thinktank.com/qdeath1.html and http://christian-thinktank.com/4157.html.

### Historical Problems with the Muslim Substitution Theory

The Muslim substitution theory has serious historical and moral problems. First, the Old Testament predicted the Messiah's death (see Isaiah 53:5-10; Psalm 22:16; Daniel 9:26; Zechariah 12:10), and in dying Jesus fulfilled these prophecies (see Matthew 4:14; 5:17-18; 8:17; John 4:25-26; 5:39). There are no predictions in the Old Testament that someone would be substituted for the Messiah; all references indicate that He would die personally.

Second, Jesus predicted His own death many times throughout His ministry (see John 2:19-21; Matthew 12:40; Mark 8:31). He never predicted that someone else would be substituted in His place. All of the predictions for Jesus' resurrection in both the Old and New Testaments are based on the fact that He would personally die (see Psalm 16:10; Isaiah 26:19; Daniel 12:2; Matthew 12:40). Obviously Jesus could not have been resurrected if someone else had died in His place. There are virtually no scholars today—that are not already committed to Islamic theology—who accept the substitution theory. In fact, even non-Christian scholars admit that Jesus' death by crucifixion is a historical certainty. In the words of non-Christian, critical scholar John Dominic Crossan, "That he was crucified is as sure as anything historical can ever be." [6]

### Resolving the Conflict: Method 2—The "Examine the Evidence" Approach

Now approach the question "Was Jesus crucified?" by examining the historical, theological, and medical evidence. There are different types of evidence and each contributes toward determining an answer to the question. The intention here is to look at the facts, records, and testimony for the readers to evaluate. Getting people to evaluate evidence that contradicts what they have made their minds up about can be challenging. Most sincere Muslims we've met and with whom we have discussed this topic are adamant in insisting that Jesus was not crucified and for the most part disregard any evidence that says otherwise. We can understand that mentality when one believes the Quran is from God and is afraid to question his own faith. However there are many who do have very sincere questions and toward that we endeavor to present the facts and details of Jesus' crucifixion.

First, a review of the definition of the word "evidence." It has several meanings, but for our theological context, the dictionary.com site defines "evidence" as "data presented in proof of the facts in issue and which may include the testimony of witnesses, records, documents, or objects."

And this is exactly the type of evidence we will be using. We'll draw from these records and documents:

- Old Testament evidence
- Quranic evidence (apart from its statement on the crucifixion event)
- New Testament evidence
- historians' writings
- medical evidence

I (Josh McDowell) debated the Muslim apologist and polemicist Ahmed Deedat and during that debate I explained the perspective of the Gospels to him:

> The point: there are some people who do not have an historical perspective of literature, who try to make an issue out of the fact that the writers of the four accounts of the gospel, Matthew, Mark, Luke and John, never signed their names. Please, men and women, we need to go back through history and see how they did it then.
>
> First of all, the manuscripts were so well-accepted as being authoritative, with everyone knowing who wrote them, they did not need names placed on them. You might say it was the writers' way of not distracting from the purpose of making Jesus Christ the central issue. Also, the work of these authors, Matthew, Mark, Luke and John, went through the apostolic age. They went through the test of the apostolic period of the first century to confirm their accuracy, authenticity and reliability. Other people, through limited reading and absence of any type of research, say that the documents of Matthew, Mark, Luke and John are hearsay because the writers were

not eyewitnesses of the events surrounding the crucifixion and resurrection of Jesus Christ.

The people who say that will often appeal to Mark 14:50. They say that within two minutes they could dismiss the argument because Jesus' followers all left Him and fled. So therefore, everything was hearsay. Men and women, this line of reasoning ignores common sense in the facts of the case. For example, read just the next four verses. It says this: "And Peter followed Him." You see they left Him in a group, but they came back individually—immediately, Mr. Deedat. [7]

We believe that the New Testament contains the testimony of many direct and indirect witnesses to the crucifixion and our intention is to categorize the comments and show from a variety of viewpoints there is a uniform declaration that points to Jesus being crucified. Finally we'll cross-examine the Islamic argument.

### Old Testament Prophets Suffered Persecution and Death

Let's start the examination by using the life stories of the Old Testament prophets related to unjust suffering and death. I've discussed the crucifixion with a number of Muslims and they have a strong reaction to Allah allowing Jesus, a good and innocent man, and one of his special messengers and prophets, to die a brutal and humiliating death by the hands of sinners. They believe that Allah is just and fair and that he would protect his messengers, including Jesus, from the hands of evil men.

This Muslim belief is sincere and understandable, but it is based upon myth. God often allowed His prophets and messengers to suffer "unjustly," to even be tortured and murdered by evil men. The Old Testament states that the prophets were rejected, persecuted, and brutalized:

> The LORD, the God of their fathers, sent word to them through his messengers again and again, because he had pity on his people and on his dwelling place. But they mocked God's messengers, despised his words and scoffed at his

prophets until the wrath of the LORD was aroused against his people and there was no remedy (2 Chronicles 36:15-16).

So clearly, Old Testament prophets suffered painful persecution. Additionally, Jewish traditions detail a number of cruel deaths suffered by their prophets. Indeed, it seems strange that Muslims would hold to the view that Allah would never let one of his prophets suffer or die because the Quran also states that the Old Testament prophets suffered painful persecution and death! Below is one out of several verses:

> But they broke their covenant, denied the revelations of God, and killed the prophets unjustly. They said: "Our hearts are sealed." It is God who has sealed their hearts, on account of their unbelief. They have no faith, except a few of them ("Women," 4:155).

Finally, Jesus taught that Old Testament prophets suffered persecution and death:

> Woe to you, teachers of the law and Pharisees, you hypocrites! You build tombs for the prophets and decorate the graves of the righteous. And you say, "If we had lived in the days of our ancestors, we would not have taken part with them in shedding the blood of the prophets." So you testify against yourselves that you are the descendants of those who murdered the prophets (Matthew 23:29-31).

The point here is that it is reasonable to believe that God could let Jesus, as a prophet or messenger, suffer persecution and die by crucifixion at the hands of sinful men. The Old Testament, the Quran, and the New Testament all state that persecution and killing of the prophets occurred. On this point we can say that Jewish, Christian, and Islamic theology agree that various prophets and messengers through the ages suffered and died at the hands of evil men.

### Old Testament Passages State That the Messiah Would Suffer

The Old Testament declares the Messiah to be a special emissary for God and there are many Old Testament passages that describe the

Messiah. Some of these passages foretell His power and ruling authority and a few foretell His sufferings. For example, the previously mentioned Isaiah 12:1-12 passage. Also, the book of Daniel foretells the
Messiah's suffering:

> Know and understand this: From the time the word goes out to
> restore and rebuild Jerusalem until the Anointed One, the ruler,
> comes, there will be seven "sevens," and sixty-two "sevens." It
> will be rebuilt with streets and a trench, but in times of trouble.
> After the sixty-two "sevens," the Anointed One will be put to
> death and will have nothing. The people of the ruler who will
> come will destroy the city and the sanctuary (Daniel 9:25-26).

These verses show that the Messiah would indeed suffer and die.
This was also reinforced by Jesus' post-resurrection statements that He
fulfilled the Scripture's predictions that the Messiah needed to suffer
before entering His glory.

This theme is elaborated on by Dr. William Campbell:

> By revelation Jesus showed his disciples that he, the Son of
> Man, was with them the first time "to be cut off" in order "to
> bear the sin of many." Secondly, in the future he would return
> from heaven with mighty power to establish his kingdom on
> earth. What the Jewish Rabbis thought of as "two messiahs,"
> we now understand to be two appearances of the "one Mes-
> siah—Jesus of Nazareth." [8]

### Jesus Foretold His Suffering and Death and Chose the Cross Willingly

Jesus was not taken by surprise when the Jews and Romans came
for Him. Jesus knew what was going to happen; in fact He predicted it!
He taught His disciples that the authorities were going to kill Him but
that He would rise three days later. Further, over and over He taught
them that He was laying His life down because He loved His people.
For example in Matthew 16:21-27 He explains His death and resurrection and the subsequent cost of discipleship (also see Luke 9:18-22;
22:37). Below is Matthew 16:21:

From that time on Jesus began to explain to his disciples that
he must go to Jerusalem and suffer many things at the hands
of the elders, chief priests and teachers of the law, and that he
must be killed and on the third day be raised to life.

The theological point here is that Jesus' crucifixion and resurrection
were part of God's plan. Jesus foretold it and He obeyed God and took
up His cross willingly. Following His resurrection He taught the disciples that the crucifixion was part of God's plan. In that, Jesus kept the
theological link between the Old and New Testaments:

He said to them, "How foolish you are, and how slow to
believe all that the prophets have spoken! Did not the Messiah have to suffer these things and then enter his glory?" And
beginning with Moses and all the Prophets, he explained to
them what was said in all the Scriptures concerning himself
(Luke 24:25-27; also see 22:44-49).

There is a continuity with all of Jesus' teaching about the Messiah's
suffering and death. Jesus used the Scriptures as a basis for His life and
He taught them to His disciples. He showed them that the Messiah's
suffering and death was prophesied in the Old Testament Scriptures
and fulfilled by Him.

### New Testament Christians Say That Jesus Was Crucified

Consistent with Jesus' teachings, Christians also taught that Jesus
had been crucified and rose from the dead. There are a number of
places throughout the New Testament that state Jesus' crucifixion and
resurrection. For example, when Peter preached his first sermon in Acts
2:29-36 he boldly declared that the Jewish Scripture foretold the Messiah's death and resurrection.

Following Jesus' death and resurrection the Christians preached
the Gospel and part of that was the message about Jesus' bearing mankind's sins and His death and resurrection. It was a consistent and uniform message that was proclaimed to the Jews first and then later to the
Gentiles worldwide. (See also Luke's writings in Acts 1:1-3 and Paul's
in 1 Corinthians 15:3-8.)

### There Were Many Eyewitnesses to Jesus' Suffering, Crucifixion, and Death

There were a number of eyewitnesses to Jesus' crucifixion detailed in Matthew 27, Luke 23, John 19, and Mark 15. They were from all walks of life and knew of Jesus. These witnesses included those who opposed Him and those who supported Him, those who were friends and family and those who were enemies, those who were Jews and those who were Gentiles, those who were civilians and those who were soldiers. Below is John 19:25-27:

> Near the cross of Jesus stood his mother, his mother's sister, Mary the wife of Clopas, and Mary Magdalene. When Jesus saw his mother there, and the disciple whom he loved standing nearby, he said to his mother, "Woman, here is your son," and to the disciple, "Here is your mother." From that time on, this disciple took her into his home.

Let's consider all of the witnesses: Jesus' mother, John the apostle, Clopas's wife Mary, Mary Magdalene, Joseph, various women disciples, Simon of Cyrene, a "large number of people," chief priests, teachers of the Law, elders, passersby, and a centurion. This is an impressive list of eyewitnesses. From high ranking officials, to normal everyday people, from those that knew Jesus personally, to those that hated Him or knew Him from a distance; all types of witnesses saw Jesus crucified. The point here is that Jesus' crucifixion did not occur in a dark corner. It was a public crucifixion witnessed by many people. These people had firsthand knowledge of what had happened.

Notice Pilate's reaction in Mark 15: Pilate did not witness the crucifixion firsthand. However, he was surprised to learn that Jesus had died so quickly. He had a hard time believing it so he sent a centurion to verify the death. The centurion was obligated to do his job properly or his life could be forfeit! Only after the centurion verified Jesus' death did Pilate release His body to Joseph of Arimathea to be buried.

Up to this point in time, just following Jesus' death, in the previous three sections above, we have presented various types of New Testament witnesses from different perspectives that directly or indirectly testify to Jesus' crucifixion. Note that the statement of crucifixion is not disputed anywhere. There were probably hundreds of witnesses to Jesus' crucifixion and as such this event of Jesus' crucifixion was accepted as fact by the people of Jerusalem, that is, Jesus' crucifixion was accepted as public knowledge.

Many weeks later, on the Day of Pentecost, Peter preached the Gospel to the Jews and declared that the people had handed Jesus over to be crucified (Acts 2:23). Note the people's response in verse 37:

> When the people heard this, they were cut to the heart and said to Peter and the other apostles, "Brothers, what shall we do?"

The people received Peter's rebuke because they knew it to be true. Nobody challenged Peter's statement. A short while later Peter was brought before the religious rulers and he accused them of the misdeed. He repeated his rebuke and not one of the authorities disputed his statement:

> Know this, you and all the people of Israel: It is by the name of Jesus Christ of Nazareth, whom you crucified but whom God raised from the dead, that this man stands before you healed (Acts 4:10).

The religious leaders did not dispute Peter's accusation because they knew they played a part in having Jesus crucified. In Acts 5:30, and Acts 7:51-53 the theme is repeated, and again, no rejection of the accusation occurs. If the Jewish leaders had been falsely accused then they would have taken immediate action to prosecute the accusers; instead, they received the accusation and did not refute it.

Therefore, even if you reject Jesus' crucifixion you must be honest and admit that the theme of His crucifixion is woven comprehensively throughout the Old and New Testament. The event of the crucifixion is not some spurious addition to the Gospel; it is not something that someone added casually. The crucifixion is rooted and entwined as part of the Gospel message. Thus, the addition of the crucifixion to the Gospel would not just be a minor corruption but a wholesale corruption that occurred during the lifetimes of the eyewitnesses. Such a widespread corruption (which the Quran does not even allow for) happening so quickly and drowning out any dissent is obviously impossible. Everyone knew Jesus was crucified. The crucifixion was a fundamental part of the Gospel message that Jesus predicted and preached and it remains a fundamental part of the Gospel message today.

### Historians' Evidence

There is other testimony from non-Christians to Jesus' crucifixion. *The Roman historian Tacitus,* who lived not long after Jesus died (AD 56–117), documented in his work "Annals" that Jesus had been killed:

> Christus, from whom the name had its origin, suffered the extreme penalty during the reign of Tiberius at the hands of one of our procurators, Pontius Pilatus, and a most mischievous superstition, thus checked for the moment, again broke out not only in Judaea, the first source of the evil, but even in Rome, where all things hideous and shameful from every part of the world find their centre and become popular. [9]

*The Assyrian writer Lucian of Samosata* lived from AD 125 to 180 and also detailed Jesus' death and how Christians lived their faith:

> The Christians, you know, worship a man to this day,—the distinguished personage who introduced their novel rites, and was crucified on that account...

> Peregrine, all this time, was making quite an income on the strength of his bondage; money came pouring in. You see, these misguided creatures start with the general conviction that they are immortal for all time, which explains the contempt of death and voluntary self-devotion which are so common among them; and then it was impressed on them by their original lawgiver that they are all brothers, from the moment that they are converted, and deny the gods of Greece, and worship the crucified sage, and live after his laws. [10]

Lucian and Tacitus were not eyewitnesses to the crucifixion. Tacitus was a serious historian and Lucian was an accomplished writer. Both men documented, not long after Jesus' death, that Jesus was crucified.

## Medical Evidence

Jesus' crucifixion has attracted interest from people in the medical field, both Christian and non-Christian. Details of Jesus' suffering and crucifixion from the Gospels are often compared to known medical facts about such torture and crucifixion. What they have found is that what the Gospels describe aligns with medical knowledge. The witnesses' details of what happened to Jesus are in line with the medical facts. This leads to a conclusion that someone was actually tortured and crucified. Below are quotes from various articles on the medical aspects of what Jesus experienced.

> In conclusion, we now have empirical evidence of a crucifixion. Death on a cross could be prolonged or swift. The crucifixion of Josephus' acquaintance who survived should not be projected to the crucifixion of Jesus. The major extra biblical paradigm for crucifixion is no longer Josephus; it is the archaeological data summarized above. The crucifixion of Jesus, who did not possess a gladiator's physique and stamina, did not commence but culminated when he was nailed to the cross. After the brutal, all night scourging by Roman soldiers, who would have relished an opportunity to vent their hatred of the Jews and disgust for Palestinian life, Jesus was practically dead. I see no reason why the Synoptic account does not contain one of the few bruta facta from his life when it reports that, as he began to stagger from Herod's palace to Golgotha, he was too weak to carry the cross; Simon of Cyrene carried it for him. Metaphors should not be confused with actualities nor faith with history. It is not a confession of faith to affirm that Jesus died on Golgotha that Friday afternoon; it is a probability obtained by the highest canons of scientific historical research. [11]

The short excerpt below is from Dr. C. Truman Davis's analysis of the crucifixion tied to Jesus' physiological experiences. He concludes with:

> Apparently to make doubly sure of death, the legionnaire drove his lance through the fifth interspace between the ribs, upward through the pericardium and into the heart. The 34th verse of the 19th chapter of the Gospel according to St. John reports: "And immediately there came out blood and water." That is, there was an escape of water fluid from the sac surrounding the heart, giving postmortem evidence that our Lord died not the usual crucifixion death by suffocation, but of heart failure (a broken heart) due to shock and constriction of the heart by fluid in the pericardium.
>
> Thus we have had our glimpse—including the medical evidence—of that epitome of evil which man has exhibited toward Man and toward God. It has been a terrible sight, and more than enough to leave us despondent and depressed. How grateful we can be that we have the great sequel in the infinite mercy of God toward man—at once the miracle of the atonement and the expectation of the triumphant Easter morning. [12]

There are many other sites and articles written about the medical aspects of Jesus' crucifixion if you wish to study the event in depth. The point here is that the New Testament writings that depict Jesus' physical experiences align with known medical facts. There is nothing unreasonable or fallacious in the medical aspects of the testimony concerning the crucifixion.

### Summary of the Evidence

1. The Old Testament, Quran, and New Testament all agree that the prophets suffered and died by the hands of evil men.

2. The Old Testament foretold that the Messiah would suffer and die.

3. Jesus stated that He would suffer and die and tied His predictions to the Old Testament prophecies describing the sufferings of the Messiah.

4. The Gospel accounts describe Jesus' suffering, death, and resurrection.

5. Postresurrection Jesus told His disciples that the Old Testament Scriptures foretold that the Messiah would suffer and die before entering His glory.

6. The disciples proclaimed that Jesus was crucified and resurrected.

7. The Jewish people accepted the disciples' assertions that they were responsible for Jesus' crucifixion.

8. Later non-Christian writers and historians recorded aspects of the Christians' lifestyles and beliefs and detailed that Jesus was crucified.

9. Medical facts corroborate the physiological sufferings experienced by Jesus detailed in the Gospels.

This evidence substantiates that the New Testament's presentation of Jesus' crucifixion bears scrutiny and is reliable.

## The Islamic Argument Cross-Examined

As stated earlier, most Muslims interpret sura 4:157-158 to mean that someone other than Jesus was crucified. They hold to stories such as Ibn Kathir's. On the surface, the Muslim argument may seem plausible to someone who is not familiar with the history of the region. But let it be cross-examined and see if it stands up to scrutiny.

Would Jesus' mother fail to recognize her own son? Ibn Kathir thinks so but we question it. Even if a substitute looked like Jesus, Mary would be able to discern the difference. Mothers can even tell their twins apart.

Further, in the Gospel account Jesus speaks to His mother and His disciple John and instructs John to care for His mother. Even experiencing a painful death a loving son would seek the welfare of his mother. Someone else would be far less inclined to care about others not intimate with him. Additionally, Ibn Kathir's account has a dead man speaking to Mary. Does that make any sense?

The Quran does not say what happened to Jesus following the crucifixion. But there the Quran mentions that Jesus was raised to God:

> I told them only what You bade me. I said: "Serve God, my
> Lord and your Lord." I watched over them while living in
> their midst, and ever since You took me to Yourself, You have
> been watching them. You are the witness of all things (5:117).

The Quran tells us that at some point during His life, Jesus was raised up to God. Some Muslims believe that He was taken up to God the day of His supposed crucifixion! What they are saying is that God allowed an innocent man to suffer and die in Jesus' place. As we showed earlier, the Quran states that many prophets suffered and died at the hands of evil men. If God intended to raise Jesus to heaven why not allow Him to bear His own cross and endure sufferings just as other prophets?

There are "tests of truth" used to evaluate conflicting testimony. One test concerns itself with the amount of detail within each account. When you compare the Gospel accounts of the crucifixion you find many details corroborating each other. The Quran fails to provide anything of substantive value other than an unclear denial of Jesus' crucifixion, and that, in and of itself, seems to divide Muslim scholars to this day. The Bible's account provides interconnected and compelling details. The Quran's account contains but two verses. This type of "test of truth" leans toward the Bible.

Kenneth Cragg raises a strong objection to the claims that it wasn't Jesus by asking a pointed question:

> What are we to say of the nature of a God Who behaves
> in this way or of the character of a Christ Who permits
> another—even if a Judas—to suffer the consequences of an

antagonism His own teaching has aroused against Himself? Is this kind of victory the worthiest in prophets of God? The antagonism is there, on the Muslim hypothesis. The question is: what does God do, what does Jesus do, with it. The answer is unmistakably that Jesus suffers it.[13]

Cragg challenges the depiction of God and Jesus—that God would allow an innocent man to endure the sufferings and death meant for Jesus. Jesus was a strong man and He made a stand. He never attempted to trick or connive His way out of a tough situation.

Indeed, it is surprising that any Muslim would respect a prophet who ran from danger and allowed someone else to suffer in His place. Jesus running from the trouble He was facing and letting another pay the penalty seems utterly unbecoming of the kind of bravery that Muslims revere in their prophets and leaders. In fact, faith in the face of martyrdom is a chief virtue for Muslims. Indeed, it makes far more sense that a Muslim would more readily believe that Jesus faced His death with dignity and purpose. The Gospels tell us that He did.

Ibn Kathir's story contains several historical errors:

1. There was no Greek king in Damascus who ruled over Jerusalem during Jesus' time.

2. Roman provincial rulers had to go through some type of trial before they could outright crucify someone.

3. Ibn Kathir's story is unable to state how many disciples were with Jesus—12, 13, or 17.

4. Why did the disciples in the house with Jesus see His ascension but the deputies outside failed to see it?

5. Why did the disciples who saw Jesus ascend fail to teach the other disciples that Jesus was taken up by God?

These errors and logical inconsistencies are enough to warrant a casting aside of Ibn Kathir's story as an imaginary tale.

Finally there seems to be an internal inconsistency within the Quran if one believes that in sura 4:157-158 Allah made someone else look like Jesus to experience the suffering, crucifixion, and death. As such, the Jews boasted of crucifying Jesus. Then, according to Ibn Kathir, Christians there believed the Jews' report and subsequently taught that Jesus had been crucified.

John Gilchrist concludes:

> ...no one can seriously believe in the substitution theory if he believes that God acts nobly and consistently at all times. If the man crucified was made to appear to be Jesus himself, is it then surprising that his disciples and followers really believed it was him and so founded the whole Christian faith on a hoax, an illusion of which God himself was the deliberate author? Many of Jesus' disciples laid down their lives preaching Christ crucified—all for nothing, all because they were deceived by the God of a prophet for whom they had left everything to be his followers (Mark 10.28)? The substitution theory implies that God is the author of the greatest fraud in history.[14]

The evaluation of Ibn Kathir's interpretation of sura 4:157-158 and his supporting story (which is based on earlier Muslim scholars' writings) shows that his story is a myth. His story contains a number of mistakes, inconsistencies, and illogical statements. It contains historical errors, it does not account for various details or logical expectations, and makes God complicit in spreading a lie.

In conclusion, when the sum total of the writings are examined we find that they agree on all primary details. From the Old Testament writings stating that the Messiah was to suffer, to Jesus forth-telling His suffering and death, to the various Gospel accounts of the crucifixion event, to Jesus' statements following His resurrection, to the apostolic proclamations of the Gospel and acceptance of responsibility by the Jewish people, the crucifixion-related statements are in harmony. There were hundreds of eyewitnesses to the event and there is no recorded challenge or contradiction to the claim of crucifixion. Many of these witnesses knew Jesus personally. Their testimony is consistent from beginning to end. The men who proclaimed the crucifixion and resurrection put their lives on the line and many died because of it. These men knew Jesus had been crucified and saw the resurrected Messiah. They lived their lives proclaiming the Gospel and died willingly for it.

# Muhammad and the Bible:
## Is He the "Counselor" Foretold by Jesus?

Muslims' question:
*"Shouldn't Christians accept Muhammad as a prophet
because the Bible mentions and prophesies his coming?"*

We want to explore the Islamic claim that the Bible foretells Muhammad. No matter where we go, in almost every dialogue with Muslims, the issue that "Muhammad is mentioned in the Bible" becomes a major point of conversation.

Before we look at the Scriptures we need to make a key point. Both Christians and Muslims need to understand that knowing a material's context or the background of a particular passage is critical to understanding that material. Context is key to understanding what religious texts mean. This is true of the Bible and of the Quran. In Islamic studies, there is an entire field of study dedicated to understanding the context behind the Quranic verses: "asbab al-nuzul" ("the occasion behind the revelation"). Without that effort the results of Quranic interpretation would be a twisting mass of confusion because the Quran contains little contextual material. No one would be able to tell what verses were spoken when, where, and why they were given. No one would know which of the apparent contradictory verses held sway over others (that is, abrogation). So in both Quranic and biblical studies knowing context is required.

One of Islam's theological concepts that links it to Christianity and Judaism is the claim that Muhammad is foretold or mentioned in the

Bible. Several important Islamic texts make this claim. The Quran 7:157 states:

> Those who follow the messenger, the Prophet who can nei-
> ther read nor write, *whom they will find described in the Torah
> and the Gospel* (which are) with them. He will enjoin on them
> that which is right and forbid them that which is wrong. He
> will make lawful for them all good things and prohibit for
> them only the foul; and he will relieve them of their burden
> and the fetters that they used to wear. Then those who believe
> in him, and honour him, and help him, and follow the light
> which is sent down with him: they are the successful.

Additionally, the Quran states that Jesus foretold that another prophet, named "Ahmad," would come:

> And when Jesus son of Mary said: O Children of Israel! Lo! I
> am the messenger of Allah unto you, confirming that which
> was (revealed) before me in the Torah, and bringing good
> tidings of *a messenger who cometh after me, whose name is the
> Praised One*. Yet when he hath come unto them with clear
> proofs, they say: This is mere magic (61:6).

Similar claims are stated in the Hadith collections of Abul-Husain Muslim[1] and Muhammad al-Bukhari.[2] Another detailed claim is found in Ibn Ishaq's *Sirat Rasul Allah*, which identifies Muhammad as the "Comforter." The book's translator, A. Guillaume, notes that Muslims have corrupted their historical texts by injecting Muhammad as the Comforter into the text in order to fulfill sura 7:157. As such, the Muslim scholars misquoted the New Testament and took it out of context. In his notes, Guillaume goes on to analyze the quote and concludes that somehow, perhaps through no fault of his own, Ibn Ishaq's theology or understanding is flawed or corrupted.

This is a sensitive subject for Muslims because the Quran is out on a limb claiming that Muhammad is foretold in the Bible. Consequently, Muslims have searched the Bible to find passages that may point to Muhammad. There are a dozen or so biblical passages cited by various

Muslim apologists and polemicists as proof behind that claim. Most of their claims are totally out of context and not based upon logical reasoning. Unfortunately, it is easy to take a bad argument and make it sound good when the audience is not well versed in the subject. However, when you take a deeper look, you find scarce discussion in those Muslim claims of the meaning of the passage or use of related biblical references.

In that light we're going to examine the two most frequently quoted Bible passages used by Muslims to prove that the Bible predicts Muhammad. These passages are 1) Muhammad is the Counselor, or the Comforter, foretold by Jesus in John 14–16; and 2) Muhammad is the prophet foretold by Moses in Deuteronomy 18. We are going to address these claims by examining the scope and the meaning of those biblical passages. We will also discuss the various aspects and implications of the Muslim claims. We are going to do this in some detail because most Muslims do not know the Bible (just as many Christians do not know the Quran) and this is a very important topic to them.

### Is Muhammad the Counselor (Comforter)?

First of all, some translations use the word "Comforter" but "Counselor," or "Advocate," in a legal sense, are more accurate translations. The New Testament passages in question are John 14–16. These are a subset of Jesus' "Farewell Discourse" which covers John 13 through 17. Jesus' discourse occurs during a special time: Jesus is sharing dinner with His disciples just before the Passover celebration. Jesus knows that His betrayal will occur soon so during this time He gives His final words to His beloved disciples. This is a sensitive time and He speaks intimately with them. As John says,

> It was just before the Passover Festival. Jesus knew that the hour had come for him to leave this world and go to the Father. Having loved his own who were in the world, he loved them to the end (John 13:1).

If you spend 20 minutes or so and read chapters 13 through 17 you'll see Christ's love for His disciples expressed over and over, from

His washing of their feet in humble service, to His prayer for them in chapter 17. His love is being expressed *to them*, His words are given specifically *to them*. You see this brought out more fully in His prayer when He prays *for them*, and for future believers: "My prayer is not for them alone. I pray also for those who will believe in me through their message" (17:20). This context then is essential for understanding this scriptural passage.

Here are the specific verses that mention or talk about the Counselor:

1. John 14:15-17
2. John 14:25-27
3. John 15:26
4. John 16:7-8
5. John 16:13-15
6. John 7:37-39 (related to the above five verses)

Take a few minutes and review those verses and their context in those chapters.

Since Muslim apologists use these very verses as proof of Muhammad predicted by the Bible (that is, these verses are not "corrupted" by their standards), we will use these verses as part of our discussion. Let's work through these scriptures, make observations, establish actual facts about these verses, and then ask counter-questions.

What do these Scriptures tell us about the identity of the "Counselor," or "Comforter"? There are 13 critical details:

1. The "Father" is giving the Counselor. Since Islamic doctrine denies that God can be a Father (Quran 5:18 and "Father" is not one of the Islamic names for God) then there is a contradiction between this "uncorrupted" verse, and Muhammad's teachings (John 14:15).

2. Several times throughout this discourse Jesus promises that the Counselor will interact with these disciples. He says that the Father will send the Comforter to "you," that the

Comforter will "come to you," and that the Comforter will "guide you into all truth." Jesus isn't talking about some 570 years later when Muhammad lived. Jesus is talking to His disciples in the present, with Him in the *now*. Muhammad never interacted with these disciples (John 14:25-27; 16:13).

3. The Counselor would be with these disciples forever. People do not live forever and Muhammad only lived to be some 63 years old (John 14:15-16).

4. Jesus identifies the Counselor as a spirit, the Spirit of truth, the Holy Spirit. Muhammad was not, and never was, a spirit (John 15:26).

5. The world could not know or see the Counselor. Everybody could see Muhammad and thousands of people knew him (John 14:15-17).

6. Jesus told His disciples that they already knew the Counselor. They did not know Muhammad (John 14:17).

7. Jesus said that the Counselor lived with these same disciples. That means that the Counselor would have to be omnipresent to be with all of them simultaneously. Muhammad would not live for another 570 years or so (John 14:17).

8. The Counselor would be "in" the disciples. Muhammad was not even a gleam in his great-great-grandfather's eye when Jesus spoke those words. Please note that the Greek word here translated as "in" means to be inside of (John 14:17).

9. The Counselor would teach these disciples what Jesus said to them earlier. Muhammad would not begin to speak the Quran until about 600 years later (John 14:25-27).

10. Jesus would send the Counselor to the disciples which were with Him. Muhammad could not have sent anything

to these disciples as he didn't live until 570+ years later
(John 15:26).

11. The Counselor goes out from the Father. Muhammad was
born to Amina and Abdullah and did not come directly
from God (John 15:26).

12. The Counselor will guide these disciples into all truth.
Muhammad could not guide anyone into all truth because
he did not know all truth. In fact, the Quran (10:94)
commands Muhammad to ask the Christians and Jews
about truth if he has any doubts (John 16:13).

13. The Counselor will testify about Jesus. Muhammad
mentioned Jesus in the Quran and Hadith to make
theological points but did not personally testify about
or glorify Jesus as Christ intended. The Quran's primary
message glorifies Muhammad, i.e., people are able to
enter Paradise if they believe in and obey Allah and his
messenger Muhammad.

### Does Muhammad Fit the Description?

Take into account the background of the passages and answer the
questions honestly. Did the Father send Muhammad to these disciples?
Did the disciples know Muhammad? Did he teach those disciples? Of
course not. We could go on and ask a number of similar questions and
the logical and honest answer to them would be a resounding "*No!*
Muhammad does not fulfill the statements about the Counselor!" It's
just not there.

In the book *The Islam Debate*, John Gilchrist and I (Josh) summa-
rize a review of this topic and present our conclusion:

> In light of the clear references in John to the fact that the
> Comforter is the Holy Spirit (John 14:17 and 26; 15:26;
> 16:13), it is hard to draw any other valid conclusion. A care-
> ful study of the passage helps identify the Comforter as the
> Spirit, and not Muhammad.

> It does seem clear from the four texts quoted that Comforter, Holy Spirit and Spirit of Truth are interchangeable terms and that Jesus is speaking of the same person in each instance. The one fact that emerges is that the Comforter is a spirit.[3]

If you are being true and honest with yourself then you'll admit that Muhammad could not be the Counselor who Jesus foretold would come to those disciples. We want to emphasize this for the readers because those who believe in a just God know instinctively that He wants complete honesty from His followers. He wants us to be true to the evidence. We appeal to the reader to consider the evidence with an open mind and heart. There is no way that Muhammad could fulfill what Jesus told His disciples about the Counselor.

On the other hand, the Holy Spirit fulfills what Jesus said. The Holy Spirit was already with them, but not "in" them. They knew the Holy Spirit for they knew Jesus. The Father would later send the Holy Spirit to indwell them. The Holy Spirit would teach, guide, and instruct them. The world could not see the Spirit and the world could not know the Spirit.

## The Larger Context: Old Testament Prophecy and Its Fulfillment

At the beginning of this chapter, we emphasized the need for the reader to take the overall context of this theme into account. Now we want to present a much broader scope, a scope that goes beyond John's passages.

To begin with there are a number of other verses that tie into the "Counselor," the Holy Spirit, that have not been reviewed. The first deals with what Jesus told the disciples in John, and it is found in the book of Acts, 1:1-8. Below are verses 7 and 8:

> He said to them: "It is not for you to know the times or dates the Father has set by his own authority. But you will receive power when the Holy Spirit comes on you; and you will be my witnesses in Jerusalem, and in all Judea and Samaria, and to the ends of the earth."

Jesus commanded His disciples to wait in Jerusalem to be baptized by the Counselor, the Holy Spirit. This was to occur *"in a few days."* The Counselor would empower these disciples to preach the Gospel throughout the world. This passage correlates to what Jesus stated in John 14:25-26.

### The Arrival of the Counselor and the Prophecy Fulfilled

How and when were Jesus' prophetic words in John fulfilled?

About ten days after Christ's ascension the disciples gathered together. Up to this point the disciples had not engaged in any public ministry. But then an extraordinary event happened—the Counselor came to them!

> When the day of Pentecost came, they were all together in one place. Suddenly a sound like the blowing of a violent wind came from heaven and filled the whole house where they were sitting. They saw what seemed to be tongues of fire that separated and came to rest on each of them. All of them were filled with the Holy Spirit and began to speak in other tongues as the Spirit enabled them (Acts 2:1-4).

The Counselor, the Holy Spirit, came to those disciples and entered them, filled them, and enabled them to preach the Gospel boldly. Peter preached to the crowd that had gathered for the Feast of Pentecost and his words are recorded in Acts 2:29-41. Below are verses 38 and 39:

> Peter replied, "Repent and be baptized, every one of you, in the name of Jesus Christ for the forgiveness of your sins. And you will receive the gift of the Holy Spirit. The promise is for you and your children and for all who are far off—for all whom the Lord our God will call."

After receiving the Comforter, Peter and the disciples were boldly preaching the Gospel to the crowd. Did you note that Peter said that those who believe would receive the "promise" of the "gift" of the Holy Spirit? Notice how this ties in to Jesus' words about the Holy Spirit:

By this he meant the Spirit, whom those who *believed* in him were later to receive (John 7:39).

While he was preaching, Peter told the people that what they saw happening was the fulfillment of prophecy from their Scriptures:

> Then Peter stood up with the Eleven, raised his voice and addressed the crowd: "Fellow Jews and all of you who live in Jerusalem, let me explain this to you; listen carefully to what I say. These men are not drunk, as you suppose. It's only nine in the morning! No, this is what was spoken by the prophet Joel:

> "'In the last days, God says,
> I will pour out my Spirit on all people.
> Your sons and daughters will prophesy,
> your young men will see visions,
> your old men will dream dreams.
> Even on my servants, both men and women,
> I will pour out my Spirit in those days,
> and they will prophesy'" (Acts 2:14-18).

This drives the theme deeper and roots it into the Old Testament. Jesus' words to His disciples about the Counselor were not new or unrelated to God's promises. Rather, they were a fulfillment of what their Jewish Scriptures predicted; a prophecy spoken by God about the last days. There is a continuity between the faith and theology of the Old Testament and that of the New Testament. God promised His people that He would pour His Spirit out upon them. Jesus promised His disciples that He would send the Holy Spirit to them. Both of these promises were fulfilled on the Day of Pentecost!

The prophecies concerning the Counselor covered more than Jesus' time and words to His disciples; they extend hundreds of years in the past. They are anchored as God's promise for those that choose to believe and obey Him.

Jesus is revealed here as more than a prophet. He said that He would send the Counselor, or Advocate:

> Very truly I tell you, it is for your good that I am going away.
> Unless I go away, the Advocate will not come to you; but if I
> go, I will send him to you (John 16:7).

No prophet ever had the power to direct the Spirit of God and send
Him. Jesus said He would send the Spirit. Jesus was indeed more than
a prophet.

## A Different Argument: "Counselor" Versus "Praised One"

Some Muslim apologists take a different approach to the passages
in John that foretell the Counselor. They assert that the Greek word
for counselor or comforter, "paracletos," has been corrupted and that
the original word was "periclytos," which translated means "praised
one." *By using this argument they state that the Muslims who claim that
Muhammad is the "Counselor" are in error,* because those Muslims
accept the word "Counselor," not "Praised One." We wonder if Muslims understand this internal division and conflict they have with each
other, centered on these arguments.

Like the Muslims who wish to validate the Quran by forcing
Muhammad into John's passages, these Muslims wish to validate the
Quran by forcing Muhammad's name, "Ahmad," into those passages.
As we mentioned earlier the name "Ahmad" ties in with the Quranic
verse 61:6, which foretells an "Ahmad" to come.

Dr. Campbell addresses this claim:

> The first thing to be understood is that in Greek, unlike Ara-
> bic, the vowels are written into the text. Thus to change from
> pErIclYtos to pArAclEtos would require the alteration of
> three written letters.

Secondly there is absolutely no textual evidence for such a reading. Not one copy of the Gospel of John, from the oldest Greek copy
of AD 200 until now, shows "periclytos" in place of "paracletos." Photograph 7 of Papyrus p75 from AD 200 shows John 14:9-26a. The last
word on the page clearly shows "PARACLETOS" from verse 26. Verse
16 has been partly destroyed, but in the middle of the line marked by
the two arrows one can still see "PARACL - N" for "paracleton" ("ON"

signifies a direct object). In the first case the whole word is visible and in the second, two of the three letters under discussion can be clearly seen.

Thirdly, although "periclytos," which means famous or renowned, was used by Homer when he wrote *The Iliad* and *The Odyssey* in the classical Greek of the tenth century BC, there is not one instance where this word, or any of the other members of its word group, are used in the Koine Greek of the New Testament or the Septuagint [that is, Greek] translation of the Old Testament.

Thus there is neither textual nor linguistic support for "periclytos."

Dr. Campbell provides some biblical background for the meaning of the Greek word:

> A paraclete is someone who can be called on for help. Therefore the meaning depends on what kind of help you need, whether defense by an "advocate—a lawyer," or comfort by a "comforter" in time of sadness…[the] dictionary defines it as (1) intercessor, (2) advocate, (3) consoler or comforter and (4) exhorter. There is no single English or French or Arabic word which includes all these meanings. So we are back to context!…
>
> "Praise be to the God and Father of our Lord Jesus Christ, the Father of compassion and the God of all comfort (paraklesis), who comforts (parakaleo) us in all our troubles, so that we can comfort (parakaleo) those in any trouble with the comfort (paraklesis) with which we ourselves are comforted (parakaleo) of God." [4]

Similarly, in the book *Answering Islam* by Norman Geisler and Abdul Saleeb, the issue of "paraclete versus periclytos" and the context of the verses in John is discussed:

> Of the over 5366 Greek manuscripts of the New Testament there is absolutely no manuscript authority for placing the word "periclytos" ("praised one") in the original, as the Muslims claim it should read. Rather, they read paraclete ("helper"). [5]

Look at it from a different perspective. Muslims would be offended greatly if we were to say that the original Quran had different words than that Quran released as Uthman's recension (critical revision) of the Quran. (The Islamic Caliph Uthman released what is considered to be the standard Quran in worldwide use today. Prior to that there were many differing Qurans in existence and Uthman ordered them all destroyed.) If we were to proclaim that today's Quran is corrupted from what Muhammad originally spoke, Muslims would be right to challenge us to produce evidence (which actually does exist). However, Muslims who claim that "periclytos" is the correct spelling need to produce evidence. Unlike the variant Qurans, there is no manuscript evidence for "periclytos." Since they cannot produce any evidence, they have an obligation to tell their readers that they have no evidence and they are only assuming what it says and means. Remember, even other Muslims disagree with them and accept the word "counselor" to be correct.

## Who Did the Early Church Think Was the Counselor?

A basic principle of interpretation of a historical text is, "how did the people of the day understand its meaning?" In their language and culture, what did it mean to them? Jesus' disciples passed on His teachings to their disciples, who passed it on to their disciples, and so on. How did the early Church Fathers (that is, leaders) view the meaning of "counselor"? Who did they think the Counselor was? Ignatius, Tertullian, and Origen all believed the Counselor was the Holy Spirit. Below is a quote from Ignatius from his letter to the Philippians:

> "What is His name, or what is His Son's name, that we may know?" And there is also one Paraclete. For "there is also," saith [the Scripture], "one Spirit," since "we have been called in one hope of our calling." And again, "We have drunk of one Spirit," with what follows. And it is manifest that all these gifts [possessed by believers] "worketh one and the selfsame Spirit." There are not then either three Fathers, or three Sons, or three Paracletes, but one Father, and one Son, and one Paraclete.[6]

Knowing what the early church believed about the Counselor is important because it illustrates a continuity of belief and theology from the time of Jesus extended into church history. You don't find the early Church Fathers saying that the Counselor was going to be a mortal man who would teach them new doctrines, rather you find the Fathers teaching the same thing that Jesus and the apostles taught: the Counselor was the Holy Spirit who now empowered the church.

## A Good Pushback Question from Muslims

In any religious discussion there will be a series of rebuttals and counter rebuttals. But there is one Muslim counter-assertion we found to be strong enough to deserve a complete answer. This is the assertion: "The Holy Spirit cannot be the Counselor because Jesus said He had to leave in order for the Counselor, or Advocate, to come: 'Unless I go away, the Advocate will not come to you; but if I go, I will send him to you' (John 16:7).

"Since the Spirit of God was already present on earth, He could not fulfill Jesus' words. Since the Holy Spirit was already present on earth before and during Jesus' time, He does not match the fact that Jesus said He must depart in order for the Counselor to come."

### Answer

Pointing out that the Holy Spirit was already present with Jesus and the disciples is a good and accurate observation. The Holy Spirit is shown to have acted in both the Old and New Testaments before Jesus' death and resurrection. But Jesus actually told them the same thing in John 14:17: "You know him, for he lives with you and will be in you"! *The Holy Spirit was with them, but later He would be "in" them!*

*The Expositor's Bible Commentary* adds this detailed comment on the Holy Spirit's ministry:

> John the Baptist had predicted that Jesus would baptize with the Holy Spirit (Matt 3:11; Mark 1:8; Luke 3:16; John 1:33). In his discussion of the new birth, Jesus had already spoken to Nicodemus of the work of the Holy Spirit (John 3:5). The ministry of the Spirit, however, would be directed primarily

to the disciples. He would direct their decisions, counsel them continually, and remain with them forever. He would be invisible to all and un-apprehended by the world at large since the world would not recognize him. To use a modern metaphor, he would not operate on the world's wavelength. His presence was already with the disciples insofar as they were under his influence. *Later, he would indwell them, when Jesus himself had departed.* This distinction marks the difference between the Old Testament experience of the Holy Spirit and the post-Pentecostal experience of the church. The individual indwelling of the Spirit is the specific privilege of the Christian believer (see John 7:39).[7]

Observe again John 7:38-39:

> "Whoever believes in me, as Scripture has said, rivers of living water will flow from within them." By this he meant the Spirit, whom those who believed in him were later to receive. Up to that time the Spirit had not been given, since Jesus had not yet been glorified.

The commentary above answers the question and explains the differences between the Holy Spirit being present on earth versus His "indwelling" the disciples. This key difference is emphasized by the prophecy in Joel. The indwelling of the Holy Spirit was a promise and a gift from God given to those who believe that Jesus is the Messiah, the Son of God.

### Conclusion on Muhammad as the Counselor

We have established several critical points regarding the Islamic claim that Muhammad is the Counselor:

1. A simple but honest reading of John's passages (verses that Muslims implicitly accept as uncorrupted) proves that the Counselor is the Holy Spirit.

2. When the context of the passages is understood there can be no doubt that the Counselor is the Holy Spirit.

3. The early Christians also believed that the Counselor was the Holy Spirit.

4. There is a continuity between the Old and New Testaments regarding the outpouring of the Holy Spirit and the fulfillment of that prophecy by the coming of the Counselor at Pentecost.

5. The Islamic claim that "periclytos" (that is, Ahmad), instead of "paracletos," is the original reading is totally without evidence. The evidence is overwhelming that "paracletos" is the original word. Not only do the oldest manuscripts contain "paracletos," but not one, not even one of the 5,366 Greek manuscripts contains the word "periclytos," which many Muslims claim is the original wording.

# Muhammad and the Bible:
# Is He the "Prophet" Foretold by Moses?

Muslims' question:
*"Moses foretold that a new prophet would come
with God's Word. Couldn't Muhammad be that prophet?"*

The most frequently cited passage found in the Old Testament that Muslims claim foretells Muhammad is based on Deuteronomy 18:14-20.

> Though these nations you are about to drive out listen to fortune-tellers and diviners, the LORD your God has not permitted you to do this.

> The LORD your God will raise up for you a prophet like me from among your own brothers. You must listen to him. This is what you requested from the LORD your God at Horeb on the day of the assembly when you said, "Let us not continue to hear the voice of the LORD our God or see this great fire any longer, so that we will not die!" Then the LORD said to me, "They have spoken well. I will raise up for them a prophet like you from among their brothers. I will put My words in his mouth, and he will tell them everything I command him. I will hold accountable whoever does not listen to My words that he speaks in My name. But the prophet who dares to speak in My name a message I have not commanded him to speak, or who speaks in the name of other gods—that prophet must die" (HCSB).

Before we proceed a couple of important points need to be understood:

1. In chapter 8 we emphasized that "context" is key to understanding the meaning of a religious text. This is relevant for this passage's meaning of "a prophet."

2. We are going to touch on a variety of doctrines, both Islamic and Christian, and our intention is not to go into deep theological discussions related to Muhammad's prophethood or Christ's divinity in this chapter, but rather to take their words at face value and discuss them as such. This may trouble both Christians and Muslims but those discussions are outside the scope of this chapter.

## Deuteronomy's Context

"Deuteronomy" means "a repeating of the Law." Moses was leading the Israelites and he retold them or "repeated" to them the Law of God. He recounted the commandments given in Exodus, Leviticus, and Numbers. Soon the Israelites were going to cross into the promised land, Canaan, and Moses was reinforcing God's word to His people. He knew that strict obedience to God was essential if the Israelites were to succeed and be victorious when they entered Canaan. He also knew that he was not going to enter the land with them, so he gave them the best encouragement and admonition he could in his last words to his people.

Moses is giving his most heartfelt words and warnings to his people, God's people, because he loved them and wanted them to succeed. He was repeating to them the commands they needed to obey to insure their success. Go back and review the passage in question, Deuteronomy 18:14-19, and take note of what stands out to you relative to the characteristics of the future prophet Moses is talking about.

## What Can We Tell About the Future Prophet from This Passage?

Several requirements for this future prophet are obvious:

1. He will be a prophet like Moses. At this point there is no definition of what "like Moses" means. But he must be like Moses in some critical aspects.

2. He is to come from "among you, from among your fellow Israelites."

3. He is to speak God's words directly: "I will put my words in his mouth. He will tell them everything I command him."

4. This prophet is being sent to the Israelites, to speak to the Israelites and to command the Israelites.

We're going to review these requirements one at a time. Although we have four good starting points we still lack enough definition to narrow the search and distinguish if it is Jesus or Muhammad who fulfills them. Finding more details about the identity or characteristics of this future prophet from the context of Deuteronomy is critically important. Just as we should establish our understanding of specific verses in the Quran by using contextually related verses in the Quran (let the Quran interpret the Quran), so we should establish our understanding of specific verses in Deuteronomy by referencing contextually related verses in Deuteronomy (let the Bible interpret the Bible). We have to examine the contextual setting for this passage, that is, can we learn more about this passage from other passages in Deuteronomy?

## Requirement One: A Prophet "Like Moses"

Deuteronomy 34:10-12 sheds a great deal of light on what it means to be a prophet like Moses:

> Since then, no prophet has risen in Israel like Moses, whom the LORD knew face to face, who did all those signs and wonders the LORD sent him to do in Egypt—to Pharaoh and to all his officials and to his whole land. For no one has ever shown the mighty power or performed the awesome deeds that Moses did in the sight of all Israel.

From this verse we can identify two characteristics that set Moses apart:

1. The Lord knew him face-to-face.

2. He performed many signs and wonders in Egypt's and Israel's sight.

### Characteristic #1: Knowing God Face-to-Face

Let's start with "The Lord knew him face-to-face." Two relevant passages shed more light on this requirement. The first is found in Exodus 33:11:

> The LORD would speak to Moses face to face, as one speaks to a friend. Then Moses would return to the camp, but his young aide Joshua son of Nun did not leave the tent.

The second related verse, Numbers 12:1-9, about Moses' office as prophet, reinforces this special "face to face" relationship. Below are verses 5-8:

> The LORD…said, "Listen to my words:
> "When there is a prophet among you,
>     I, the LORD, reveal myself to them in visions,
>     I speak to them in dreams.
> But this is not true of my servant Moses;
>     he is faithful in all my house.
> With him I speak *face to face*,
>     clearly and not in riddles;
>     he sees the form of the LORD.
> Why then were you not afraid
>     to speak against my servant Moses?"

Let's review these religious texts and ask, "Did Jesus and Muhammad know God face-to-face?" Let's start with Muhammad. The Quran says that God cannot be seen in 6:103 and 42:51. Further there are a number of Hadith (for example, Sahih Muslim, volume 1, #337, and

Sahih Bukhari, volume 6, #378), that state that Muhammad did not see God. Muhammad saw angels but not Allah. The Quran and the Hadith state clearly that Muhammad could not and did not see God; therefore, Muhammad did not know God face-to-face as Moses knew Him.

What about Jesus? Did He know God face-to-face?

John's Gospel 1:15-18 states that Jesus not only had seen God, Jesus was with God from eternity. Later Jesus would say that He had seen the Father (John 6:43-51), and when Jesus prayed to the Father (John 17:1-5), He stated He was with the Father before the world began.

The *New International Version Study Bible* makes a pertinent comment regarding seeing God and John 1:18:

> "[Jesus] has made him known." Sometimes in the OT people are said to have seen God (e.g. Ex 24:9-11). But we are also told that no one can see God and live (Ex 33:20). Therefore, since no human being can see God as he really is, those who saw God saw him in a form he took on himself temporarily for the occasion. Now, however, Christ has made him known.[1]

*The New International Commentary on the New Testament* makes a similar comment:

> The emphatic declaration, "No one has ever seen God" (notice that the word "God" is in an emphatic position) is in line with the words of the Lord, "no one may see me and live" (Exodus. 33:20; cf. John 5:37; 6:46). Yet there are other passages that explicitly affirm that some people have seen God (for example, Exodus. 24:9-11). What then does John mean? Surely that in his essential being God has never yet been seen by people. Some had had their vision of God, but these were all partial. The theophanies [an appearance of God in human form] of the Old Testament did not and could not reveal God's essential being. But Christ has now made such a revelation. As Calvin puts it, "When he says that none has seen God, it is not to be understood of the outward seeing of the physical eye. He means generally that, since God dwells in

inaccessible light, He cannot be known except in Christ, His lively image." [2]

Jesus Himself says that He was with God before He came to earth, and that He has seen God (John 6:46) and knew God (John 10:15). Moses saw a "theophany," that is, an appearance of God in human form, but Jesus was with the Father and saw Him fully in heaven.

**Conclusion on characteristic #1 (knowing God face-to-face).** Jesus did know and see God face-to-face and thus He fulfills the requirement. On the other hand, the Quran and the Hadith state clearly that Muhammad did not see God, either as a theophany, or in His fullness of glory, but at most Muhammad saw God metaphorically, "with the eyes of his heart."

### Characteristic #2: "He Performed Many Signs and Wonders"

Did Jesus or Muhammad perform many signs and wonders in the eyes of their native populations, both believing and unbelieving?

*Let's start with Jesus.* Yes, Jesus did perform many miracles in the eyes of those who believed in Him and those who did not. Healing the paralytic in Luke 5:18-26 and raising a child from the dead in Matthew 9:18-26 are examples. Even the Quran in 3:48-50 says Jesus performed miracles.

Jesus' miracles in front of believers and nonbelievers fulfills the requirements of Deuteronomy 18. Both His followers and those who doubted Him saw the miracles He performed. Nobody challenged Him on His ability to work miracles. We can safely conclude that Jesus fulfills the prophetic requirements.

**Did Muhammad perform miracles in front of believers and disbelievers?** To answer this question accurately we have to consider the source materials of Islam: the Quran, Hadith, and Sira. The Quran states that Muhammad did not perform any miracles in the sight of the nonbelievers. In many passages throughout the Quran (for example, 6:37; 13:7; 28:48; 10:20; 17:90-93; and others), the nonbelievers challenge Muhammad on his lack of miracles or "portents." Below is 17:90-93:

And they say: We will not put faith in thee till thou cause a spring to gush forth from the earth for us; Or thou have a garden of date-palms and grapes, and cause rivers to gush forth therein abundantly; Or thou cause the heaven to fall upon us piecemeal, as thou hast pretended, or bring Allah and the angels as a warrant; Or thou have a house of gold; or thou ascend up into heaven, and even then we will put no faith in thine ascension till thou bring down for us a book that we can read. Say (O Muhammad): My Lord be Glorified! Am I aught save a mortal messenger?

Examine the challenges the non-Muslims issued against Muhammad in suras 6:37, 13:7, 24:48, 10:20, 17:59. He had not been able to confirm his calling from God by "portents," that is, miracles. However, Jesus confirmed His ministry by miracles.

Examine how the Quran identifies Muhammad. In 17:93 he is identified as a "mortal messenger." In 13:7 he is identified as a "warner." As only a mortal messenger and warner Muhammad was not supposed to be able to perform miracles. The point made throughout the Quran is that Muhammad was sent to be a "messenger" to warn people. In sura 28:48 the people compared Muhammad to Moses and said that Muhammad was *not* performing miracles like Moses.

But when there came unto them the Truth from Our presence, they said: Why is he not given the like of what was given unto Moses? Did they not disbelieve in that which was given unto Moses of old? They say: Two magics that support each other; and they say: Lo! in both we are disbelievers.

And in sura 17:59 Allah confirms to Muhammad that he did *not* perform miracles.

Naught hindereth Us from sending portents save that the folk of old denied them. And We gave Thamud the she-camel—a clear portent save to warn.

An easier to understand translation of sura 17:59 is from Dawood:

> Nothing hinders us from giving signs except that the ancients
> disbelieved them. To Thamud We gave the she-camel as a
> visible sign, yet they laid violent hands on her. We give signs
> only by way of warning. [3]

The Quran states that Muhammad did *not* perform miracles in the eyes of the believers or nonbelievers.

However, when we turn to the Hadith we do find Muhammad performing miracles. Here are three examples:

1. water flowing from Muhammad's fingers (Bukhari, volume 4, #779)

2. increasing available water (volume 1, #340)

3. multiplying food (volume 5, #428)

Miracle 3 fulfills part of the prophetic requirement in that it was performed in front of believers, but it does not fulfill the requirement of being performed in front of disbelievers.

We are left with having to make a choice between three options.

1. Take the Quran at face value in that Muhammad was not sent to, and could not, perform miracles.

2. Take the Hadith as true in that Muhammad performed miracles in front of believers and nonbelievers, thus fulfilling the prophetic requirements of Deuteronomy.

3. Synthesize the Quran and Hadith and conclude that Muhammad did perform miracles, primarily for his followers, but rarely in the sight of nonbelievers.

The Quran is part of the foundation of Islam. Based upon the fact that verses in the Quran repeatedly state that Muhammad performed no miracles, we believe that Muhammad did not perform any miracles. Various scholars have suggested that the Hadith miracles are fabrications—New Testament copycat miracles created to embellish Muhammad to make him equal to Jesus.

Further, Jesus' ministry lasted 3 years, and many miracles are linked to His ministry. Muhammad's ministry lasted 23 years, and the Quran was revealed over that 23-year period, yet it contains no references to any miracles performed by Muhammad.

**Conclusion on characteristic #2 (signs and wonders).** Jesus clearly fulfills the requirement of performing miracles while it is doubtful that Muhammad did. However, based upon the Hadith, we do not think Muhammad can be ruled out entirely. There are both Muslims and Christians who will disagree with us on this point but we think it fair to take into account the Hadith's evidence. Both Jesus and possibly Muhammad fulfill this requirement.

### Conclusion on Requirement One: A Prophet "Like Moses"

We have now examined both parts of requirement 1, knowing God face-to-face and performing miracles in front of believers and non-believers. Jesus fulfills both requirements. He knew God face-to-face, and he performed miracles in front of everyone. Muhammad does *not* fulfill both of those requirements. He did not know God face-to-face, and he probably didn't perform miracles although the Hadith establishes that he did.

### Requirement Two: The Prophet Must Be "from Among Your Own Brothers"

Deuteronomy 18 does not define what "among their brothers" means. Therefore we have to look for additional content in Deuteronomy. We should allow Deuteronomy to interpret, or to present the context for Deuteronomy if possible. The first thing we should search for is the use of the same phrase for clues to its meaning. This exact phrase is actually used elsewhere in Deuteronomy.

Here is one use of the phrase:

> When you enter the land the LORD your God is giving you, take possession of it, live in it, and say, "We want to appoint a king over us like all the nations around us," you are to appoint over you the king the LORD your God chooses.

> Appoint a king from your brothers. You are not to set a for-
> eigner over you, or one who is not of your people (Deuter-
> onomy 17:14-15 HCSB).

This passage in Deuteronomy does define its term "among your own brothers" as being a fellow Israelite. No one outside of an Israelite could be king.

Another use of the phrase occurs in chapter 18, actually before the passage in question:

> The Levitical priests, the whole tribe of Levi, will have no
> portion or inheritance with Israel. They will eat the LORD's
> fire offerings; that is their inheritance. Although Levi has no
> inheritance among his brothers, the LORD is his inheritance,
> as He promised him (Deuteronomy 18:1-2 HCSB).

Again the definition and meaning is clear, "brothers" here means fellow Israelites, no one else. If we take into account that the reference discussed above uses "brothers," we see that they are all God-directed ministries: king, priest, and prophet. God was directing His chosen people to institute positions of leadership that could only be filled by "His people." Outsiders, non-Israelites, could not fulfill those positions.

Therefore if we take the context of these two passages into consideration we can arrive at no other conclusion but that "among your own brothers" means a fellow Israelite. Moses did not need to redefine the term by adding "brother Israelite" because the Israelites already understood the meaning of "among your own brothers." It meant a fellow Israelite.

However, Muslim apologists have argued that a legitimate definition of "among your own brothers" signifies races or tribes of non-Israelite people but who have a blood relation with the Israelites, that is, he cannot be an Israelite, but has to be someone descended from Abraham. Since Muslims believe that Muhammad is descended from Ishmael (a claim that is disputed), he fulfills that part of the passage. This seems historically to be a "real stretch of the imagination."

When you take into account the actual context of "brothers" and determine from the Bible who Israel's "brothers" were, you find that this term is only extended to the Edomites. The Edomites were actually cousins to the Israelites because they descended from Isaac's son Esau, brother to Jacob. No other race or group of people descended from Abraham is identified as Israel's "brothers."

### Conclusion on Requirement Two: "From Among Your Own Brothers"

If we take the related verses and the Deuteronomy context into account we can only logically and honestly conclude that an "Israelite" could fulfill Moses' prophetic words about the future prophet. Consequently, Jesus can fulfill that requirement; Muhammad cannot.

### Requirement Three: "I will put my words in his mouth. He will tell them everything I command him."

This requirement is similar to the first, that is, knowing God face-to-face. But this concept has some theological ramifications because of the nature of how Jesus and Muhammad received revelations or God's words. (A Christian could argue that Jesus gave revelations and He did not necessarily receive them. But for the sake of this discussion we have to compare and contrast the modes of revelation for Jesus and Muhammad.)

So then, how did God speak with Muhammad, and how did God speak with Jesus?

Let's start with Jesus. There are several passages, such as John 7:16-17, John 8:28, and John 14:24, that state that God spoke directly with Jesus and Jesus repeated God's words to the people. Below is John 7:16-17:

> Jesus answered, "My teaching is not my own. It comes from him who sent me. Anyone who chooses to do God's will will find out whether my teaching comes from God or whether I speak on my own."

Even the Quran in 5:110-111 states that God spoke directly to Jesus.

One must conclude that Jesus fulfills the requirement of God putting His words in His mouth, and He will tell them everything God commanded Him.

What was Muhammad's mode of revelation? God in the Quran commands Muhammad to speak the revelation to the people. But when we look at the details in the Quran and Hadith we find a catch: All of the words that Muhammad learned as "revelation" were not revealed to him directly by God, but rather by a spirit Muhammad believed was the angel Gabriel. The Quran states that Gabriel taught Muhammad the Quran:

> Say (O Muhammad, to mankind): Who is an enemy to Gabriel! For he it is who hath revealed (this Scripture) to thy heart by Allah's leave, confirming that which was (revealed) before it, and a guidance and glad tidings to believers…(2:97).

Also, Bukhari's Hadith states that it was Gabriel who interacted with Muhammad:

> Narrated Masruq:
>
> I asked Aisha "What about His Statement:—'Then he (Gabriel) approached And came closer, And was at a distance Of but two bow-lengths Or (even) nearer?'" (53.8-9) She replied, "It was Gabriel who used to come to the Prophet in the figure of a man, but on that occasion, he came in his actual and real figure and (he was so huge) that he covered the whole horizon." [4]

There are also Hadith that state that the person who taught Muhammad the Quran was Gabriel (for example, Bukhari, volume 1, #4).

> Muhammad learned the entire Quran not via personal contact with God, but through personal contact with a spirit who he believed to be the angel Gabriel. Gabriel spoke the Quran to Muhammad. Muhammad did not learn the Quran from God via inspiration or revelation, but rather from Gabriel as Gabriel spoke to him. In fact, when Gabriel forced

Muhammad to recite the very first verses of the Quran (96:1-5), Muhammad became so terrified by this first encounter with Gabriel that he thought he had gone mad or become demon possessed and moved toward suicide![5]

### Conclusion on Requirement Three: "I will put my words in his mouth. He will tell them everything I command him."

We conclude that Jesus spoke the words that God wanted spoken and thus fulfills the requirement. But we cannot make the same conclusion about Muhammad because there was a medium between God and Muhammad, a spirit that Muhammad believed was the angel Gabriel. Of course Muslims believe that Gabriel was repeating God's words to Muhammad and thus Muhammad was speaking God's words. But that does not fulfill the requirement Moses laid out, of having God Himself putting His words into the prophet's mouth.

### Requirement Four: The Prophet Is Sent to the Israelites

The following is a quick review of the context of this passage. Moses was pouring his heart out to his people and telling them what to expect in the future. He was telling them that another mighty prophet would come to be God's voice to them and lead them. This was a prophet whose primary focus and ministry was going to be to the Israelites! Moses was telling the Israelites, God's people, who would come to them in the future. How do Jesus and Muhammad stack up against this requirement?

Let's start with Jesus. In Matthew 15:21-28 Jesus said that His primary ministry was to the house of Israel. Additionally, in Matthew 10:5-8 when Jesus sent out His apostles to minister, He sent them only to "the lost sheep of Israel." However, Jesus knew that His work would continue and spread throughout the world, that is, to the Gentiles. That is why He commanded His disciples to preach the Gospel to the whole world:

> Go and make disciples of all nations, baptizing them in the name of the Father and of the Son and of the Holy Spirit, and

teaching them to obey everything I have commanded you. And surely I am with you always, to the very end of the age (Matthew 28:19-20).(Also see John 17:20.)

Paul comments on this in the book of Romans:

I tell you that Christ has become a servant of the Jews on behalf of God's truth, so that the promises made to the patriarchs might be confirmed and, moreover, that the Gentiles might glorify God for his mercy (Romans 15:8-9).

Paul is saying that Christ was sent primarily to the Jews to fulfill God's promises to the house of Israel, and this power and blessing would be witnessed by the Gentiles and as a result they too would believe in the true God and put their faith in Christ. The case is easily made that Jesus fulfills requirement four.

What about Muhammad? Does he fulfill requirement four?

Muhammad was born in Mecca and grew up in the region of the Arabian peninsula known as the Hijaz—the western region bordering the Red Sea and including the cities of Mecca and Medina. Although paganism was entrenched there, Christianity and Judaism were also well known in the region. (Contrary to what some writers on the topic have asserted, many communities of Christians and Jews existed throughout the Arabian peninsula, including the Hijaz, and their religious stories were spread throughout. In fact, pictures of Jewish prophets, and of Jesus and Mary, were inside the Kaaba!)

Muhammad was about 40 when he began his ministry. He focused his ministry upon his friends and family at first, then later to his tribesmen and the various clans within Mecca. Later on he began to preach to visiting groups of Arabs coming on religious pilgrimages to the Kaaba.

During this time Muhammad challenged, and even insulted, the various Meccan clans and their pagan beliefs. As a result they persecuted him. Over time the persecution became severe. Out of concern for his followers' safety he sent them north to live with a group of Muslim converts in Yathrib (Medina) and eventually Muhammad fled for his life to Medina. (This is known as the Hijrah—*hegira* in English. It marks the formation of a physical, geopolitical community of Muslims, and their calendar starts with this emigration.)

This period of time covered about 13 years. During this time Muhammad focused primarily upon the Arabs in his vicinity. After he arrived in Medina he began to preach Islam to the various Jewish tribes that happened to live in the area. Almost to a man they rejected him as a false prophet.

Thus, it can be said that Muhammad did not intend to go to the Jewish tribes in the Hijaz. It was only after he was forced to flee to Medina that he began to preach Islam, and himself as a prophet, to the Jews who happened to live there.

### Conclusion on Requirement Four: The Prophet Is Sent to the Israelites

Accordingly, Muhammad does not fulfill the intent of Deuteronomy 18. He did not come with a focus on the house of Israel. His focus was upon the Arabs in his hometown. Later, because of forced migration, circumstances not of his own choosing, he preached Islam to the Jews. Muhammad intended that his message be carried throughout the entire world, but the house of Israel was not his primary focus. As such, it appears that Muhammad does not fulfill requirement four.

## Other Related Verses That Affect the Overall Context

Now we are not left with only the verses from Deuteronomy as material by which we can determine who the prophet is that Moses foretold. There are New Testament passages that also comment on this very topic and *declare Jesus to be the prophet foretold by Moses.*

Jesus said that Moses wrote about and predicted Him in John 5:45-47. The disciple Philip also declared the same thing in John 1:44-45. Other people also believed Jesus to have been the prophet that Moses foretold (John 6:14; 7:37-40). Why were the people saying this? Because they had seen the miracles that Jesus performed, just as Moses foretold.

Further, following His ascension, His disciples proclaimed that Jesus was the prophet foretold by Moses. In Acts 3:17-23, Peter proclaims:

And now, brothers, I know that you did it in ignorance, just as your leaders also did. But what God predicted through the mouth of all the prophets—that His Messiah would suffer—He has fulfilled in this way. Therefore repent and turn back, that your sins may be wiped out so that seasons of refreshing may come from the presence of the Lord, and He may send Jesus, who has been appointed Messiah for you. Heaven must welcome Him until the times of the restoration of all things, which God spoke about by the mouth of His holy prophets from the beginning. Moses said:

> The Lord your God will raise up for you a Prophet like me from among your brothers. You must listen to Him in everything He will say to you. And it will be that everyone who will not listen to that Prophet will be completely cut off from the people (Acts 3:17-23).

Also, in Acts 7:37-38, Stephen, who was soon to be martyred, preached to the Jewish leaders that Jesus was the prophet that Moses foretold. So there is additional testimony from people and from Jesus' disciples that He was indeed the prophet foretold by Moses in Deuteronomy 18.

## Good Pushback Questions from Muslims

When the Jews questioned John the Baptist, they asked the following:

> Now this was John's testimony when the Jewish leaders in Jerusalem sent priests and Levites to ask him who he was. He did not fail to confess, but confessed freely, "I am not the Messiah." They asked him, "Then who are you? Are you Elijah?" He said, "I am not." "Are you the Prophet?" He answered, "No" (John 1:19-21).

The pushback question is: "The Jewish priests and Levites identified the Messiah to be someone other than the prophet that Moses foretold. They were held to be two separate individuals. If Jesus was the Christ, how could He then be the prophet that Moses foretold?"

This is a good question because it shows that people are studying the biblical text and taking it at face value. The premise of the question is accurate, that is, that the priests and Levites believed that the Messiah and the prophet that Moses foretold were two separate people.

### Answer

Jesus fulfilled both roles. Just as Muslims understand that Muhammad fulfilled several roles as a prophet, political leader, military leader, and so on, so too did Jesus fulfill various Old Testament prophecies that pointed out specific details about a future leader. They pointed to the same person, but that was not obvious to the religious leaders of that time.

### What About Physical Similarities That Are "like Moses"?

In the vein of "a prophet like me" Muslims have developed lists of physical similarities between Muhammad and Moses and use them as evidence for Muhammad, not Jesus, being the foretold prophet. Below are some of them:

1. Moses and Muhammad were military leaders; Jesus never led men in combat.

2. Moses and Muhammad began their ministries at age 40; Jesus began around the age of 30.

3. Moses and Muhammad ruled politically; Jesus ruled no one.

That is a good set of similarities. But Christian apologists have also come up with physical similarities. Below are some of them.

1. Moses and Jesus were born into a people who were being oppressed by foreign rulers; Muhammad was born into an un-oppressed society.

2. Moses and Jesus were moved for their own safety and were saved by divine intervention; Muhammad grew up in safety in his tribal areas in and outside of Mecca.

3. Moses and Jesus mediated new covenants between God
and the people; Muhammad brought new laws but not a
new covenant.

### Answer

Even more similarities can be generated on either side. Do you see
the problem here? Both Muslims and Christians can pick various characteristics about Muhammad or Jesus and parallel them to Moses based
on a prior bias. In fact, without an objective standard for judging parallels, it is quite easy to draw parallels between any two people or things
based on someone's predetermined goal. Rather than looking for parallels based on subjective criteria and bias, we should rely on the biblical
criteria required to be "like Moses." Remember, the "like Moses" mentioned previously requires the criteria found in Deuteronomy 34:10-12:

> Since then, no prophet has risen in Israel like Moses, whom
> the LORD knew face to face, who did all those signs and won-
> ders the LORD sent him to do in Egypt—to Pharaoh and to
> all his officials and to his whole land. For no one has ever
> shown the mighty power or performed the awesome deeds
> that Moses did in the sight of all Israel.

What did Moses have that many other prophets did not have? He
knew the Lord "face to face," he performed "signs and wonders" that
both believers and nonbelievers witnessed. So whether or not Jesus
and Moses were threatened as children, or Muhammad and Moses
began their ministry at age 40 is irrelevant and arbitrary. It is as relevant as if saying Moses, Jesus, and Muhammad all loved grapes or liked
to fish. Those physical similarities have no bearing on the discussion
whatsoever because they are not related to the requirements given in
Deuteronomy.

### Conclusion: Is Muhammad the "Prophet" Foretold by Moses?

We have reviewed the claims that either Jesus or Muhammad was
the prophet foretold by Moses. We have examined Deuteronomy's

context and determined the requirements that Moses laid down for this prophet to meet. Four requirements were defined and presented and we compared Jesus and Muhammad against those requirements. Jesus fulfilled all four requirements but Muhammad did not fulfill any of the requirements completely. Jesus not only fulfilled what Moses laid down for the future prophet, Jesus exceeded the requirements! Jesus Himself says that He was with God before He came to earth, and that He has seen God (John 6:46). Moses saw a "theophany," that is, an appearance of God in human form, but Jesus was with the Father and saw Him fully, in heaven. No biblical prophet has ever made that claim. Jesus was greater than the other biblical prophets.

# 10

# The Reliability of the New Testament (Part 1)

Muslims' question:
*"The Bible has been corrupted,
so how can I believe its story of Jesus?"*

This is an appropriate question because to answer our earlier question—"Who is Jesus?"—we need a reliable and detailed record of His life. The most extensive record that fulfills this criteria is the New Testament. To justify the use of the New Testament we must show that it is reliable. If the New Testament is reliable we can accurately know and present Jesus' teachings, mission, and identity, the very identity that Peter proclaimed as "Messiah" and "Son of God."

On the other hand, if the New Testament is not reliable, then Jesus' identity is lost because no valid and substantial record of His life exists. You might say to yourself, "Don't other books, like the Qur'an, tell me about Jesus' life?" But as you read those accounts, written far later than the New Testament, you will find that they don't provide us with rich detail about His life, teachings, and actions.

The *Baker Encyclopedia of Christian Apologetics* states:

> Without a reliable New Testament we have no objective, historical way to know what Jesus said or did. We cannot establish whether he was God, what he taught, or what his followers did and taught. There are two basic steps in the argument for the reliability of the New Testament documents. First, we must show that the manuscripts were written early enough and with enough attention to detail to be faithful records. A side issue, also important, is whether the

New Testament books have been passed down accurately, so that we can know for sure what was written in the original copies or autographs. Second, we must know if the sources or witnesses used by the authors were reliable. [1]

Proving the reliability of the New Testament involves many disciplines and they cannot be covered comprehensively in a single chapter or two. However, we can present and discuss the primary evidence for the New Testament's reliability. We will see how the New Testament was developed, compiled, and standardized, and discuss some seeming contradictions, textual variants, and related scholars' statements.

## The Earliest New Testament Writings

Dr. Bruce Metzger presents details about the early history of the New Testament writings in *The Canon of the New Testament*:

> In the oldest Christian communities there was also another authority which had taken its place alongside the Jewish Scriptures, and that was the words of Jesus, as they were handed down in oral tradition. During his public ministry Jesus had claimed to speak with an authority in no way inferior to that of the ancient Law, and had placed his utterances side by side with its precepts by way of fulfilling or even correcting and repealing them...
>
> At first Jesus' teachings circulated orally from hearer to hearer, becoming, so to speak, the nucleus of the new Christian canon. Then narratives were compiled recording the remembered words, along with recollections of his deeds of mercy, and healing. Some documents of this kind underlie our Gospels, and are referred to in the preface to the Third Gospel (Luke 1:1-4). [2]

Likewise Scottish professor and biblical scholar Dr. F.F. Bruce affirms:

> Jesus wrote no book: he taught by word of mouth and personal example. But some of his followers taught in writings as well as orally. Often, indeed, their writing was a second-best

substitute for the spoken word. In Galatians 4:20, for example, Paul wishes that he could be with his friends in Galatia and speak to them directly so that they could catch his tone of voice as well as his actual words but, as he could not visit them just then, a letter had to suffice...

If Jesus wrote no book, what he said was treasured and repeated by those who heard him, and by their hearers in turn. To those who confessed him as Lord his words were at least as authoritative as those of Moses and the prophets. They were transmitted as a most important element in the "tradition" of early Christianity, together with the record of his works, his death and resurrection. These were "delivered" by the original witnesses and "received" in turn by others not simply as an outline of historical events but as the church's confession of faith and as the message which it was commissioned to spread abroad. [3]

New Testament biblical scholars agree that Jesus did not write any texts. Those who followed Him repeated what He taught, that is, the message was transmitted orally. Over time those teachings were written down and the disciples began to put together details of His life coupled with His teachings. The written texts of Jesus and the apostles' teachings were later quoted by the early Church Fathers. F.F. Bruce states that Jesus' words were on par, if not superior to, the Old Testament. This gave Jesus' and the apostles' teachings the status of Scripture. [4]

## The End of the Age of the Apostolic Fathers

Over time Jesus' apostles and disciples, that is, those who knew Him personally, began to die and church leadership passed to the disciples of the apostles and other prominent Christians. The writings that were later to become the New Testament were familiar to them, and began to be recognized as authoritative. Metzger summarizes the apostolic Fathers' development of the New Testament:

In short, we find in both the Jewish and the Hellenistic groups a knowledge of the existence of certain books that later will comprise the New Testament, and more than once they express their thoughts through phrases drawn from these writings. These reminiscences tend to show that an implicit authority of such writings was sensed before a theory of their authority had been developed—in fact, before there was even a consciousness of their authority. This authority, moreover, did not have, to any degree, an exclusive character.

On the other hand, we see that the words of Jesus are taken as the supreme authority. Sometimes these quotations are similar to what we find in the four Gospels; at other times they differ. Already at the time of Papias we find the beginning of a movement, unconscious at first, that will tend to subordinate the authority of the words of Jesus to the warranty arising from the fact that these words are preserved in such and such books which deserve the reader's confidence.[5]

## The Reliability of the Oral Tradition Underlying the Gospels
### Memorization in Antiquity

One of the first challenges against the reliability of the New Testament is that much of the original teachings could have been lost through oral transmission. Did the disciples remember correctly? Did they add or take away words? Did they interpret or spin Jesus' original words to fit current purposes? In an era where rote memorization is essentially a lost art, it is easy to wonder how reliably the initial information about Jesus could have been passed along during the first forty years or so before the composition of the Gospels. Critics even compare such oral transmission to playing the "telephone game"! Consider the comments of professor and author Dr. Bart Ehrman:

> What do you suppose happened to the [Jesus] stories over the years, as they were told and retold, not as disinterested news stories reported by eyewitnesses but as propaganda meant to convert people to faith, told by people who had themselves heard from fifth- or sixth- or nineteenth-hand? Did you or your kids ever play the telephone game at a birthday party? The kids sit in a circle, and one child tells a story

to the girl sitting next to her, who tells it to the next girl, who tells it to the next, and so on, until it comes back to the one who first told the story. And it's now a different story…Imagine playing telephone not among a group of kids of the same socioeconomic class from the same neighborhood and same school and of the same age speaking the same language, but imagine playing it for forty or more years, in different countries, in different contexts, in different languages. What happens to the stories? They change.[6]

The critics say that the Gospels reflect the distorted transmission of 40 years of oral tradition rather than that of reliable, eyewitness testimony. While such a claim could make some sense on the surface, when their position is examined more carefully, we find it is weak and contains important flaws. This is because through thorough research the details of early church culture and disciplines of memorization are brought to light.

For example, in a world where only a minority of the population could read, the cultivation of memory was a major point of emphasis in oral cultures. New Testament scholar Dr. Craig Keener notes:

Many cultures orally pass on information for centuries, maintaining accuracy in the points transmitted. (Even in the transmission of Balkan ballads, where this pattern has been disputed, the basic story is fixed at the oral stage long before the words are fixed at a written stage.)…

Like some other societies, the ancient Mediterranean world highly prized oral memory. Bards recited Homeric epics and other poets from memory, though intellectuals generally regarded these bards as low-class, engaging in elementary exercise. Centuries before the Gospels, the best professional reciters could recite all of Homer by heart; in the general era of the Gospels, Dio Chrysostom even claims a people who no longer were able to speak Greek well but most of whom knew "the Iliad by heart." Many poems remained fluid, but the Iliad remained textually constant, because it became canonical for Greek culture. Such feats of memory appear in some other oral societies. [7]

We don't have to rely solely on studies of ancient uses of memory to see that people are capable of accurately recording and passing on information orally. Studies have been done on largely nonliterate societies today that do not pass on information through writing, but through oral performances.

Indeed, for centuries, Muslims have prided themselves on the ability to memorize the entire Quran, a document roughly the size of the New Testament, and in Islam's earliest days, the Quran was transmitted largely by those who memorized it in its entirety. So, it is an anachronism at best to speak of an impossibility of maintaining the accuracy of traditions through oral media.

However, that the New Testament writers could preserve accurate traditions regarding Jesus through oral tradition does not guarantee that they did so. What reasons do we have for believing that the Jesus traditions specifically were preserved by the early church up until the composition of the Gospels?

### Memorization in the Church

Consider some reasons offered by New Testament scholar Dr. Craig Blomberg as to why the church would have desired to preserve Jesus' teachings:

> Similar to the OT prophets, Jesus proclaimed the "Word of the Lord" that would have garnered respect and a concern among his followers to safeguard what was considered to be revelation from God. "Just as many parts of Old Testament prophecy are considered by even fairly skeptical scholars to have been quite well preserved, so Jesus' words should be considered in the same light."
>
> 1. Jesus' claim to Messiahship would have provoked concern for his followers to preserve his words, particularly as "one fairly consistent feature in an

otherwise diverse body of first-century expectations was that the Messiah would be a teacher of wisdom."

2. More than 90 percent of Jesus' sayings are depicted in forms that were used to facilitate memory.

3. The Gospels betray abundant evidence of Jesus commanding his disciples to "learn specific lessons and to transmit what they learn to others, even before the end of his earthly ministry (for example, Mark 6:7-13, Luke 10:1-17; Mark 13:28; Luke 11:1; Mark 9:10; Acts 2:42)."

4. Teachers in both Jewish and Greco-Roman contexts in Jesus' day gathered disciples in order to perpetuate their teachings. Given the scholarly certainty that Jesus gathered disciples, we may take it for granted that this would have been the case for him as well. [8]

If the accurate preservation of oral traditions was not only possible, and in the case of Jesus desired, then we may take it as probable that the New Testament traditions would have been passed along accurately by Jesus' followers. More evidence of this stems from certain aspects of the Jesus tradition as it is found in the New Testament.

Paul's letters in many areas reflect a concern to pass along apostolic traditions. Similarly, the early church placed emphasis on the importance of teachers. Teachers, having served as apparently the first paid ministers (see Galatians 6:6; Didache 13:2), likely functioned by transmitting the oral traditions of the early church to converts.

Of course, the Gospels indicate that Jesus was considered to be a teacher, serving as the ultimate model for the earliest disciples:

If we come to the ministry of Jesus as first-century historians, and forget our twentieth-century assumptions about mass media, the overwhelming probability is that most of what Jesus said, he said not twice but 200 times, with (of course) a myriad of local variations.

Jesus is constantly identified as a teacher by both his deeds and his words. In his ministry, he clearly followed the Old Testament models of prophets and their followers, the inter-testamental pupil-teacher relationships, as well as the models of discipleship used by the Essenes and other Jewish teachers of the day. In addition, Jesus expected his disciples to obey and imitate him (Matt. 10:38; 11:28-30; 16:24; 20:26-28; 23:11), a demand reiterated throughout the New Testament by Jesus' disciples who used Jesus as a model. Again, the very fact that Jesus is posed as a teacher means that it is the burden of the critic to explain why the words and deeds of Jesus would not immediately or rapidly be formed or collated for preservation—if not by someone like Matthew or Mark, then by Jesus himself. The critic must suppose that Jesus taught and spoke with little or no concern that his words and deeds be carried on and transmitted.[9]

Furthermore, similar to antecedent Judaism, the early church ubiquitously placed great emphasis on the importance of eyewitness testimony. Consider the following comments of Dr. Paul Rhodes Eddy and Dr. Gregory Boyd:

> ...it is significant to note that—beginning with its Scriptures—the Jewish tradition as a whole put strong emphasis on the role of eyewitnesses. Only by appealing to credible eyewitnesses could one certify a claim as factual (e.g., Jeremiah 32:10,12; Ruth 4:9-11; Isa. 8:2). Correlatively, bearing false witness was considered a major crime in ancient Judaism. Indeed, this was one of the explicit prohibitions of the ten primary stipulations of the Sinai covenant (Exodus 20:16). The Jewish law of multiple witnesses reflects the life-or-death importance of this command (Deut. 17:6-7; Num. 35:30).
>
> It seems that this emphasis on the importance of eyewitnesses was quite explicitly carried over into the early church. The Sinai principle regarding multiple witnesses was retained

(Mark 14:56,59; John 5:31-32; Heb. 10:28) and made the basis of church discipline (Matt. 18:16; 2 Corinthians. 13:1; 1 Tim. 5:19). More broadly, the themes of bearing false witness, giving a true testimony, and making a true confession are ubiquitous in the tradition of the early church…As Robert Stein observes, the sheer pervasiveness of these themes in the early church testifies to "the high regard in which eyewitness testimony was held."

More specifically, certain key individuals are singled out in the New Testament for their roles as faithful witnesses, teachers, and preservers of the Jesus tradition, for example, Peter, James, and John, as well as James the brother of Jesus… This emphasis on key individuals is not only consistent with ancient Judaism, but it is precisely what we should expect, given what we have learned from orality studies about the central role individual tradents play in orally dominant cultures. [10]

Above we discussed the issue of memorization in antiquity. Numerous researchers have cited a number of memorization techniques detectable within the sayings of Jesus. Holding summarizes these proven techniques:

What of the New Testament as a whole? The NT is filled with "verbal clues" that indicate that it was composed of documents intended to be transmitted and understood orally, and, in turn, easily memorized. As with the teachings of Jesus, we find examples of puns, alliteration, repetition, and parallelisms. None of this should be surprising, for the authors of the NT documents knew that the majority of their audience was illiterate and would first encounter their material by having it read aloud to them. The only way the NT authors could be sure that their message would be instilled in the hearts and minds of their audience would be to encourage the process of memorization. [11]

### Conclusions About Memorization in Antiquity

Hopefully by now you can appreciate the difference in the careful transmission of oral tradition and playing the telephone game. Holding notes what he touts as the "two critical differences":

> First, unlike telephone, where the message is repeated from one ear to another in whispers, oral transmission—in a particularly didactic setting like that of the ministry of Jesus—is more akin to a teacher openly and loudly repeating the message to be passed along to the entire class, and doing it as many times as is needed for the students to get the message right. Then, each time a student repeated the message, other students (and the teacher) would jump in to make necessary corrections. Finally, only those students who mastered the message and got it right would be permitted to teach the message.

> Second, the message itself is not something trivial…Didactic oral transmission is all about passing along information critical to a group's identity and purpose, and preserving it for future generations so that the group itself, and its beliefs, survive. [12]

In light of the early church's desire to preserve Jesus' message, Ehrman's illustration of the "telephone game" is an inappropriate and inaccurate metaphor. It does not bear on the actual case. In the telephone game, the fun comes from seeing how the story changes as it is being told to each person. So the people playing it don't really care if the message is changed. In fact, they want to see just how much it did change. That's far different from the circumstances of ancient and modern oral cultures and the early church, who had an interest not in changing the message, but making sure it stayed the same.

## Gospel Aramaisms

Confirming the conclusion that the Jesus traditions were in fact well preserved from the beginning is the presence of Aramaisms within the

Gospel material. Within the greater Greek-speaking world of the time, Aramaic is universally considered among scholars to have been the language of the earliest Jerusalem church. Dr. Craig Keener elaborates:

> Material from Masada indicates that bilingualism (and even trilingualism) was common, but Aramaic was the common tongue for most Judeans, though Hebrew could be used in priestly and purity matters. Aramaic was the dominant language for the masses even in Jerusalem. Even Greek composition in Judea reflects abundant Aramaisms, especially for those scribes and translators whose Greek was weaker. The Aramaic tradition apparently remained important enough that Paul seems to have taught some Aramaic words to his churches (Rom 8:15; 1 Corinthians 16:22; Gal 4:6). [13]

As such, this is also the language through which the oral traditions were considered most likely to have been originally formulated and passed on by the church before eventually having been translated into Greek. Thus, if Aramaic originals are detectable behind what we find in the Greek New Testament, we have good reason to believe that much of what we read in the Gospels was translated directly from very early material, so early it takes us back to the time just after the genesis of the church. Keener writes in this regard:

> Although our extant Gospels are written in Greek, that they contain Aramaic figures of speech also tends to suggest authentic Jesus material, especially if the first translators into Greek frequently sought word-for-word fidelity as some scholars suggest. Although reconstructing Aramaic behind gospel traditions seems more complex than often allowed, some have argued that the Aramaic original of as much as 80 percent of the Synoptic sayings material appears to fit a poetic or rhythmic form helpful for memorization. Jesus' common phrase "Son of Man" (literally, "the son of the man") makes no more sense in Greek than it does in English, but such a phrase makes perfect sense in Hebrew

or Aramaic, where it frequently occurs. Some divergences in Jesus' sayings in different Gospels may reflect different possible translations of these sayings from Aramaic. (Various Semitic structural features of many sayings also suggest their antiquity, and perhaps that their sage uttered them in easily memorized form.) [14]

Maurice Casey devoted a book-sized study to the Aramaic sources underlying the Gospel of Mark. The scholarly study is very technical in some areas, though he is successful in recovering the Aramaic original behind a number of passages in the New Testament. In the conclusion of his study, he writes the following:

> All this would be to no avail if Mark's Gospel were really Greek fiction, or if all of it had been so heavily edited that Aramaic sources were irrecoverable. We have found substantial and decisive evidence that parts of Mark's Gospel are literal translations of written Aramaic sources. This follows from an argument of cumulative weight, which is dependent on evidence of several different kinds. First of all, we found clear evidence that Aramaic was the lingua franca of Jesus' environment, the language which he would have had to use in teaching normal Jews, and the natural language for his first followers to use when they reported on his life and teaching. Secondly, we found many reasons for supposing that the passages studied are generally accurate accounts of what Jesus said and did. They are therefore just the sorts of passage to be transmitted in Aramaic, quite different from the secondary narratives of the fourth Gospel, many of which originated in Greek. Thirdly, we found many details of the selected passages which are explicable only if they are part of the translations of written Aramaic sources. [15]

The data we have surveyed thus far indicates that the early church was successful in memorizing the Jesus traditions and accurately preserving them through the medium of oral transmission. In fact, that the Gospel authors had at their disposal and utilized very early material in composing their Gospels is demonstrable.

However, we should note one disclaimer prior to moving on. The establishment of eyewitness testimony is not enough, by itself, to guarantee the accuracy of the testimony. It is certainly a priori more likely that an eyewitness would tell a story more accurately than a non-eyewitness. However, due to a number of potential factors such as faulty memory, a propensity for exaggeration, or even fabrication (depending on a given situation) it is certainly possible (but not probable) that eyewitness claims could be inaccurate. On the other hand, a non-eyewitness who carefully examines the data for a given event may well be able to piece together what actually happened in a perfectly accurate manner. In the case of the Gospels, however, we have noted several reasons throughout this chapter as to why the apostolic tradents would have had the means and desire to preserve as accurately as possible the Jesus traditions. Moreover, certain features of the Gospel content strongly suggest that they had successfully done so.

## Addressing Inaccurate Assumptions

During the investigation I (Josh McDowell) made of the Bible, I discovered a number of "false assumptions." The following are just a few of them:

### False Assumption #1: The Bible is just another man-made book.

If you want to liven up the conversation at your next tailgate party, throw out this question: What is the Bible? The answers you get could be all over the map. Some people view the Bible as just another book about philosophy, ethics, and how to live a meaningful life. But calling the Bible just another book is like calling the great Vince Lombardi just another football coach. The Bible is in a class by itself.

### Fact #1: The Bible is God's unique message about who He is and how you can know Him.

Consider the Bible's unique qualifications:

- It was written over a span of 1500 years—40 generations.
- It was penned by more than forty authors from different walks of life, including kings, peasants, philosophers, fishermen, poets, statesmen, scholars, military leaders, a doctor, a tax collector, and a rabbi.
- The authors wrote from three continents: Asia, Africa, and Europe.
- The authors wrote in three languages: Hebrew, Aramaic, and Greek.
- Its prophecies have proven 100 percent accurate.

Key evidence for the accuracy of the Bible is in the scores of specific prophecies about nations and events that were fulfilled hundreds of years later. The Bible takes the accuracy of these prophecies very seriously. The prophet's very life was on the line! One single prophecy that did not come true would be disastrous for a prophet: He was to be stoned to death on the spot.[16] During the days of the Old Testament, people were not recklessly jumping onto the prophetic bandwagon. They knew they had to be right 100 percent of the time.

Jesus often appealed to the Old Testament prophets about His life and ministry (Luke 24:25-27). So let's take a look at just some of the hundreds of biblical prophecies that have been fulfilled.

The Bible contains amazingly specific predictions about who would be the Messiah. Scholars have demonstrated that some three hundred Old Testament predictions were literally fulfilled in the life of Jesus Christ. Dr. Peter Stoner and Robert Newman, in their book *Science Speaks*, say that by applying the science of probability to just eight of those prophecies, "we find that the chance that any man might have lived down to the present time and fulfilled all eight prophecies is 1 in $10^{17}$."[17] That's one chance in 100,000,000,000,000,000.

Here is an example of eight (out of more than 300) messianic prophecies and their fulfillment in Jesus Christ.

| The Prophecy | The Fulfillment | The Time Span |
|---|---|---|
| Born of a virgin<br>Isaiah 7:14 | Luke 1:26-38 | 700 years |
| Born in Bethlehem<br>Micah 5:2 | Matthew 2:1;<br>Luke 2:4-7 | 700 years |
| The time of His<br>appearance<br>Daniel 9:24-27 | Luke 19:44;<br>Galatians 4:4 | 538 years |
| Abandoned by His<br>disciples<br>Zechariah 13:7 | Matthew 26:31;<br>Mark 14:50 | 520 years |
| Pierced in His side<br>Zechariah 12:10 | John 19:34,37 | 520 years |
| His resurrection and<br>exaltation<br>Psalm 16:10; Isaiah 52:13;<br>53:10-12 | Acts 2:25-32 | 1000 years<br>(Psalms)<br>700 years (Isaiah) |
| His ascension into heaven<br>Psalm 68:18 | Acts 1:9;<br>Ephesians 4:8 | 1000 years |
| A forerunner prepares<br>His way<br>Isaiah 40:3-5; Malachi 3:1 | Matthew 3:1-3;<br>Luke 3:3-6 | 700 years (Isaiah)<br>450 years<br>(Malachi) |

If you agree that these fulfilled messianic prophecies bear the stamp of the divine, you should seriously consider the Bible as the Word of God—a book worthy of your investigation, especially as it makes claims about your eternal destiny.

The Bible treats hundreds of controversial subjects with harmony and continuity from Genesis to Revelation and focuses on one consistent theme: God's love and plan for His human creation.

One of the New Testament writers, the apostle Paul, writes, "All Scripture is God-breathed and is useful for teaching, rebuking, correcting and training in righteousness, so that the servant of God may be thoroughly equipped for every good work" (2 Timothy 3:16-17). God is not trying to restrict you or bully you with His instructions. He always has your best interests at heart, and His Word is intended to protect you and provide for you.

If the Bible is really God's written message to the human race, it must be accurate and reliable. If it were just a collection of nice thoughts, it wouldn't matter if parts of it had been left out or changed over the centuries. If it's only one of many versions of truth, who cares whether it's accurate? But if the Bible is really what God wants to tell you about Himself and your relationship with Him, it is extremely important for you to know that it was recorded exactly as God gave it and has been accurately passed down to you today.

### False Assumption #2: The Bible is full of myths and legends.

When people claim that the Bible is full of myths and legends, they are usually referring to the New Testament—especially the accounts of the life, death, and resurrection of Jesus Christ recorded in Matthew, Mark, Luke, and John. The arguments typically sound something like this:

- The virgin birth of Jesus is just an invention to explain away Mary's getting pregnant before the wedding.

- The miracles of Jesus, such as walking on water, are explainable natural events that got exaggerated over time.

- Jesus' resurrection was made up by His grieving followers after His brutal death.

Because Christians base their faith on these so-called incredible and unbelievable stories, skeptics assume that nothing in the Bible can be accepted as truth.

*Fact #2: The Bible can be trusted because Jesus' disciples staked their lives on its truth.*

If Jesus' followers made up the "legend" of His resurrection, they paid for that lie with their lives. History tells us that ten of Jesus' original twelve disciples suffered violent deaths as a result of boldly proclaiming that He was the risen Son of God.

Would these men have died for a lie? Though it's true that thousands of people throughout history have died for a lie, they did so only if they thought it was the truth. If the resurrection of Jesus was a lie and the disciples knew it, certainly one or two at least—and probably several—would have cracked under the pressure and confessed the conspiracy to save their lives.

But it wasn't a conspiracy based on a lie. The disciples saw Jesus alive after His death and burial. Luke writes, "After his suffering, he [Jesus] presented himself to them [the disciples] and gave many convincing proofs that he was alive" (Acts 1:3).

Why did the followers of Jesus need "many convincing proofs"? Because when Jesus died, they thought it was all over—the movement, the cause, the kingdom. When Jesus was arrested, they ran and hid (Mark 14:50). And when they were told that His tomb was empty, at first they didn't believe it (Luke 24:11). They needed serious convincing, especially a guy by the name of Thomas (John 20:24-25). Can you identify with him? I sure can.

What was the result of their seeing Jesus alive? The disciples were transformed from cowardly to courageous—overnight! In fact, we know from early biblical and nonbiblical historical sources that the disciples faced torture and death for their belief in Jesus' resurrection. Summarizing the evidence, historians Gary Habermas and Michael Licona note:

> In all, at least seven early sources testify that the original disciples willingly suffered in defense of their beliefs. If we include the sufferings and martyrdoms of Paul and James the brother of Jesus, we have eleven sources. Even the highly critical New Testament scholar Rudolf Bultmann agreed that historical criticism can establish "the fact that the first disciples came

to believe in the resurrection" and that they thought they had seen the risen Jesus. Atheistic New Testament scholar Gerd Lüdemann concludes, "It may be taken as historically certain that Peter and the disciples had experiences after Jesus' death in which Jesus appeared to them as the risen Christ." Paula Fredriksen of Boston University comments, "I know in their own terms what they saw was the raised Jesus. That's what they say and then all the historic evidence we have afterwards attest to their conviction that that's what they saw. I'm not saying that they really did see the raised Jesus. I wasn't there. I don't know what they saw. But I do know that as a historian they must have seen something." [18]

The disciples could not have faced torture and death unless they were totally convinced of Jesus' resurrection. Jesus' life, death, and resurrection form the central theme of the Bible. The boldness and courage of His once cowardly followers is powerful evidence for the reliability of the Bible as a whole.

### False Assumption #3: The Bible was written and copied by hand, so it is full of mistakes.

The documents included in the Bible were originally written with pen and ink on papyrus, many centuries before the printing press was invented. As the ink faded and the papyrus deteriorated, copies were made of the original manuscripts, and copies were made of the copies.

None of the original manuscripts of the Bible has been found. What we have are copies of copies ranging in size from scrolls to scraps of papyrus. The Bible today is a translation of the most reliable existing manuscript copies, but how can we be sure that the words in our modern-day Bibles are the same as what God originally said?

### Fact #3: Overwhelming evidence proves that the Bible has been accurately preserved.

To determine the reliability of the Bible manuscript copies we have today, we can ask two questions that historians ask to test the reliability of any ancient literature:

**How many manuscript copies still exist?** Like the Bible, other ancient writings have been passed down through the centuries as manuscript copies. Checking multiple copies against each other allows scholars to find copying mistakes and determine the author's original words. Obviously, the more copies you have of a manuscript, the closer you will get to the original.

Modern editions of classic ancient books are often based on just a handful of existing copies. Yet scholars are confident that the present versions accurately reflect the authors' originals.

By comparison, trusting that the Bible has been preserved and passed down to us accurately is a slam dunk. Take the New Testament, for example. We're not talking about mere hundreds or even a few thousand handwritten manuscript copies still in existence. Libraries and museums around the world today hold close to twenty-five thousand copies of portions of the New Testament.

The following chart illustrates the stark contrast in manuscript authority between a numbers of volumes of ancient literature and the New Testament.

| Author/Book | Date Written | Earliest Copies | Time Gap | Number of Copies | Most Recent Numbers |
|---|---|---|---|---|---|
| Homer *The Iliad* | 800 BC | c. 400 BC | c. 400 yrs. | 643 | 1757 |
| Thucydides *History* | 460-400 BC | c. A.D. 900 | c. 1300 yrs. | 8 | 96 |
| Caesar *Gallic Wars* | 100–44 BC | c. AD 900 | c. 1000 yrs. | 10 | 251 |
| Livy *History of Rome* | 59 BC– AD 17 | c. AD 1000 | c. 1000 yrs. | 19 (most) | 150 |
| Pliny the Elder *Natural History* | AD 61–113 | c. AD 850 | c. 750 yrs. | 7 | 200 |
| The New Testament | AD 50–100 | c. AD 114–325 | c. 50–225 yrs. | 24,000+ | |

**How much time passed between the original writing and the earliest copies we have?** Obviously, the closer the copies are to the originals, the more reliable the copies will be. The earliest copies of most classic ancient writings are 400 to 1,400 years removed from the originals. The earliest copies we have of New Testament documents, however, are only 50 to 225 years removed from the original documents.

The evidence is overwhelming. "In the variety and fullness of the evidence on which it rests, the New Testament stands absolutely and unapproachably alone among ancient prose writings," [19] writes New Testament scholar F.J.A. Hort. Theologian Norman Geisler adds, "The abundance of manuscript copies makes it possible to reconstruct the original with virtually complete accuracy." [20] Christian apologist Ravi Zacharias writes, "In real terms, the New Testament is easily the best attested ancient writing in terms of the sheer number of documents, the time span between the events and the document, and the variety of documents available to sustain or contradict it. There is nothing in ancient manuscript evidence to match such textual availability and integrity." [21]

Dr. Dan Wallace, manuscript scholar, comments on the earliest manuscript of the New Testament recently discovered:

> Seven New Testament papyri had recently been discovered—six of them probably from the second century and one of them probably from the first.

> It was dated by one of the world's leading paleographers. He said he was "certain" that it was from the first century. If this is true, it would be the oldest fragment of the New Testament known to exist. Up until now, no one has discovered any first-century manuscripts of the New Testament. The oldest manuscript of the New Testament has been P52, a small fragment from John's Gospel, dated to the first half of the second century. It was discovered in 1934.

> Not only this, but the first-century fragment is from Mark's Gospel. Before the discovery of this fragment, the oldest manuscript that had Mark in it was P45, from the early third century (c. AD 200–250). This new fragment would predate that by 100 to 150 years.

How do these manuscripts change what we believe the original New Testament to say? We will have to wait until they are published next year, but for now we can most likely say this: As with all the previously published New Testament papyri (127 of them, published in the last 116 years), not a single new reading has commended itself as authentic. Instead, the papyri function to confirm what New Testament scholars have already thought was the original wording or, in some cases, to confirm an alternate reading—but one that is already found in the manuscripts.

These new papyri will no doubt continue that trend. But, if this Mark fragment is confirmed as from the first century, what a thrill it will be to have a manuscript that is dated within the lifetime of many of the eyewitnesses to Jesus' resurrection![22]

**Quotations by the early Church Fathers.** The early Fathers quoted Scripture in both their sermons and in their letters to churches. We have been able to document 36,289 quotations of just the New Testament (often one quote equals an entire chapter or two). Metzger and Ehrman say:

> Besides textual evidence derived from New Testament Greek manuscripts and from early versions, the textual critic has available the numerous scriptural quotations included in the commentaries, sermons, and other treatises written by the early Church fathers. Indeed, so extensive are these citations that if all other sources for our knowledge of the text of the New Testament were destroyed, they would be sufficient alone for the reconstruction of practically the entire New Testament.[23]

### False Assumption #4: The Bible's reliability cannot be proved from outside sources.

Many people assume that the Bible's claim to be the inspired, reliable Word of God is hollow because the only evidence for such a claim is the Bible itself. This would be like arguing that the Bible is God's infallible word because the Bible says it is God's infallible Word. Put another way, it would be kind of like claiming to be the world's number one authority on anything. If you're the only one saying it, who's going to believe you?

### Fact #4: The Bible's reliability is substantially supported by external sources.

Mountains of persuasive evidence outside of the Bible confirm the truth of what is inside the Bible. Here are just a few examples of the evidence, and these barely scratch the surface.

**The writings of early Christians.** Extensive quotations of Scripture by leaders, writers, and theologians in the early church confirm the reliability of our modern-day Bible. We can document approximately thirty-six thousand quotations from these sources, and these range from single verses to entire passages. All but eleven verses of the New Testament can be verified from these secondary quotations.

Norman Geisler writes, "Early Christian writers provide quotations so numerous and widespread that if no manuscripts of the New Testament existed today, the New Testament could be reproduced from the writings of the early Fathers alone." [24]

- Clement of Rome (AD 95) quotes from Matthew, Mark, Luke, Acts, 1 Corinthians, 1 Peter, Hebrews, and Titus.

- Ignatius (AD 70–110) quotes from thirteen New Testament books, including Matthew, John, Acts, Romans, Galatians, James, and 1 Peter.

- Clement of Alexandria (AD 150–212) quotes 2,400 times from all but three books of the New Testament.

- Cyprian (died AD 258) quotes 740 times from the Old Testament and more than 1,000 times from the New Testament.

**The writings of early non-Christians.** Even many non-Christians from early centuries of the modern era authenticate the people, places, and events of the New Testament in their writings. Their records help substantiate that the world at large was well aware of the events of the New Testament and the claims of Scripture.

Tacitus, a first-century Roman historian, wrote about the death of Jesus and alluded to a "mischievous superstition" (likely a reference to Jesus' resurrection).

The writings of Josephus, a first-century Jewish historian, contain many statements that verify the historical validity of both the Old and New Testaments.

In a letter to Emperor Trajan in about AD 112, Pliny the Younger, a Roman author and administrator, describes early Christian worship practices, which confirms that Christians worshipped Jesus as God from an early date.

**The evidence of archaeology.** The *Baker Encyclopedia of Christian Apologetics* states: "The science of archaeology has brought strong confirmation to the historicity of both the Old Testament and the New Testament. Archaeological evidence for the reliability of the New Testament is overwhelming." It then goes on to provide details of the accuracy of Luke's Gospel, testimony of secular historians, and physical evidence related to Christ's crucifixion. One notable testimony from the archaeologist Sir William Ramsay is provided:

> I began with a mind unfavorable to it (Acts), for the ingenuity and apparent completeness of the Tubingen theory had at one time quite convinced me. It did not lie then in my line of life to investigate the subject minutely; but more recently I found myself often brought into contact with the book of Acts as an authority for the topography, antiquities, and society of Asia Minor. It was gradually borne in upon me that in various details the narrative showed marvelous truth. [25]

Archaeological discoveries, especially in the last half century, strongly attest to the reliability of the Bible. "Discovery after discovery has established the accuracy of innumerable details, and has brought increased recognition to the value of the Bible as a source of history," archaeologist William F. Albright has written. [26]

For example, for centuries, no archaeological evidence existed to support that Pontius Pilate ever lived. Then in 1961, two Italian archaeologists uncovered a Latin inscription referring to Pilate by name as a Roman governor.

Evidence from outside the Bible resoundingly supports the Bible's historical reliability. It is the most thoroughly documented collection of writings in all of history. Thus, you have every reason to trust the Bible.

# The Reliability of the New Testament (Part 2)

Muslims' question:
*"Who determined what books would be in the Christian
New Testament? Weren't the choices biased?"*

Thus far we've examined the transitions from Jesus' teachings, to the apostles' teachings, to the initial writing of texts, to the informal to formal recognition of those texts. We now come to the development of the New Testament canon—the group of books that have been recognized as God's inspired revelation. This is a broad subject and branches into several fields of Christianity. This subject is interwoven with early church history, Christian theology, the works of the early Church Fathers, textual criticism, and so on. A major difficulty for this development was that the early church was persecuted brutally and this inhibited the church's organization, communication, and stability. However, there is a very broad and strong agreement amongst the various scholars, Catholic, Protestant, and Orthodox, and others, on the formation of the New Testament canon and of its reliability today.

## The Process of the Development of the New Testament canon

As stated earlier, the early church esteemed, copied, and distributed the writings of Paul, Matthew, Mark, Luke, John, and others and began to view these as Scripture. However, it took time for the letters and Gospels to circulate and it took time for the early church to develop its theology and doctrine. But in general, the canon of the New Testament was recognized, compiled, and established during the first four centuries of Christianity. It is very important to understand that this was a process, not an event! (Controversy regarding some New Testament books continued through the early Reformation [1500s] but it was not widespread and was resolved subsequently.) On the other hand, F.F. Bruce notes that by the early second century the Church Fathers had informally recognized most of the books that make up the New Testament today:

> In the first half of the second century, then, collections of Christian writings which were due one day to be given canonical status were already taking shape—notably the fourfold gospel and the corpus of Pauline letters. [1]

Church Fathers, and others, compiled lists of the recognized writings. For example for the most part these lists agreed with each other. Through councils and dialogue, conflict with false teachers and false doctrine, the early Church Fathers began to settle on what should, and should not, be regarded as Christian Scripture, that is, the New Testament canon.

> By the late second century, collections of early Christian documents would certainly have been well underway. Marcion was already making a limited collection of Paul and Luke… Iraenaeus and Tertullian show extensive knowledge of a wide assortment of NT books. If the Muratorian canon is to be dated in the second century rather than the fourth, it provides clear evidence at this time of a canonical list (in Rome?) which contains many NT books… [2]

Referring to the general recognition of the writings that would eventually be regarded as the New Testament, Metzger writes:

> Certainly there is little enough recognition of their being regarded as "holy Scripture." By the close of the second century, however, we can see the outline of what may be described as the nucleus of the New Testament. Although the fringes of the emerging canon remained unsettled for generations, a high degree of unanimity concerning the great part

of the New Testament was attained among the very diverse and scattered congregations of believers not only throughout the Mediterranean world but also over an area extending from Britain to Mesopotamia. By the end of the third century and the beginning of the fourth century, the great majority of the twenty-seven books that still later came to be widely regarded as the canonical New Testament were almost universally acknowledged to be authoritative. [3]

Metzger then goes on to describe how conflicts with several groups led the church to take a formal stand and develop and define its Scriptures and doctrines. For example, Gnostics invented rival Gospels and unorthodox doctrine. Marcion invented his own particular unorthodox doctrines about God and Jesus. And the Montanists claimed to produce new prophecies and teachings.

Another pressure brought against the church was Roman persecution under Diocletian. This persecution caused the destruction of many Christian writings, many regarded as Scripture by the Christians. Metzger recounts one such incident:

> In the account of the martyrdom of Agape, Irene, and Chione, at successive hearings the three women were interrogated by the prefect Dulcitius of Thessalonica, who inquired, "Do you have in your possession any writings, parchments, or book of the impious Christians?"...On the next day when Irene was once again brought before the court, the prefect asked, "Who was it that advised you to retain these parchments and writings up to the present time?" "It was almighty God," Irene replied, "who bade us love him unto death. For this reason we did not dare to be traitors, but we chose to be burned alive or suffer anything else that might happen to us rather than betray them (i.e., the writings)."

> After sentencing the young woman to be placed naked in the public brothel, the prefect gave orders that the writings in the cabinets and chests belonging to her were to be burned publicly. The account concludes by describing how in March and

April of the year 304, the three became martyrs for their faith by being burned at the stake. [4]

Metzger comments on the initial establishment of the New Testament canon:

> After the period of the Apostolic Fathers we enter a new era in the history of the books of the New Testament in the Christian Church. Now the canonical Gospels come to be regarded as a closed collection, and are accepted under this form throughout the whole Church. The Epistles of Paul likewise come to be known and accepted as inspired Scripture, and here and there the same is true for the Acts of the Apostles and the Book of Revelation. Several other books are still on the fringe of the canon, not recognized by all, such as the Epistle to the Hebrews and the Epistles of James, of Peter, of John and of Jude. [5]

The canonization of the final books of the New Testament continued for some time longer. From AD 367 through 405, several councils were held that detailed and continued to recognize the books that made up the New Testament. As Andreas Köstenberger and Michael Kruger explain:

> Any suggestion that the church creates the canon, or that the canon is simply and solely the outcome of a long period of "choosing" by the established church, would not only unduly reverse the biblical and historical order but would have been an idea foreign to the earliest Christians. This is why the early church fathers speak consistently of "recognizing" or "receiving" the books of the New Testament, not creating or picking them. In their minds, scriptural authority was not something they could give to these documents but was something that was (they believed) already present in these documents—they were simply receiving what had been "handed down" to them. [6]

In other words, they were ratifying what had become the mind of the church.

## Tests for Canonicity

What did the church leaders use to determine what texts should, or should not, be regarded as Scripture? The decision-making process that the early church used has directly impacted the entire Christian world! This process then needs to be understood in order for us to have confidence in their determinations.

F.F. Bruce explains:

> The earliest Christians did not trouble themselves about criteria of canonicity; they would not have readily understood the expression. They accepted the Old Testament scriptures as they had received them; the authority of those scriptures was sufficiently ratified by the teaching and example of the Lord and his apostles. The teaching and example of the Lord and his apostles, whether conveyed by word of mouth or in writing, had axiomatic authority for them. [7]

But as stated previously, as time wore on, external and internal pressures bore upon the church; various writings proliferated, false Gospels were written, false claims were made, and she needed to define which texts were authoritative and which were not.

Metzger lists several "tests" or criteria used by the early church to determine if Christian writings deserved to be given special status or deemed as Scripture. However, Metzger notes that "inspiration" was not a criterion because Christians believed that much of what they did could be "inspired." Here are the three criteria Metzger lists:

1. *Rule of faith*: Does the text agree with the fundamentals of the Christian faith?

2. *Apostolic authorship*: Was the text written, or purported to be written, by an apostle?

3. *Church acceptance*: Was the text received and utilized by the church at large?

Metzger then concludes:

These three criteria (orthodoxy, apostolicity, and consensus among the churches) for ascertaining which books should be regarded as authoritative for the Church came to be generally adopted during the course of the second century and were never modified thereafter. [8]

F.F. Bruce provides a similar list of criteria: [9]

1. *Apostolic authority*: Were the writings reputed to be written by an apostle or someone associated with them?

2. *Antiquity*: Was the text old enough to be ascribed to the apostolic age?

3. *Orthodoxy*: Does the text teach correct doctrine about Christ, His life, and His teachings?

4. *Catholicity*: Was the text received and recognized by the catholic (universal) church?

5. *Traditional use*: Has the text been used and practiced by the church for an established time?

There were four books, respected and considered by the early Christians to be Scripture, that did not make the final cut: 1 Clement, the Epistle of Barnabas, the Shepherd of Hermas, and the Didache. The Shepherd of Hermas was found in one of the earliest complete sets of the New Testament—the Codex Sinaiticus, and the Didache is considered to be a catechism for the early church.

Conversely, several books took longer to be recognized as Scripture by the entire church.

The only books about which there was any substantial doubt after the middle of the second century were some of those which come at the end of our New Testament. Origen (185-254) mentions the four Gospels, the Acts, the thirteen Paulines, 1 Peter, 1 John and Revelation as acknowledged by all; he says that Hebrews, 2 Peter, 2 and 3 John, James and Jude, with the "Epistle of Barnabas," the Shepherd of Hermas, the Didache, and the "Gospel according to the Hebrews," were disputed by some. Eusebius (c. 265-340) mentions as generally acknowledged all the books of our New Testament except James, Jude, Peter, 2 and 3 John, which were disputed by some, but recognized by the majority. Athanasius in 367 lays down the twenty seven books of our New Testament as alone canonical; shortly afterwards Jerome and Augustine followed his example in the West. The process farther east took a little longer; it was not until c. 508 that 2 Peter, 2 and 3 John, Jude and Revelation were included in a version of the Syriac Bible in addition to the other twenty two books. [10]

By the mid-300s, the canon of the New Testament was established firmly, although minimal disagreements, and reviewing councils, continued for hundreds of years.

## Noncanonical Books

On the other hand, there were a number of other books written by Christians (both of the proto-orthodox and unorthodox, that is, heretical varieties) aside from those that eventually found their way into the New Testament canon. Many of these other books were Gospels. Some critics are quick to ask the question of why the canonical Gospels (that is, Matthew, Mark, Luke, and John) should be accorded more authority or be considered more historically trustworthy than those that were not included in the New Testament canon. Why should the Gospel of Mary or the Gospel of Philip, for instance, be excluded from the canon or be considered any less reliable than the canonical Gospels?

First of all, as stated above, they did not meet the criteria of antiquity. While the canonical Gospels are universally regarded by modern New Testament scholars to have been penned no later than about AD 70 to 105,* the non-canonical Gospels are considered by most scholars to have been written from about the first quarter of the second century and later. For example, the Gospel of Peter is typically cited as one of the earliest noncanonical Gospels, commonly dated to around AD 125. The Gospel of Thomas is dated between about this time and about

---

* Some would argue substantially earlier; see Robinson 1976 and Wenham 1992.

AD 170 by the majority of scholars. The Gospel of Judas is thought by most to have been composed in the final quarter of the second century. Other Gospels are still later in the third and fourth centuries and beyond. Because of the late dates of composition as well as the content of these Gospels, most scholars do not believe that such Gospels allude to authentic traditions (at least by and large), much less can they truthfully lay claim to direct apostolic testimony.

Specifically because of some of the criteria listed above, none of the noncanonical Gospels ever received serious consideration for canonicity. Unlike the canonical Gospels, they were not heavily quoted, were not the subject of early Christian commentaries, and did not demonstrate the kind of antiquity that made these Gospels' connections to apostolic authority probable. In fact, the heterodox nature of many of these Gospels betrayed their inconsistency with apostolic teaching. They did not fit in with or belong to the family of New Testament texts. They were spurious, foreign, even cancerous.

This kind of recognition, even by official councils, should in no wise cause Muslims to raise objections to the New Testament's canonicity. Indeed, Islamic historical sources reveal to us that the Quran was given an official form after: (a) Uthman ordered Zayd ibn Thabit to collect the variant Quranic copies spread throughout the Islamic empire; (b) the variant copies were compared to what the Muslims thought were more accurate copies; (c) Uthman ordered the variants burned; and (d) Uthman's officially recognized recension became the standard Quran for all Muslims.

## Dating the Books of the New Testament

The New Testament books were written in the mid to late first century. The *Baker Encyclopedia of Christian Apologetics* cites two scholars on New Testament dating: [11]

- *William F. Albright*. "We can already say emphatically that there is no longer any solid basis for dating any book of the New Testament after about AD 80…In my opinion, every book of the New Testament was written by a baptized Jew between the forties and the eighties of the first century (very probably sometime between about AD 50 and 75)."

- *John A. T. Robinson.* Robinson places Matthew at 40 to after 60, Mark at about 45 to 60, and John at from before 40 to after 65.

The *Encyclopedia* continues to give additional evidence for the New Testament's first-century dating:

> Other Evidence. Early Citations.
>
> Of the four Gospels alone there are 19,368 citations by the church fathers from the late first century on…This argues powerfully that the Gospels were in existence before the end of the first century, while some eyewitnesses (including John) were still alive.[12]
>
> Early Greek Manuscripts.
>
> The earliest undisputed manuscript of a New Testament book is the John Rylands papyri (P52), dated from 117 to 138…Whole books (Bodmer Papyri) are available from 200. Most of the New Testament, including all the Gospels, is available in the Chester Beatty Papyri manuscript from 150 years after the New Testament was finished (ca 250).[13]

Jesus died around AD 33 and all of the original New Testament texts were written within one generation from that point. The fact that the original texts were written at such an early date gives credibility to the argument that even with minor variation in oral transmission, there was not a great deal of time for material to be added or subtracted.

Another consideration favors dating the Gospels having been written before AD 70. Consider the following hypothetical: In 20 years, someone finds a book about the history of New York City buried in a pile of books, but the book is not dated. The book does not contain any account of the attack on the World Trade Center buildings in 2001. Given that the World Trade Center attack is one of, if not the most, important event in New York's history, when would you surmise the book was written? Naturally, you would deduce that it was written before 2001, otherwise the author would have included the event. Now, consider these historical facts: The Jewish Temple was the centerpiece of Jewish culture and civilization in first-century Palestine. Scholars unanimously agree that the Romans under Emperor Vespasian destroyed it in AD 70. Now, none of the Gospels records the Temple's destruction, even though it was one of the most important events in the first century. Given that the Gospels record historical information, it seems far more likely that the Gospels were written before the Temple's destruction. Otherwise, at least one of them would have mentioned it. John is the latest Gospel written, and because he does not mention the Temple's destruction, we can surmise that his Gospel was written before AD 70, and the other Gospels were even earlier. This seems especially so when it comes to Matthew and Luke because Matthew 24:1-8 and Luke 21:5-6 record Jesus' prophecy that the Temple would be destroyed. If Matthew and Luke were written after AD 70, we would naturally expect them to record the destruction of the Temple as a fulfillment of Jesus' prophecy. But because they don't record it, we can conclude they were written before AD 70.

## Textual Variants and New Testament Manuscripts

There exist over 5000 Greek New Testament manuscripts dating from the second through the ninth centuries. However, there are between 300,000 to 400,000 variants, that is, anytime the New Testament manuscripts have alternate wordings. Like with other ancient literature, the many manuscript copies that we have today are at variance with one another in literally hundreds of thousands of places. As far as ancient documents are concerned, the more copies of a work that we have the more variants there will be (which makes sense as more copies open the door to more variability), and the New Testament has by far and away more manuscript copies than any other classical Greco-Roman literature or any type of literature in history. The larger number of New Testament variants is directly related to the extremely large number of manuscripts. Simply put, the more manuscripts, the more

variants. *Scholars agree that the vast majority of these variants are irrelevant being spelling or grammatical differences, or "nonsense" errors.*
There are three large categories of variants:

1. *Spelling differences*: The name John, for example, may be spelled with one "N" or with two. Clearly, a variation of this sort in no way jeopardizes the meaning of the text. Spelling differences account for roughly 75 percent of all variants. That's between 225,000 and 300,000 of all variants.

2. *Proper names*: Some manuscripts may refer to Jesus by His proper name, while others may say "Lord" or "he." This should hardly call the meaning of the text into question.

3. *Translation of text*: Roughly 1 percent of all variations involved the meaning of the text. Even this can be an overstatement. For example, disagreement on "our" versus "your" in 1 John 1:4:

> We write this to make *our* joy complete.
>
> *or*
>
> We write this to make *your* joy complete.

The short answer to the question of what theological truths are at stake in these variants is—*none*.

There are a number of important variants that do impact the meaning and understanding of the text. However, in the end no crucial Christian doctrine is in doubt by the results of more than two centuries' worth of New Testament textual criticism.

Dan Wallace categorized the variants and stated:

> The final—and by far the smallest—category consists of variants that are both meaningful and viable. Only about 1 percent of all textual variants fit this category. But even here the situation can be overstated. By "meaningful" we mean that the variant changes the meaning of the text to some degree. It may not be terribly significant, but if the variant affects our

understanding of the passage then it is meaningful. To argue
for large-scale skepticism because we cannot be certain about
a very small portion of the text is a careless overstatement...[14]

New Testament textual critics of virtually all stripes agree that
the vast majority of the original New Testament text can be reconstructed with virtual certainty from the tens of thousands of manuscripts in existence. In the remaining places where the text is in doubt,
it is believed that with perhaps a few rare exceptions, the original text
is intact among the known variants, or that if the original text cannot
be known for certain then the original meaning is intact.

## Variants: The How, Who, and Why

But why are there variants or how did they get there? Who made
them? Why did they make them? There are many important questions
regarding the variants and these variants are critical to the Christian
faith. *The variants are important and should not be summarily dismissed
because they can shed light into understanding the finer details about a
New Testament passage.* Commenting on the initial copies of the original documents and how various errors were introduced into the earliest copies, Metzger writes:

> In the earlier ages of the Church, biblical manuscripts were
> produced by individual Christians who wished to provide for
> themselves or for local congregations copies of one or more
> books of the New Testament. Because the number of Chris-
> tians increased rapidly during the first centuries, many addi-
> tional copies of the Scriptures were sought by new converts
> and new churches. As a result, speed of production some-
> times outran accuracy of execution.[15]

This type of production, with the greater amount of errors occurring earlier in Christian history, rather than later, continued into the
middle of the fourth century. Metzger writes:

> When, however, in the fourth century Christianity received
> official sanction from the State, it became more usual for

commercial book manufacturers, or scriptoria, to produce copies of the books of the New Testament. [16]

Even with the errors, the degree of accuracy was excellent. Metzger notes that the scribes were diligent:

> In view of the difficulties involved in transcribing ancient books, it is the more remarkable how high was the degree of achievement of most scribes. The fact is that in most manuscripts the size of the letters and the ductus of the script remain surprisingly uniform throughout even a lengthy document. [17]

Complementing the New Testament texts were the writings of the early Church Fathers. As early as the second century they were quoting from New Testament texts. Metzger writes:

> Besides textual evidence derived from New Testament Greek manuscripts and from early versions, the textual critic has available the numerous scriptural quotations included in the commentaries, sermons, and other treatises written by early Church Fathers. Indeed, so extensive are these citations that if all other sources for our knowledge of the text of the New Testament were destroyed, they would be sufficient alone for the reconstruction of practically the entire New Testament. [18]

The quality of the Church Fathers' quotations can be challenged; at times their quotations did not agree with other Fathers' quotations, and at times (probably for many different reasons), they presented different versions of the same quotation! But the point is that they had a viable record they were quoting from, despite their paraphrasing or their quotation inconsistency. In sum, writing about the reliability of the New Testament, Dr. Craig Blomberg states:

> All kinds of minor variations distinguish these manuscripts from one another, but the vast majority of these variations have to do with changes in spelling, grammar, and style, or accidental omissions or duplications of words or phrases.

Only about 400 (less than one per page of English translation), have any significant bearing on the meaning of the passage...*But overall, 97-99 percent of the NT can be reconstructed beyond any reasonable doubt,* and no Christian doctrine is founded solely or even primarily on textually disputed passages...

There is absolutely no support for claims that the standard modern editions of the Greek NT do not very closely approximate what the NT writers actually wrote. [19]

### How Were the Variants Introduced?

There were a number of causes of error in the transmission of the New Testament text. Metzger classifies these in two categories: [20]

*Unintentional errors:*

• errors arising from faulty eyesight

• errors arising from faulty hearing

• errors of the mind

• errors of judgment

*Intentional changes:*

• changes involving spelling and grammar

• harmonistic corruptions

• addition of natural compliments and similar adjuncts

• clearing up historical and geographical difficulties

• conflation of readings

• alterations made because of doctrinal considerations

• addition of miscellaneous details

But in his final comments on the cause of errors Metzger writes:

Lest the foregoing examples of alterations should give the impression that scribes were altogether willful and capricious in transmitting ancient copies of the New Testament, it ought to be noted that other evidence points to the careful and painstaking work on the part of many faithful copyists…

Even in incidental details one observes the faithfulness of scribes…These examples of dogged fidelity on the part of scribes could be multiplied, and serve to counterbalance, to some extent, the impression which this chapter may otherwise make upon the beginner in New Testament textual criticism. [21]

The scribes' accuracy has been noted, challenged, and discussed, but Philip Comfort also notes a distinct case of where the scribe's work has been exemplar: the case of the papyri manuscript P75 correlation to Codex Vaticanus:

The text produced by the scribe of P75, however, is a very "strict," accurate MS. In fact, it seems to have been the kind of MS used in formulating Codex Vaticanus—for the readings of P75 and B (Codex Vaticanus) are remarkably similar… Prior to the discovery of P75, certain scholars thought that Codex Vaticanus was the work of a fourth-century recension; others (chiefly Hort) thought it must trace back to a very early and accurate copy. Hort said that Codex Vaticanus preserves "not only a very ancient text, but a very pure line of a very ancient text."…P75 appears to have shown that Hort was right.

Prior to the discovery of P75 many textual scholars were convinced that the second- and third-century papyri displayed a text in flux, a text characterized only by individual independence…But P75 has proven this theory wrong. What is quite clear now is that Codex Vaticanus was simply a copy (with some modifications) of a MS much like P75, not a fourth-century recension. This does not automatically mean, however, that P75 and B represent the original text. What it does mean is that we have a second-century MS showing great affinity with a fourth-century MS whose quality is highly esteemed. [22]

The point of the P75 correlation to Codex Vaticanus is that they were fathered by different, earlier manuscripts, yet both of them are "remarkably similar." This proves an instance in which the scribes took their job seriously, and did excellent work. This also proves that at least some parts of the earliest manuscripts were nearly identical.

### Significant Variants

There are significant variants that prove that some copyists took liberties and willfully introduced words, verses, or entire passages into the New Testament! These changes were a willful corruption (meaning a changing) of the manuscript they copied. None of these variants has a right to be considered to be part of the original, or earliest, New Testament manuscripts. These variants could be classified as "meaningful and viable."

F.F. Bruce states:

> In the "received text" of the New Testament there are some passages which find no place in modern critical editions of the Greek Testament (or in translation based on these). Should such passages be recognized as canonical? There is no person or community competent to give an authoritative ruling on this question; any answer to it must be largely a matter of judgment.
>
> There is, for example, the text about the three heavenly witnesses which appears in AV/KJV [the King James Version and the American Standard Version] at 1 John 5:7. This passage is a late intruder; it has no title to be considered part of the New Testament or to be recognized as canonical.
>
> What of the last twelve verses of Mark's Gospel (Mk. 16:9-20)? These verses—the longer Marcan appendix—were not part of Mark's work. That in itself would not render them uncanonical—as we have seen, canonicity and authorship are two distinct issues—but their contents reveal their secondary nature...The right of these twelve verses to receive canonical recognition is doubtful.

Then there is the story of the woman taken in adultery (John 7:53–8:11). This certainly does not belong to the Gospel of John. It is an independent unit of gospel material, of the general character as the Holy Week incidents in the temple court recorded in Mark 12:13-37. The account has all the earmarks of historical veracity, and as a genuine reminiscence of Jesus' ministry is eminently worthy of being treated as canonical. [23]

Bruce is saying that none of these passages are original but perhaps the John passage could be considered genuine. The point is that there is evidence of New Testament manuscript corruption, but, as a text critic does his job, he is able to define what was, and what was not original, or near to the original. It is not a guessing game, but rather it is a hunt, a defining investigation. As such, scholars are able to identify (and they continue to identify) the earliest text of the manuscripts. Part of the rewards of this labor is that they are able to prove that the "meaningful and viable" variants do not affect Christian doctrine, however lightly they may shade it.

## Summary on the Impact of the Variants

Dan Wallace sums up the effect that the meaningful and viable variants have upon the New Testament and Christianity:

> First, there is virtually no need for conjecture about the original wording. That is, the wording of the original text is almost always to be found in the extant (remaining) copies. Second, any uncertainty over the wording of the original New Testament does not have an impact on major teachings of the New Testament. The deity of Christ certainly is not affected by this.

> There is simply no room for uncertainty about what the New Testament originally taught. Whether one chooses to believe it is a different matter, and that is taken up in other chapters. Our concern here is simply to show that the fundamental teachings of the New Testament are undisturbed by viable textual variants. [24]

Complementing Wallace's work, the *Baker Encyclopedia of Christian Apologetics* states:

> Whereas there are many variant readings in the New Testament manuscripts, there are a multitude of manuscripts available for comparison and correlation of those readings in order to arrive at the correct one. Through intensive comparative study of the readings in 5686 Greek manuscripts, scholars have carefully weeded out errors and additions from "helpful" copyists and discerned which early manuscripts are most accurate. Textual issues remain, but today's Bible reader, and especially those who read a recently edited Greek New Testament from the United Bible Society, can be confident that the text is extremely close to the autographs. [25]

## Assumed Contradictions

Alongside the issue of the variants there is the matter of assumed contradictions within the New Testament. Skeptics of all varieties will often point out the many apparent discrepancies or perceived errors within the New Testament in order to discount its reliability. Christians have for centuries countered such alleged difficulties by providing appropriate resolutions and honest skeptics have admitted that many of the problems dissolve once they are subject to scholarly scrutiny. But other skeptics, having a hardened bias, are unlikely to be convinced that such difficulties can be resolved. We're not saying that every question or challenge can right now be answered satisfactorily, but the majority have been. Further, most of the purported discrepancies in the Gospels are in matters of secondary details. Consider one of Ehrman's examples regarding why Judas Iscariot betrayed Jesus:

> The four accounts differ on why Judas did the foul deed. There is no reason stated in Mark, although we are told that he received money for the act, so maybe it was out of greed (14:10-11). Matthew (26:14) states explicitly that Judas did it for the money. Luke, on the other hand, indicates that Judas did it because "Satan entered into him" (22:3). In other

words, the devil made him do it. In John, Judas is himself called "a devil" (6:70-71), and so presumably he betrayed his master because he had an evil streak. [26]

Let us ask you, is harmonization an unreasonable exercise in this case? The different reasons for Judas's betrayal are complementary. That Judas would be willing to betray the Messiah for money and that he is "a devil," or as Ehrman puts it "had an evil streak," certainly go hand in hand: Judas was willing to take money to betray Jesus because he had an evil streak. Luke's argument about the devil entering Judas fits quite nicely with the reasons cited by the other Gospels for Judas's betrayal. It is certainly not a novel concept in Christianity to believe that evil acts committed by men are at least partially the result of satanic influence. Religious and nonreligious people have attributed the incredible brutality of the atheists Stalin and Mao Tse-Tung, the occult-follower Hitler, and the nominal Muslim Saddam Hussein, and so on, to some type of demonic power.

This type of harmonization is a simple exercise and anyone who has lived into their teens should be able to understand that people can do a specific act for a variety of reasons, or that different motivations can cause someone to perform an act.

Thus most discrepancies among the Gospels are similarly addressed. Further, some scholars actually see a benefit or a support for reliability when a single story is told from differing perspectives that offer differing details. In fact, according to Abdu Murray, a trained trial lawyer, this kind of testimony is often used in a court of law to test whether two or more witnesses are telling the truth. Sometimes, when two witnesses tell the same story in exactly the same way, it damages their credibility because it appears that the witnesses collaborated to get their stories straight. In other words, it looks like they are conspiring to tell a story. But, if two witnesses give an account of the same event, but with different facts that complement each other's account, their credibility is enhanced because their facts fit together, yet they do not appear to have colluded to fabricate a story. Lawyers often make that very case in closing arguments to illustrate to a jury why they should believe certain witnesses' testimony.

Applying that kind of analysis to the Gospels, we see that far from the surface-discrepancies bringing into question the Gospels' general historical reliability, they in fact enhance it, because different witnesses of a significant event will present different viewpoints, different details, different perspectives of that event. Different does not necessarily mean contradictory. Most often, in the case of the Gospels, these details complement, not contradict, each other.

Here is an example of two accounts that tell the same story with different, but complementary information. In Matthew 26:57-68, we see that those who seized Jesus spit on Him and struck Him and told Him to prophesy about who had hit Him. This seems strange, since it would be obvious to Jesus who had hit Him. So why tell Him to prophesy about it? When we read Luke 22:63-64, we get the answer. Luke tells the same story, but he includes the detail that Jesus was blindfolded when they struck Him, so it would be difficult to tell who had struck Him.

Rather than conclude on one extreme that Matthew and Luke offer contradictory accounts, or go to the other extreme and conclude that they conspired to get their stories exactly the same (or that later Christians copied material from one and put it in another), we can see that they offer different, but complementary accounts of the same event, making it more likely that they were telling the truth. This is but one of the many examples of complementary accounts tending to show the Bible's veracity.

## Other Points to Consider

Dr. James White debated Bart Ehrman and made a significant point:

> I asked a computer program to compare for us two different texts; the Westcott and Hort text and the Byzantine majority platform text. I was not saying that there was a 95% agreement in the comparison of the two manuscripts...I said very clearly, "We are looking at printed texts here," that is: What does the Byzantine manuscript tradition look like, what does the Alexandrian look like, and let's compare the

various places using computer technology to do so. And I gave you the exact number—it's just under 6,600 differences between the Byzantine Majority Text and the Modern Critical Text. That's a number—put it into the math for yourself—it's about a 95% agreement, there's about a 4.7% variation between those printed collations. [27]

White's point that two manuscript traditions, at opposite ends of the manuscript tradition, agree in 95 percent of the text is impressive! For all of the variants, once the manuscript traditions are collated there is significant uniformity. This point should not be lost or missed for those who wish to understand the big picture, that is, "Do we have what Jesus and the early apostles did and taught?" This led Dr. White to frame the real issue: "...the issue is not if God preserved His Word, but how." Dr. White's challenge to those who insist on perfect copying, that is, no variants allowed during transmission, is that no copying of the New Testament texts would have been possible until the invention of the printing press some 1500 years later, or perhaps until the twentieth century when the photocopier was invented.

There is another way to look at the textual variants. There are copies of copies of copies of copies out there. When they are compared to each other there is great similarity. If the wholesale deviation that some critics claim took place these copies of copies of copies would not resemble each other, however, the opposite is true. The Gospel message is the same.

## Conclusion

We have focused on the reliability of the New Testament and discussed a number of relevant topics and shown the following:

- The early church took the oral transmission of Jesus and the apostles' teaching seriously which insured the integrity of those teachings. Further, the inclusion of Aramaisms in the Gospels indicates that the oral transmission was recorded.

- Church tradition almost uniformly declares that the Gospels were written by the apostles or their associates. Even if the Gospels were not written by the apostles they could still provide accurate accounts.

- The majority of texts that were to become the New Testament canon were known to the early church by the first part of the second century. Early lists of the recognized texts were made in the early to mid-second century and the New Testament canon began to take shape. By the middle of the third century it had taken shape; through various tests and discussions, the church formally recognized what she had informally recognized for many years.

- The genre of the Gospels supports the goal of recording accurate historical information, and archaeology supports the historical reliability of the Gospels.

- Textual variants occurred early in the copying of the manuscripts but 97 to 99 percent of those variants *are not* meaningful and viable. The remaining 1-3 percent of the variants do affect the texts but do not affect cardinal Christian doctrine. Most of the assumed contradictions can be dealt with fairly and rationally by harmonizing different versions of the same event.

To the Muslims' question, "Can I believe the Bible's story of Jesus—hasn't it been corrupted?" a Christian can confidently conclude with a resounding "Yes, you can trust the New Testament."

Dan Wallace's conclusion sums up the credibility and reliability of today's New Testament:

> The Gospels are historically credible witnesses to the person, words, and deeds of Jesus Christ. What the evangelists wrote was based on a strong oral tradition that had continuity with the earliest eyewitness testimony. In essence, the gospel did not change from its first oral proclamation to its last written production.

The original documents of the New Testament have been lost, but their contents have been faithfully preserved in thousands of copies. Today we are certain of about 99 percent of the original wording. In no place is the deity of Christ or his bodily resurrection called into question by textual variants. Although much of the wording of the text has undergone change over the centuries, the core truth-claims of Christianity have remained intact. [28]

**Further reading on archaeological support for the reliability of the New Testament:**

www.carm.org/can-we-trust-new-testament-historical-document

www.christianitytoday.com/ct/2003/septemberweb-only /9-22-21.0.html

# An Evaluation of the Quran

The Quran is Islam's primary theological text and it is loved, cherished, and venerated. Many proclaim that the Quran is Muhammad's only or greatest miracle and some view it as the greatest miracle in history.

Volumes have been written on the Quran by Muslim, Christian, and atheist scholars. Topics such as its historical development, primary doctrines, and key themes have taken up entire books. We cannot cover all details in one chapter, but we will present basics and examine it from a Christian perspective.

In some respects the Quran has a great deal in common with the Bible. Christians may be surprised to learn that the Quran is full of Old and New Testament references. It pays great respect to various biblical figures and heroes. One chapter is named "Mary" after Jesus' mother and another is named "Jonah" after the Jewish prophet.

There are some beautiful and moral passages in the Quran. An example is 2:177:

> It is not righteousness that ye turn your faces to the East and the West; but righteous is he who believeth in Allah and the Last Day and the angels and the Scripture and the prophets; and giveth wealth, for love of Him, to kinsfolk and to orphans and the needy and the wayfarer and to those who ask, and to set slaves free; and observeth proper worship and payeth the poor-due. And those who keep their treaty when they make one, and the patient in tribulation and adversity

and time of stress. Such are they who are sincere. Such are the Allah-fearing.

One favorite is 91:1-10 (from Arberry's translation):

By the sun and his morning brightness and by the moon when she follows him, and by the day when it displays him and by the night when it enshrouds him!

By the heaven and That which built it and by the earth and That which extended it! By the soul, and That which shaped it and inspired it to lewdness and godfearing! Prosperous is he who purifies it, and failed has he who seduces it. [1]

Some Christians have a weak and superstitious approach to reading the Quran. They view it as a black magic book that will deceive them and cause them to leave the faith and so avoid reading it at all costs. (We have Muslim friends who take a similar approach to reading the Bible.) It is no good if Christians cannot engage the Quran if they wish to engage in dialogue with Muslims. Muslims all over the world are coming to Christ and many Christian workers in this field know the Quran well. If we are going to be effective, we should know and understand the Quran to some degree.

## Key Observations About the Quran

1. Muhammad began to proclaim the Quran following the angel Gabriel's first visitation. This occurred when he was about 40 (AD 610), and Quranic revelation ended when he died 23 years later (AD 633). Throughout this time he claimed to receive the various passages that comprise the Quran from Gabriel.

2. The Quran today consists of 114 chapters, or "suras," generally arranged in order of length. The Quran is not arranged chronologically or arranged according to topic. Suras are named after key figures or subjects or simple references found in the chapter. For example, the sura

named "Women" is named so because much of the sura deals with women.

3. Scholars do not agree on the exact chronological order of the Quran. However suras 9 or 5 are often identified as the last sura while the first passage of the Quran to be revealed is the first part of sura 96.

4. "Quran" means "Recitation" or "Reading" in English.

5. The 23-year period of revelation occurred in both Mecca and Medina. Most of the individual suras were revealed in Mecca. The longest suras were revealed in Medina. Sura 2 is a reflection of Muhammad's conflicts with the Jews of Medina.

6. Most suras consist of verses revealed in one respective town (Mecca or Medina) or the other, but some suras contain a mix of passages revealed in both Mecca and Medina.

7. Many Muslim scholars believe that the Quran is an uncreated, eternal attribute of Allah. It is the final revelation from God to man.

8. The Traditions (Hadith) and Biographical (Sira) literature are additional Islamic source texts which are used to establish Islamic theology but the Quran stands above those.

9. Muhammad often received Quranic revelations in response to immediate challenge, conflict, or controversy and in this the Quran was revealed as guidance to aid him. The Quran does not usually provide the context behind those revelations (this is where the Hadith and Sira help greatly). An entire branch of Islamic theological study, "Asbab al-nuzul" (reasons or circumstances of the revelation), exists to provide passages' context.

10. The Quran addresses many themes including Allah's greatness, prayer, alms, points based on biblical and

apocryphal Jewish and Christian stories, theological conflicts, military battles, civil relations, interactions with non-Muslims, marriage, heaven, hell, slavery, and so forth.

11. There were dozens of early compilations of the Quran. Although they were fairly uniform and had much in common there were also differences: Some had more suras, some had less, verses had significant differences (more than just pronunciation or dialect differences), verses were missing, different words were used, and so on. Despite these differences, none of Islam's theological tenets are threatened.

Arthur Jeffery, one of the top Christian scholars of the Quran, comments in *The Qur'an as Scripture:*

> Every Sacred Book, just because it is sacred, is certain to make a deep impression on the cultural life of the community which reveres it, yet in some ways the Qur'an has entered even more deeply into the life of the Muslim community than any other Scripture has done in the older religious groups. To Christians Jesus Himself was the Word of God, so that in the life of the Church He, rather than the written documents, was the Gospel, the "good news," making Scripture of less importance to the Church than the risen Lord ever present and active among them through the Spirit. So we find in the Coptic Manichaean texts that Mani himself is "the Illuminator," the "Master of the Writings," whose person was for the Manichaean community, as that of the Buddha for the various Buddhist communities, far more important than any Scripture. But in Islam Muhammad is only the mouthpiece of revelation. The Qur'an is the word of Allah. Later Muslim piety, it is true, has made much of the person of the founder, but it was the Book, the Qur'an, not the person Muhammad, which was the significant factor in forming the mould in which the Islamic system took shape. [2]

Jeffery stresses the importance of the Quran in Islam's life. It is often the central focus of a Muslim's life just as Jesus is our central focus.

## Development of the Quran

During Muhammad's ministry of 23 years, he encountered many challenges, battles, obstacles, and changing circumstances. He had successes and failures. Often the words he received from Gabriel often addressed these challenges and changes. The Quran as it stands today did not come all at once in a nice, neat package. Rather, over these 23 years, it often came when these challenges and new circumstances arose. The Quran revealed to Muhammad developed theologically over this period.

In *Introduction to the Qur'an*, Watt states:

> In a sense, then, there has been development in the Qur'an but it is not really change. The new aspects are present from the beginning in the conception of the warner. It was the change in the circumstances of Muhammad and the Muslims that made it necessary for these aspects to become explicit. The process of development, therefore, is not to be taken as exposing an inconsistency in the Qur'an but as showing the adaptation of its essential teaching to the changing ideas and changing needs of the Muslims.[3]

Note here that Watt is addressing the developing theology of the Quran. He is not addressing the Islamic doctrine of "abrogation," which will be addressed shortly.

## A Christian Examination of the Quran

Muslims claim that today's Quran is Allah's pure, uncreated, accurate, literal word. The *Reliance of the Traveller*, a Shafi'i manual of Islamic law, states:

> The Koran is recited with tongues, written in books, and memorized in hearts despite being beginninglessly eternal, an

attribute of the entity of Allah Most High, unsubjects to dis-
severance and separation by conveyance to hearts or pages. [4]

Keep that in mind as we proceed. Muslims believe that the Quran
in their hands today is a copy of the heavenly Quran. It is eternal,
uncreated, an attribute of Allah. This is not an inspired book; it is a
word-for-word replica of what has existed in heaven eternally with
Allah.

However both intra-Islamic sources and external analysis prove this
is not the case. The evidence shows that today's Quran is the work of
men. The Quran's history is very similar to the New Testament's history. Arthur Jeffery commented:

> Like other Scriptures the Qur'an passed through various
> stages of textual history till there emerged a standard text
> which came to be regarded as sacrosanct. [5]

Later Jeffery states:

> It is from beginning to end the product of one man and from
> one period. It was the community which did the formal gath-
> ering together of the material after the founder's death and
> prepared it for use by the community, but its content had
> been given to them as Scripture before his death. It was not
> the product of the community in the sense that they decided
> that this was the collection of writings which had grown up
> in the community and in which they heard the authentic
> voice of religious authority, but it was formed by one man
> and given to the community on his authority as a collec-
> tion of "revelations" which was to be regulative for their reli-
> gious life as a community. Thus it resembles the Scripture
> which Mani set himself to provide as the sacred writings for
> his community, or such modern pseudo-Scriptures as the
> Book of Mormon, or [Newbrough's] Oahspe [A New Bible],
> or the writings of Baha'u'llah, each of which was the work of
> one man, and consciously produced for the purpose of being
> used by a community as a Holy Book. It also has in common

with these the fact that it is conscious of the existence of earlier Scriptures, which were authoritative for religious communities, and was produced in deliberate imitation of them. [6]

Below are several categories of evidence that prove that today's
Quran is not the supernatural, pristine text many Muslims believe it
to be. We cannot go into each category in great detail but we will provide references for your further study.

### 1. Quran Variants

During Muhammad's lifetime his companions wrote down various
parts of the Quran on scraps of parchment, bones, stone, and so on.
Following Muhammad's death some compiled their own collections
of what they knew of the Quran. Also following Muhammad's death,
during Abu Bakr's reign, thousands of people who were coerced into
becoming Muslims while Muhammad lived rebelled and left Islam.
Abu Bakr sent armies out to either kill these people or have them re-
convert to Islam (these were called the "Wars of Apostasy"). Great battles were fought and thousands on each side died. Following that, Abu
Bakr realized that so many men who had memorized portions of the
Quran had died and thus was worried that part of the Quran might
have been lost. He asked Zaid, a "companion" of Muhammad, who
was capable and knowledgeable of the Quran, to undertake its compilation. Zaid commented that this was an incredibly difficult task but
would undertake it nonetheless. Bukhari's Hadith, volume 6, number
509 details all of this.

However, other prominent Muslims, such as Ibn Masud and Ubay
ibn Kab (and many others), had also compiled their own versions of
the Quran. Some, like Ibn Masud, taught Quranic schools in different Islamic regions and propagated the use of their own versions of the
Quran. As Islam spread, conflict arose as to which Quran was correct.
Muslims were ready to fight with other Muslims over the differences.

This prompted the third Caliph, Uthman, to set into motion the
compilation of an official Quran. He asked Zaid and several other
Muslims to do the work. Once Zaid's work was finished, Uthman had

several copies made and sent to the primary Islamic provinces. But more importantly, Uthman ordered that all other competing Quran versions be burned and destroyed. Bukhari's Hadith, volume 6, number 510 details this.

This destruction did not sit well with the other notable Muslims who had compiled their own Qurans. Prominent "companion" Muslims, like Ibn Masud, protested and said they knew more of the Quran than Zaid. Some stated that Zaid's Quran was inaccurate and contained flaws. Further they declared that Uthman was destroying Allah's word! Nevertheless, Uthman was the ruler and his command was put into effect. Those that disobeyed were punished.

**Problems with Uthman's compilation.** The problem here is that there were notable differences between the Qurans. Some Qurans had more chapters than Uthman's; others had less. The chapters were arranged differently. Some prominent Muslims claimed that verses were missing in Uthman's Quran, or different than what they learned from Muhammad.

It took time for all of the competing Qurans to be destroyed and other Muslims compared them and noted or compiled differences with respect to Uthman's Quran recension. Using these types of writings (primarily of Abi Dawud's "Kitab al-Masahif" [book of the manuscripts]) Arthur Jeffery in his *Materials for the History of the Text of the Qur'an*, categorized and analyzed the numerous different versions and collections of the Quran that existed before Uthman issued the version that is used today. (Note, even today there are variants in existence.) There were dozens of Qurans in use before Uthman's and there are thousands of differences. The majority of them are minor, but there are others that are noteworthy.

However, "noteworthy" is in the eye of the beholder. Most Islamic scholars, Muslim or non-Muslim, admit there were variants. The level of importance ("noteworthy") that a person assigns to these variants often depends on their personal theology or bias. While most non-Muslim scholars agree that today's Quran is not a perfect replica of

Muhammad's original words, they also agree that the differences are not that great.

For example, while noting that there are differences, these differences do not affect the overall doctrines of the Quran or of Islam. Watt comments:

> Thus on the whole the information which has reached us about the pre-Uthmanic codices suggests that there was no great variation in the actual contents of the Qur'an in the period immediately after the Prophet's death. The order of the suras was apparently not fixed, and there were many slight variations in reading; but of differences there is no evidence.[7]

But, when argued against the Islamic belief in the existence of a perfect Quranic replica, these differences are great, and many ardent Muslims have a difficult time dealing with challenges to even a single word found in today's Quran. To suggest to them that today's Quran is not a perfect replica of Muhammad's Quran invites a harsh reaction.

None of Uthman's original Qurans exist today; only early copies of them exist. Some claims have been made that an original version exists here or there at a prominent museum or Islamic school but evaluation and dating of those show that they are not from Uthman's time.

Commenting on Islamic responses to the variant difficulties, that is, that the variants represent personal notes or simple errors, Jeffery states:

> Modern scholarship naturally cannot accept so easy a way out of the difficulty, for it is quite clear that the text which Uthman canonized was only one out of many rival texts and we needs must investigate what went before the canonical text. On the one hand it seems likely that in canonizing the Madinan text-tradition, Uthman was choosing the text that had all the chances of being nearest the original. On the other hand there is grave suspicion that Uthman may have seriously edited the text that he canonized.[8]

Recent discovery of ancient Quranic manuscripts in Sana'a, Yemen, strengthens Jeffery's argument. The discovery has yielded a huge amount of ancient manuscript material to work with, much of which predates Uthman's Quran. Various German Islamic scholars, such as Dr. Gerd Puin, have worked with these and have found more proof that today's Quran is likely not a word-for-word replica of what Muhammad proclaimed. There are numerous variants, irregularities, omitted punctuations, and differences between the Sana'a manuscripts and Uthman's Quran used today.

Puin noted that the omissions of diacritical marks, which helped to determine vowels and consonants, rendered the original Quran vague:

> The vowels between the consonants—in this example—are only to be deduced from the context! One can imagine easily that such a defective writing is a most unfavourable condition for the recording of a demanding text as that of the Koran! The Cairo printed edition, today considered as authoritative, with its rich inventory of diacritical points, doubling, stretch, correction and recitation signs gives an impression of what an effort is necessary, to make the original text, deprived of all these signs, to the "to be read," which it is today. [9]

Watt was also aware of the addition of the diacritical points and stated:

> By the time of the caliph 'Abd-al-Malik (685–705), the inadequacy of the existing script was clear to leading Muslims, and improvements began to be made. The problem of the incorrect copying of the defective script had also to be dealt with. The traditional accounts of the passage to the *scriptio plena* do not tally with one another, nor with the finding of paleography. It is virtually certain that the *scriptio plena* did not come into existence all at once, but gradually by a series of experimental changes. [10]

The fact that the earliest Qurans did not have the diacritical marks meant that words were poorly identified because they lacked defined vowels and consonants, and assumptions were made as to what word was meant. The diacritical marks were added much later during the historical development of the Quran. Of course, this is the root of much of the variant problem. Different words can be formed by changing the vowels and consonants, based upon the opinion of one Muslim to another. This then can change the passage's context and meaning, and this is what the variants show.

Of course Muslims work to provide answers to these challenges. However Dr. Campbell, in *The Qur'an and the Bible in the Light of History and Science*, sums this whole topic up accurately:

> With this information in our minds we must now ask the following question. How do you know that the Qur'an was accurately transmitted when there were only 150 strong believers? Maybe some pieces of leather parchment were lost? Maybe a shoulder blade with two Suras written on it fell off a camel? Do not think that I am laughing or making a joke. This is serious. HOW DO YOU KNOW THAT THERE WEREN'T ANY CHANGES?
>
> You will no doubt say to me, "But they memorized the Qur'an; and some of those 150 believers were present when Muhammad first repeated the Suras; and anyway Muhammad was still with them to correct them."
>
> I do not say "No" to this, but I want you to realize something. You can't prove this. You don't have even one original sura written on a shoulder blade. You BELIEVE it. This is A BASIC ASSUMPTION. [11]

It is only a belief, a "basic assumption," that the Muslims who compiled today's Quran got it right. The actual evidence shows implicit disagreement and proves that today's Quran is man-edited and man-compiled. The ancient manuscript evidence demonstrates that today's Quran evolved over time as different Muslim scholars added diacritical marks to define words. While scholars agree that today's Quran is close to what Muhammad spoke, the evidence of competing manuscripts, thousands of variants, conflicting verses, missing verses, however proves that it is doubtful that today's Quran is an exact and 100 percent accurate compilation.

## 2. The Quran Borrows from Other Religious Works

There were many Jewish and Christian towns in and around the Hijaz during Muhammad's lifetime. J. Spencer Trimingham's *Christianity Among the Arabs in Pre-Islamic Times*[12] records details of Christianity throughout the Arabian peninsula before Islam. This peninsula was not a bastion of paganism as some have suggested, instead Christianity and Judaism flourished there before and during Muhammad's time. Muhammad had contact with Jews and Christians there and the Sira records Muhammad's interactions with them. Muhammad's wife's cousin, Waraqa, was reputed to be a Christian scholar who translated parts of the Bible into Arabic, and Muhammad attended caravan trips where he interacted with Christian monks. Muhammad could not have avoided direct, personal contact with Christians and Jews. Through his conversations with them he heard and learned their religious teachings and stories.

While Muslims believe that the Quran exists in heaven and has come down and been revealed from Allah, through Gabriel, and then to Muhammad, the evidence of his borrowing and using other religious stories shows that this material did not pre-exist in heaven with Allah. There are texts within the Quran from Jewish, Christian, and even pagan sources that reveal the human component within the Quran. This borrowing shows that Muhammad learned and accepted these religious stories as truthful and recited them as part of the Quran. Several books have been written detailing much of the borrowed material. Below is one example of many.

**Cain and Abel—the Quran and the Mishnah.** The Mishnah is a compilation and redaction of Jewish oral traditions that comment upon and present legal rulings. It can be viewed as the printed collection of Jewish oral Law. It was developed around AD 220 and codified years later. It predates Muhammad by hundreds of years.

In 5:27-32 the Quran comments on Cain and Abel and Allah's view against murder. Below is verse 32:

For that cause We decreed for the Children of Israel that whosoever killeth a human being for other than manslaughter or corruption in the earth, it shall be as if he had killed all mankind, and whoso saveth the life of one, it shall be as if he had saved the life of all mankind. Our messengers came unto them of old with clear proofs (of Allah's Sovereignty), but afterwards lo! many of them became prodigals in the earth.

Compare this to the quote from the Mishnah Sanhedrin 4:5:

> For so we find it in the case of Cain, who slew his brother, as it is written: THE VOICE OF THE BLOODS OF THY BROTHER CRIES TO ME FROM THE GROUND;— not the *blood* of thy brother, but the *bloods* of thy brother— his blood and that of his posterity...

> For this reason man was created one and alone in the world: to teach that whosoever destroys a single soul is regarded as though he destroyed a complete world, and whosoever saves a single soul is regarded as though he saved a complete world.[13]

John Gilchrist comments on this (quoting Tisdall's *The Sources of Islam*).

> Once again, as in the case of the misunderstanding about the statement in Genesis 15.7 which led to the story of Abraham being brought out of "the fire" of the Chaldees, we find that the passage in the Mishnah, repeated in the Qur'an, is derived from an interpretation of a biblical verse. Because the word for blood is in the plural in Genesis 4.10, an ingenious rabbi invented the supposition that all Abel's offspring had been killed with him which signified that any murder or life-saving act had universal implications. Clearly Muhammad had no knowledge of the source of the theory set out in the Mishnah but, hearing it related, simply set out the rabbi's suppositions as the eternal decree of God himself!

Now if we look at the thirty-fifth verse of the text above

quoted, it will be found almost exactly the same as these last words of this old Jewish commentary. But we see that only part is given in the Coran, and the other part omitted. And this omitted part is the connecting link between the two passages in the Coran, without which they are unintelligible (Tisdall, *The Sources of Islam*, p. 16).

The former part of the passage as it stands in the Mishnah is omitted in the Qur'an, possibly because it was not fully understood by Muhammad or his informant. But when it is supplied, the connexion between verse thirty-five and the preceding verses becomes clear (Tisdall, *The Original Sources of the Qur'an*, p. 66).[14]

Gilchrist shows this as yet another example of Muhammad repeating what he had learned from other faiths as part of the Quran.

In the light of the Quran's many references to the Old and New Testament characters, Gilchrist comments:

That Muhammad derived much of his knowledge of the prophets from those around him is backed up further by the fact that many of the names it gives to these prophets are not in their original form but rather in the form we find in the Greek texts of the New Testament, which is most significant because Arabic is a Semitic language in many respects closely related to Hebrew while it is considerably different to Greek. The prophets Jonah and Elijah are called Yunus and Ilyas respectively in the Qur'an, and the New Testament Greek forms of their names are likewise Yunas and Elias. The names of these prophets, therefore, as well as others (ea. Ishaq for Isaac) in the Qur'an, are given in neither their proper Hebrew nor Arabic forms but in the corresponding Greek form.

But the point is most important, especially as the Quran claims to be an Arabic Quran and a revelation to the Arabs in plain unequivocal language (Guillaume, *Islam*, p. 62).

It seems fair to conclude that, in all these instances, the Qur'an records nothing more than information which Muhammad received respecting the Biblical prophets, not through a divine revelation from heaven, but purely through communications between himself and the Jews and other knowledgeable folk he chanced to meet. [15]

Muhammad's borrowing may be a legitimate religious act, but one cannot claim that the Quran is a pure, pristine, eternal word of Allah when it borrows from and incorporates religious stories and languages.

### 3. Gabriel's Visitation

From a Christian and Jewish perspective there is reason to doubt that the real angel Gabriel visited Muhammad. The first encounter was anything but a magnificent, awe-inspiring, reverential experience for Muhammad.

Gabriel's initial appearance and interaction terrified Muhammad. Gabriel commanded him to "recite!" three times and Muhammad replied that he did not know how or what to recite. After the third time Gabriel gave Muhammad the first words of the Quran, which are now part of sura 96.

Here are excerpts taken from Islamic source materials concerning the first visitation. First from Bukhari:

> Then Allah's Apostle returned with the Inspiration, his neck muscles twitching with terror till he entered upon Khadija and said, "Cover me! Cover me!" They covered him till his fear was over and then he said, "O Khadija, what is wrong with me?" Then he told her everything that had happened and said, "I fear that something may happen to me."...

> But after a few days Waraqa died and the Divine Inspiration was also paused for a while and the Prophet became so sad as we have heard that he intended several times to throw himself from the tops of high mountains and every time he went up the top of a mountain in order to throw himself down,

Gabriel would appear before him and say, "O Muhammad! You are indeed Allah's Apostle in truth," whereupon his heart would become quiet and he would calm down and would return home. And whenever the period of the coming of the inspiration used to become long, he would do as before, but when he used to reach the top of a mountain, Gabriel would appear before him and say to him what he had said before...[16]

Similar details are recorded in Ibn Ishaq's biography of Muhammad, *Sirat Rasul Allah*:

I thought, Woe is me poet or possessed—Never shall Quraysh say this of me! I will go to the top of the mountain and throw myself down that I may kill myself and gain rest.[17]

Tabari's *History* also provides related details:

The inspiration ceased to come to the messenger of God for a while, and he was deeply grieved. He began to go to the tops of mountain crags, in order to fling himself from them; but every time he reached the summit of a mountain, Gabriel appeared to him and said to him, "You are the Prophet of God." Thereupon his anxiety would subside and he would come back to himself.[18]

And Ibn Sad's biographical material *Kitab al-Tabaqat al-Kabir* provides Muhammad's statement concerning his experience with Gabriel:

O Khadija, I see light and hear sounds and I fear I am mad.[19]

The concern here is that Muhammad's nightmarish visitation experience has no parallel in either the Old or New Testaments. There, those who experienced angels sent from God, or who had personal encounters with God (such as Isaiah, Mary, Moses, Paul) may have been initially startled, and may have received challenging and distressing messages, but they were not left terrified and self-doubting. Rather, they were comforted and confident, knowing they were dealing with a God who supported them. Daniel had several extraordinary encounters that overwhelmed him, not because he doubted who this experience was with, but because he knew he was dealing with God and His angels. In turn, they strengthened him.

Muhammad, on the other hand, had the opposite experience, and he initially thought something terrible had happened to him. Similarly, people during his time also thought he was plagued by a demon. The Quran addresses these assertions by affirming that Muhammad was neither demon-possessed nor mad:

> And your comrade is not mad. Surely he beheld Him on the clear horizon. And he is not avid of the Unseen. Nor is this the utterance of a devil worthy to be stoned (81:22-25).

This initial experience differs significantly from how God interacted with His people in the Bible. This first experience left Muhammad in a depressed and doubtful state. The Bible says that "God is not a God of disorder but of peace…" (1 Corinthians 14:33) and "the Spirit God gave us does not make us timid, but gives us power, love and self-discipline" (2 Timothy 1:7). Following this first visitation Muhammad was confused and distressed greatly.

### 4. Scientific Inaccuracies in the Quran

The Quran is not a book of science but that has not stopped various Muslims from proclaiming that science proves the Quran and that the Quran contained many scientific ideas and facts that were ahead of its time. Most of their claims are conjecture and when examined objectively they are found empty. When the Quran is scrutinized, various science-related statements are found to be inaccurate. Below are two of them.

**Development of the human fetus.** The Quran states in several places (96:1,2; 75:37-39; 40:67; 22:5; 23:12-14) that during its development a human fetus becomes a "clot" (alaqa). "Clot of blood" is what is meant here. Below is 23:12-14:

> Verily We created man from a product of wet earth; Then placed him as a drop (of seed) in a safe lodging; Then

fashioned We the drop a clot, then fashioned We the clot a little lump, then fashioned We the little lump bones, then clothed the bones with flesh, and then produced it as another creation. So blessed be Allah, the Best of creators!

Dr. Campbell writes:

As every reader who has studied human reproduction will realize, there is no stage as a clot during the formation of a fetus so this is a very major scientific problem. [20]

**Talking ants.** The Quran 27:17-19 presents King Solomon having a discussion with ants.

And there were gathered together unto Solomon his armies of the jinn and humankind, and of the birds, and they were set in battle order; Till, when they reached the Valley of the Ants, an ant exclaimed: O ants! Enter your dwellings lest Solomon and his armies crush you, unperceiving. And (Solomon) smiled, laughing at her speech, and said: My Lord, arouse me to be thankful for Thy favour wherewith Thou hast favoured me and my parents, and to do good that shall be pleasing unto Thee, and include me in (the number of) Thy righteous slaves.

Ants do not have the ability to communicate with humans through speech. Ants communicate through chemicals and smell, they do not communicate through sound. Solomon in all his greatness did not have the ability to hear them. Yet this is what the Quran states. Some Muslims have claimed that this is an allegorical statement. However, if you read the context of the entire passage (27:15-30) in which Solomon also has a detailed discussion with a bird, then the only conclusion is that the Quran states that Solomon overheard the ants talking.

There are a number of books and websites that examine the scientific errors within the Quran. These errors present the Quran's origin as being more human than divine.

## 5. Abrogation: The Quran Cancels Itself

Another problem with the Quran being purely from God is the doctrine of abrogation. This doctrine allows one verse or passage of the Quran to cancel, override, replace, or supersede another verse or passage. The Quran mentions this self-cancellation doctrine in several places. Below is one example.

> Nothing of our revelation (even a single verse) do we abrogate or cause be forgotten, but we bring (in place) one better or the like thereof. Knowest thou not that Allah is Able to do all things? (2:106).

This is a problem for Islamic scholars because it is not clear which verses are canceled out. They have followed a chronological rule of thumb in which later verses cancel out earlier verses. For example, Mustansir Mir, in his *Dictionary of Qur'anic Terms and Concepts*, states that 24:2 canceled out 4:15-16. Below are the two verses.

> The adulterer and the adulteress, scourge ye each one of them (with) a hundred stripes. And let not pity for the twain withhold you from obedience to Allah, if ye believe in Allah and the Last Day. And let a party of believers witness their punishment (24:2).

> As for those of your women who are guilty of lewdness, call to witness four of you against them. And if they testify (to the truth of the allegation) then confine them to the houses until death take them or (until) Allah appoint for them a way (through new legislation). And as for the two of you who are guilty thereof, punish them both. And if they repent and improve, then let them be. Lo! Allah is ever relenting, Merciful (4:15-16).[21]

The problem with the chronological rule of thumb is that much of the Quran's chronology is unknown. Consequently different scholars have different opinions as to which and how many verses are abrogated.

Some mention only a few, others mention over 100 verses have been abrogated. The authentic (sahih) collections of Hadith also identify a number of abrogated verses. For example,

> 'A'isha (Allah be pleased with her) reported that it had been revealed in the Holy Qur'an that ten clear sucklings make the marriage unlawful, then it was abrogated (and substituted) by five sucklings and Allah's Apostle died and it was before that time (found) in the Holy Qur'an (and recited by the Muslims). [22]

(Note: The parenthetical words in the above quote were added by the translator.) This doctrine had been problematic for Muhammad and the Muslims. Muhammad defended himself by receiving various revelations from Gabriel that justified the concept of Allah changing his law. Today the Quran has come under greater scrutiny and various Muslims have produced differing arguments on the doctrine of abrogation. Some say abrogation was progressive revelation to better suit the needs of the community, others say it applies to other religions, others say that it is not understood well enough to incorporate as a theological tenet.

This puts Allah in a very human light. This book exists through eternity yet Allah has to change his word multiple times to fit the needs of the Muslims at a given time, over the course of a few years or even days? God did not change His Law for the Jews over thousands of years. But in Islam's case it is odd, even doubtful, that Allah would have to change his law, based on the predicament of believers, over such a short period of time.

John Gilchrist believes that part of Muhammad's reasoning for inventing the doctrine of abrogation was that Muhammad's Meccan opponents, the Quraysh, charged that Muhammad was changing, or forgetting, parts of the Quran that he proclaimed. Commenting on 2:106, he states:

> This verse, therefore, clearly teaches that Allah substitutes one verse of the Qur'an for another, and it was this claim that

made the Quraysh allege that Muhammad was "but a forger," for it appeared to be a very expedient way of explaining the anomaly of earlier verses being "substituted" or "forgotten." [23]

Norman Geisler and Abdul Saleeb, in *Answering Islam: The Crescent in the Light of the Cross,* quote Gerald Nehls and comment:

> We should like to find out how a divine revelation can be improved. We would have expected it to be perfect and true right from the start…We find it unacceptable that within the space of 20 years a need for change or correction can become necessary. This surely suggests that God is not all-knowing or else the recorder made corrections. This seems particularly true in view of the fact that the corrected verses are often near the ones being corrected. [24]

The doctrine of abrogation presents Allah as *not* all-knowing, lacking foreknowledge, and changing his words per the changing ability and circumstances of Muhammad and the Muslims. God would not bend and change His Word to make life easier for His followers, while their circumstances change from good to bad to good again. A being such as that is not God.

### 6. Internal Evidence of Revision and Alteration

Chapter 6 of Watt's *Introduction of the Qur'an* is titled "The Shaping of the Qur'an." In that chapter Watt investigates and highlights many internal inconsistencies in the Quran's passages and verses, such as…

- the before-mentioned abrogation
- inconsistent rhyme and assonance
- unexpected, illogical, or inconsistent changes in subject, wording, and grammar
- unevenness and change in style
- apparent additions of text

and so forth. As a summary of the above, Watt states:

The great volume of evidence, of which what has been presented here is only a sample, shows that the qur'an is far
from being a straightforward collection (out of chronological order) of short passages of a revealed text. The matter is
too complex for any simple explanation of this kind. The vast
number of dislocations and the roughness of some of them
cannot simply be ascribed to "the Qur'anic style." The modern scholar may seldom be able to give a correct solution of
the problems raised by the dislocations, but it can surely be
no longer denied that here are problems of this kind.[25]

## Conclusion

There are numerous books and websites now available that go into
greater detail than we can go here. Here we can only provide general
summaries of the arguments. When the sum of the evidence is evaluated, the only conclusion that can be drawn is that the Quran today is
the work of men. It was compiled by men, edited by men, and revised
by men. There were notable disagreements between the leading Muslims concerning its words, passages, and chapters. The evidence shows
that it has borrowed and incorporated stories from all local religions.
Further it contains obvious scientific errors.

Although the Quran is adored by millions of Muslims its message conflicts with both the messages given to the Jewish prophets and
with Jesus' teachings. It opposes and denies most of Christianity's par-
amount doctrines: Jesus is the Son of God, the Trinity, Jesus' death,
atonement, and resurrection, and God's commands to those that love
and obey Him. While it has many similarities to the Bible, it also has
significant differences and Christians cannot accept it as the Word of
God.

**Further reading on the Quran and its variants**

William Campbell, *The Quran and the Bible in the Light of History
and Science,* http://answering-islam.org/Campbell/contents.html

Arthur Jeffery, *Materials for the History of the Text of the Qur'an*
http://www.bible.ca/islam/library/Jeffery/Materials/index.htm

John Gilchrist, *Jam' Al-Qur'an: The Codification of the Qur'an Text*
http://answering-islam.org/Gilchrist/Jam/index.html

A collection of dozens of articles on Quranic variants:
http://answering-islam.org/Quran/Text/index.html

**Further reading on sources of the Quran**

W. Goldsack , *The Origins of the Qur'an*

Abraham Geiger, *Judaism and Islam*

Charles Cutler Torrey, *Jewish Foundations of Islam*

W. St. Clair Tisdall, *The Original Sources of the Qur'an*

**Further reading on scientific errors in the Quran**

William Campbell, *The Quran and the Bible in the Light of History
and Science*, http://answering-islam.org/Campbell/contents.html

Pervez Hoodbhoy, *Islam and Science*

# The Quran Confirms the Christian Scriptures

Muslims' question:
*"We believe that the Quran is the pure Word of God and
teaches us the truth from God. Since the Quran rejects
the Bible, how can we trust the Bible?"*

Christians do not believe that the Quran is the Word of God. However the Bible and the Quran proclaim similar (and dissimilar) themes, and the Quran contains beautiful passages. But similarity, good moral guidelines, and poetry do not the Word of God make. Even atheists encourage men to love one another. A Christian's use of the Quran does not imply we believe it to be God's Word, but since our primary objective is to proclaim Christ to Muslims, we use it as a reference because the Quran speaks to Muslims.

Many Muslims are taught today that the Christian Scriptures have been corrupted. But this was not what Muhammad and the early Muslims taught. Muhammad and the early Muslims believed that the Bible was the Word of God. The confirmation of the Bible is made repeatedly in the Quran, and we are going to review a number of passages that establish that confirmation.

From the Muslim's perspective, the questions we've faced regarding the disagreement between the Quran's and the Bible's statements can be summed in the question at the head of this chapter: "We believe that the Quran is the pure Word of God and teaches us the truth from God. Since the Quran rejects the Bible, how can we trust the Bible?"

In response, what we are going to do here is use the Quran, and other Islamic source materials, to show that the Quran does not reject the Bible, rather it confirms the reliability of the Bible! We will examine what the Quran says about the Bible because it reveals Muhammad's mind and attitude toward the Bible. Let's also ask, "What did Muhammad really think about the Bible?"

We'll review the many Quranic verses which support the Bible's integrity (and conversely, the fact that there are no Quranic verses which charge corruption against the Bible), and we'll examine some of the more common claims of corruption made by Muslims who seek to absolve themselves of the Quran's command to respect the Bible.

## The Quran's High Regard for the Christian Scriptures

We have known some ex-Muslims who prior to their conversion were very devout and studied the Quran in depth. They were always troubled by how it supports the Bible. They questioned, "Why does the Quran teach that the Bible is the Word of God?" And, "How can both be true if they give conflicting messages?" The excuses that various Muslim apologists have made were flimsy and sincere people can see through them.

The point that the Quran confirms the Bible is not new; it has been made long ago by various Christians working in Islamic ministry. Below are a few quotes from various references.

About 155 years ago the great Christian scholar Sir William Muir wrote what should be considered the flagship of books on the theme of the Quran confirming the Bible. He identified some 131 Quranic verses, presented them in chronological order, and commented upon their significance in confirming the Bible. Not a single verse challenges the Bible. All of them, either explicitly or implicitly, confirm the Bible's integrity. Consider that! This theme in the Quran is not obscure; rather, it is oft pronounced and repeated. Our argument is not built upon one or two unclear verses that cause scholars to scratch their heads in puzzlement; rather, it is built upon a substantial amount of verses spoken by Muhammad during his 23 years of ministry. His "confirmation" of the Bible is repeated over and over. We encourage anyone who wants to study this subject in depth to acquire this book and read through it. You can read it at Google books as well as at Answering Islam (http://answering-islam.org/Books/Muir/Coran/index.htm). Below Muir comments on this theme:

> The Old and New Testaments are everywhere in the Corân referred to as extant and in common use; Jews and Christians are exhorted to follow the precepts of their respective Scriptures; and from first to last both portions of the Bible are spoken of in terms of reverence and homage consistent only with a sincere belief in their genuineness and authenticity. The expression noticed in the foregoing paragraph can naturally and properly be construed in accordance with this view; and hence it is obligatory that they should be so construed, and not in a sense which would run counter to the rest of the Corân. [1]

And John Gilchrist wrote:

> No one can read through the Qur'an without being struck by the attention it pays to the scriptures that preceded it. The Jews and the Christians are constantly described as Ahl al-Kitab ("People of the Book") and their scriptures are called the Tawraat and Injil respectively. Although the Qur'an speaks of the Zabur of David (presumably the Psalms, though once again said to be a book revealed to the prophet—Surah 17.55) so that Muslims generally believe that there were four major books (the Tawraat, Zabur, Injil and Qur'an), nevertheless the Jewish Scriptures is universally described in the Qur'an as the Tawraat and the Christian Scriptures as the Injil. Throughout the book the two former scriptures are always very highly regarded. [2]

Muslims believe that the Quran is the pure Word of God, like it is an entire "red letter" edition of God's Word. These are not men's words or inspirations, rather they are God's literal words. These are "no kidding around" pronouncements! And those pronouncements highly regard the Christian Scripture!

## Key Quranic Passages That Support the Bible

Let us examine a number of Quranic passages and find out what Muhammad really believed about the Christian Scriptures. You'll see that the quotations all confirm the Bible's reliability. While the Quran contradicts various Christian doctrines (perhaps due to Muhammad not knowing the Bible's doctrines very well), no challenge to the Bible's integrity is made. We are only listing a portion of them.

**5:36-38.** And We caused Jesus, son of Mary, to follow in their footsteps, confirming that which was (revealed) before him in the Torah, and We bestowed on him the Gospel wherein is guidance and a light, confirming that which was (revealed) before it in the Torah—*a guidance and an admonition unto those who ward off (evil). Let the People of the Gospel judge by that which Allah hath revealed therein. Whoso judgeth not by that which Allah hath revealed: such are evil-livers. And unto thee have We revealed the Scripture with the truth, confirming whatever Scripture was before it, and a watcher over it. So judge between them by that which Allah hath revealed, and follow not their desires away from the truth which hath come unto thee. For each We have appointed a divine law and a traced-out way...* (5:46-48).

This verse makes a strong statement about Jesus. He "confirms" the Torah, already revealed. Jesus was also given the Gospel, which corroborated the Torah. Muhammad then admonishes the Christians and Jews to judge according to what God has revealed. This shows that the Christians and Jews had existing Scriptures in their hands, they were admonished by Allah to follow those extant Scriptures, and the Quran confirms and supports those Scriptures. There is no word of corruption, no word of "lost" Scriptures.

**35:31.** As for that which We inspire in thee of the Scripture, it is the Truth confirming that which was (revealed) before it. Lo! Allah is indeed Observer, Seer of His slaves.

**3:3.** He hath revealed unto thee (Muhammad) the Scripture with truth, confirming that which was (revealed) before it, even as He revealed the Torah and the Gospel.

**12:111.** In their history verily there is a lesson for men of understanding. It is no invented story but a confirmation of the existing (Scripture) and a detailed explanation of everything, and a guidance and a mercy for folk who believe.

**29:46.** And argue not with the People of the Scripture unless it be in (a way) that is better, save with such of them as do wrong; and say: We believe in that which hath been revealed unto us and revealed unto you; our Allah and your Allah is One, and unto Him we surrender.

**10:37.** And this Qur'an is not such as could ever be invented in despite of Allah; but it is a confirmation of that which was before it and an exposition of that which is decreed for mankind—Therein is no doubt—from the Lord of the Worlds.

**5:66.** If they had observed the Torah and the Gospel and that which was revealed unto them from their Lord, they would surely have been nourished from above them and from beneath their feet. Among them there are people who are moderate, but many of them are of evil conduct.

**2:113.** And the Jews say the Christians follow nothing (true), and the Christians say the Jews follow nothing (true); yet both are readers of the Scripture. Even thus speak those who know not. Allah will judge between them on the Day of Resurrection concerning that wherein they differ.

**3:78-79.** Lo! those who purchase a small gain at the cost of Allah's covenant and their oaths, they have no portion in the Hereafter. Allah will neither speak to them nor look

upon them on the Day of Resurrection, nor will He
make them grow. Theirs will be a painful doom. And lo!
there is a party of them who distort the Scripture with
their tongues, that ye may think that what they say is
from the Scripture, when it is not from the Scripture.
And they say: It is from Allah, when it is not from Allah;
and they speak a lie concerning Allah knowingly.

Also see the Quran 16:43, 5:68, and 10:94.

### Discussion of Quranic Passages Confirming the Christian Scriptures

The sets of verses above show that the Scriptures that the Christians and Jews studied were extant, in their hands, and revered by Muhammad. The Christians "read," "studied," "taught," "judged," and "observed" these existing Scriptures. Verse 10:94 commands Muhammad to ask the Jews and Christians about his revelations! Would Allah tell Muhammad to seek advice from a people who studied a corrupt Scripture? Would Allah "confirm" repeatedly, ascribe respect for, and command people to obey a corrupted Scripture, all the while never warning them of the corruption? Of course not!

An expanded definition of the Arabic word for "confirm" is that it means to give credibility to, to believe in, to accept as true. Muhammad knew that Allah was telling him that the Scriptures that the Jews and Christians had were from him and true. The Quran was confirming those Scriptures as true, as God's previous words.

Allah does not put stipulations upon those Quranic passages. There are no caveats that state: "I confirm only that which agrees with the Quran." There are no options to take what Muhammad likes and leave the rest. There is no partial confirmation. Instead, Muhammad is told over and over again that Allah is confirming the Scriptures of the Christians and the Jews.

The senior Christian missionary and scholar Ernest Hahn also wrote a booklet on the Quran confirming the integrity of the Christian Scriptures. He addresses the charge of willful corruption of the Scriptures (al-tahrif al-lafzi), and goes into some depth to show that it carries no weight. He summarizes his study of the Quran's statements regarding the Scriptures of the People of the Book as follows: [3]

1. The great reverence and esteem in which the Qur'an holds the earlier Scriptures.

2. The repeated references within the Qur'an to the existence and worth of these earlier Scriptures.

3. Though there were several references to the effect that the Jews had changed their Holy Books, and though such references in isolation could possibly be construed as actual changes within the text itself they held in their possession, yet:

    a.  Even these references separated from their context need not necessarily be interpreted or understood as written corruptions within the actual text itself.

    b.  The abundance of evidence within the immediate context of these verses, as well as the total general witness of the Qur'an to the contrary, nullifies the charge of tahrif al-lafzi.

    c.  Even if a specific case of tahrif al-lafzi could be established, this would hardly offer authoritative evidence for a general worldwide corruption of Scriptures by Jews and Christians.

4. Though the Qur'an alleges that Christians have forgotten or have concealed a part of their Holy Books, the Qur'an does not charge them with altering their texts.

5. As there is no conclusive Quranic evidence to substantiate the charge of tahrif al-lafzi , so also there is no Quranic evidence to show that the previous books have been abrogated or taken into heaven.

Another Christian author, Dr. William Campbell, sums up his in-depth study of the Quran's statements on the Bible. Dr. Campbell broke the related Quranic verses up into subgroups, each group having a definite theme. His conclusion follows:

> The only possible conclusion from our study of the Qur'an is that copies of THE TRUE TORAH AND THE TRUE GOSPEL were present in Mecca and Medina at the time

of Muhammad. Furthermore, since no Muslim has brought forth from one of the great Islamic libraries an ancient manuscript of a different Torah or a different Gospel, and since no archaeological discoveries have shown any carved quotations which differ from the Torah and Gospel present WITH US now; I am firmly convinced that the books which were available in Mecca during the lifetime of Muhammad were identical to THE TORAH AND THE GOSPEL WHICH WE READ TODAY. [4]

Take a look at this point from another perspective: If the Scriptures of the Jews and Christians were corrupted, wouldn't Allah have told Muhammad to proclaim it? Muhammad spent many years of his life challenging idol worship and pointing out falsehood. Why would Allah, or Muhammad, have been so silent regarding corruption of sacred Scriptures? Wouldn't Allah have voiced his displeasure over the corruption of his word? Wouldn't Allah have commanded Muhammad to proclaim this great evil and warn men of this great satanic deceit? But actually the reverse is true. Both the Quran and Muhammad repeatedly confirm the integrity of the Bible.

Further, if you believe that God allowed the New Testament to be thoroughly corrupted by added themes such as Jesus' divinity, Jesus as the Son of God, Jesus' crucifixion and resurrection, and so on, then what guarantee do you have that God could protect the Quran from corruption? As we shall see in a later chapter, the Quran was edited many times during its compilation into the form it has today.

## Key Questions About the "Corruption" of the Injil

Fouad Masri, in his research on Islam and Christianity, realized there are several pivotal questions about the "Gospels" being corrupted:

*Why was the Injil changed?*

If the Injil was changed, why would God allow early Christians to live in ignorance of God's will for nearly six hundred years (the time between the Injil's supposed corruption and the coming of the prophet of Islam)? People are in a continual quest to know God's will; why destroy that sought-after treasure for many generations?

*Did the Injil's corruption take place before the coming of Prophet Muhammad or after?*

Since the Prophet Muhammad commanded all Muslims to read the Injil, it must have been corrupted after his death. He wouldn't have instructed us to believe and read a corrupted book, would he?

On the other hand, if the Injil was corrupted before his time—or during his life—he surely would have mentioned it. If the Injil has been corrupted since then, we need to go back in history and see when.

*Which parts were changed?*

Many imams claimed corruption has found its way into the Injil, but few would tell me which specific parts were affected.

Was the corruption thorough in that it affected the entire revelation of the Injil? If so, is there any benefit to reading the message of the Injil? If all of it is corrupted, why does the Qur'an require believing in it and reading it?

Perhaps only portions of the Injil were changed. If only parts are corrupted, how can I discern truth from error? Was God able to protect some parts and not others? [5]

Fouad Masri explains his acute observation:

> To my surprise, I learned that many imams are teaching what is contrary to the Qur'anic verses above. They say Al-Tawat [Books of Moses] was corrupted so God sent Az-Zubur [The Psalms of David]. When Az-Zubur was corrupted, God sent Al-Injeel[The New Testament]. Finally, the Injeel was corrupted so God sent the Qur'an. The Qur'an is incorruptible, for it is the word of God. [6]

Masri responds to the accusation that the Quranic verses declare that Jews and Christians "changed the words of God":

Those unto whom We gave the Scripture recognize (this revelation) as they recognize their sons. But lo! A party of them knowingly conceal the truth. Al-Baqara 2:146

O followers of earlier revelation! Why do you cloak the truth with falsehood and conceal the truth of which you are [so well] aware? Al-Imran 3:71

Those who conceal the clear (Signs) We have sent down, and the Guidance, after We have made it clear for the people in the Book, "on them shall be Allah's curse, and the curse of those entitled to curse." Al-Baqara 2:159

The above verses are not referring to people who changed the words of God, but those who concealed it. God is stronger than any human, and while humans may try to conceal God's word, His truth still stands out clearly from error. [7]

## Various Counter-Arguments

Some Muslims have not appreciated seeing their book used to confirm Christian Scriptures. They have sought a way out from the dilemma and made some counter-arguments, alluded to earlier. These counter-arguments usually fall under a main theme: The Quran is performing only a "partial" confirmation.

### *"Partial" Confirmation*

The original Scriptures that the Jews and Christians had were uncorrupted initially, say Muslim scholars, but later they were corrupted by various groups for various reasons. Therefore the Quran is a standard to measure the other Scriptures against. Those Scripture verses that agree with the Quran (for example, Jesus is the Messiah) are true and confirmed and those that disagree with the Quran (for example, that Jesus is the Son of God) were corrupted at some point by various Christians and Jews for various reasons, and are now therefore rejected.

This approach is found in Islamic theological textbooks today. Below is a quote from an older Islamic theological textbook that contains a modern comment inserted as a note to bias the text away from what the Quran teaches. The insertion (denoted following the letter "A") was done by Sheikh Abd Al-Wakil Durubi, from Syria, during the translation of the text into English.

> u3.4 To believe in His inspired Books means those which He revealed to His messengers, believe meaning to be convinced that they are the word of Allah Most High, and all they contain is truth.
>
> (A: The obligation of belief applies to the original revelation, not the various scriptures in the hands of non-Muslims, which are textually corrupt in their present form.)
>
> Scholars differ as to how many Books there are. Some hold they number 104, and some say otherwise. [8]

The Muslim arguments are not strong. It is not our intention to go into depth refuting these arguments since the work has already been done by men like Hahn and Campbell. But we will spend a couple of pages on them.

The weakness in the charge of eventual corruption is that the Scriptures that Muhammad confirmed in the Quran are the Scriptures we have today. Muhammad lived from 570 to 633 and we have an abundance of biblical manuscripts that predate Muhammad. Muhammad confirmed those extant Scriptures. Further, as was stated earlier, Muhammad was in contact with Byzantine Christians whose Bible is the same one we have today. So it is no good to claim that the Scriptures Muhammad confirmed were corrupted later. This argument is a no-win argument. Either the Muslim apologists themselves put Muhammad in a bad position (by claiming he confirmed corrupted Scriptures) or they ignore the Bible's textual history and manuscript evidence.

The fact is that all of the various Bibles and Bible manuscripts that we have from before that time all agree on key doctrines which Islam rejects: Jesus is the Son of God, He is divine, He died and was resurrected, and so forth.

Sir William Muir addressed this counter-argument as well. His response bears repeating. Remember he wrote this some 155 years ago.

There are now extant Manuscripts of an earlier date than the era above-mentioned, and open to the most scrupulous examination of any enquirer. There are Versions of the Old and New Testaments, translated before the period in question. The Septuagint translation of the Old Testament was executed prior to the Christian era. There are still remains of the Octapla of Origen, drawn up four centuries before Mahomet, in which the various versions of the Old Testament were compared in parallel columns. Of the New Testament there are the Latin, Syriac, Coptic, and Armenian versions, made long anterior to Mahomet, by a reference to which the Mussulman investigator will be able to satisfy himself that there have been no alterations in the original text since the time of his Prophet. [9]

### Muhammad Confirms the Bible

The argument that the Quran only confirms what agrees with it also bears no weight and is not supported by the Quran. Over and over again Muhammad confirmed those pre-existing Scriptures. In not one Quranic verse does he ever say anything remotely close to, "The Bible has been corrupted." The Christian doctrines mentioned previously are challenged by the Quran in various verses, but the context of the challenge is that the Quran assumes those doctrines are man-made, and are *not* doctrines found in the Scriptures:

> The Jews say Ezra is the son of God, while the Christians say the Messiah is the son of God. Such are their assertions, by which they imitate the infidels of old. God confound them! How perverse they are! (9:30)

Muhammad did not believe the Scriptures to be corrupt, rather he believed the Christians were making or repeating man-made falsehood. You see Muhammad's error here. He thought Christians were making false claims up and repeating them ("their assertions"). The fact was that the Bible states that Jesus is the Son of God. If Allah/Muhammad were to say it as the Muslim apologists want it to say, the Quran in 9:30 would read, "Their Scriptures are corrupted!" Instead the finger is pointed at men making up false doctrines and speaking them.

The claim that the Quran only confirms what it agrees with is a reflection of what verse 9:30 says. Muslim apologists are making up a doctrine not found in the Quran!

We also want to point out that Muhammad had many a chance to expose this corruption if he thought it were so. Outside of the Quran, there are the Hadith and the Sira. Both classes of texts are used as Islamic source materials. Below are quotes from these sources that show that Muhammad believed the Christians' and Jews' Scriptures to be God's truth, God's Word.

Earlier we asked, "What did Muhammad think about the Bible?" Below are Muhammad's own words. This reference is from the Sira. Ibn Ishaq, in the *Sirat Rasul Allah* (translated by Guillaume), tells the story of Jewish men coming to Muhammad.

> Rafi b. Haritha and Sallam b. Mishkam and Malik b. al-Sayf and Rafi b. Huraymila came to him and said: "Do you not allege that you follow the religion of Abraham and believe in the Torah which we have and testify that it is the truth from God?" He replied, *"Certainly."*[10]

A similar version of this story is found in the Hadith collection of Abu Dawud.

> Narrated Abdullah Ibn Umar:
>
> A group of Jews came and invited the Apostle of Allah to Quff. So he visited them in their school.
>
> They said: Abul Qasim, one of our men has committed fornication with a woman; so pronounce judgment upon them. They placed a cushion for the Apostle of Allah who sat on it and said: Bring the Torah. It was then brought. He then withdrew the cushion from beneath him and placed the Torah on it saying: *I believed in thee and in Him Who revealed thee.*[11]

When Muhammad encountered the Christian Scripture he believed it to be the Word of God. His belief is found throughout the Quran, and is supported by both the Sahih Hadith and Sira.

## Conclusion

Our intention was to show that the Quran does indeed confirm the New Testament. We do not believe that Muhammad knew the contents of the New Testament. We do believe that he heard many stories with Christian themes but he never understood biblical doctrines. As a religious and moral man living in his time, raised in a culture that was infused with and surrounded by Jewish and Christian cultures, he would naturally be raised with a respect for those faiths. And his respect and esteem for the Scriptures of those faiths is displayed over and over again in the Quran. As such, he confirmed the existence and integrity of those Scriptures. He even commanded that they be read, studied, adhered to, and obeyed.

Muhammad's Quran testified to the validity of those Scriptures that existed during his time. He did not speak one word of their corruption. Muhammad may not have understood what those Scriptures taught, he may not have understood that his own teachings contradicted those Scriptures, but he did believe that those Scriptures were truth from God.

We conclude with Muir's words on the topic:

> Lastly; all honest Moslems are called on to believe for they cannot consistently disbelieve, that these Scriptures are the inspired "Word of God"...Let them search the Scriptures diligently, and they will find the whole tenor of those sacred Books to be "that God is in Christ reconciling the world unto Himself";—that Jesus is "the Way, the Truth, and the Life"; "This is life eternal, that they might know Thee, the only true God, and Jesus Christ whom Thou hast sent." [12]

# A Christian Evaluation of Muhammad

How do you evaluate the life of a man who lived 63 years, 23 of which shaped the world's history? What standard of measure should you use? Spiritual, physical, moral, worldly, political, military, all of the above? Obviously Muhammad can be evaluated from many different perspectives.

From a worldly point of view he was eminently successful. Initially in Mecca he endured suffering and persecution, lived through fearful times, persisted in his purpose, and in the end triumphed magnificently. He bled for his cause and eventually caused his opponents to bleed more. He suffered setbacks and defeats yet defeated and vanquished his enemies. He was a good father and husband. Friends were devoted and followers loved him to the extent that they would die or kill for him. They trusted, believed, and venerated him utterly. At the end of his life he obtained most of his desires and enjoyed the fruits of power and pleasure: wealth, dominance, fame, respect, sex with beautiful wives and slaves. Certainly then from the world's point of view Muhammad was an outstanding success and a man to be envied.

From a generic religious point of view Muhammad should also be considered eminently successful. He prayed consistently, he held fast to what he believed were the words of God, and proclaimed them boldly. He fasted, shared his possessions, and shared in his followers' sufferings. As a result of his labor Islam is the second largest religion in the world, numbering over 1 billion followers. Islamic theological schools have existed for over a thousand years and are found throughout the world. Millions of Muslims practice the disciplines of Islam daily through prayer, fasting, dawa (proclaiming Islam), and religious study. Muslims are moral and Islamic morality parallels Christian morality in several respects: Muslims are honest, truthful, hospitable, and circumspect in manners and dress. Like Christianity, they view murder, theft, abortion, homosexuality, adultery, and sexual promiscuity as sinful.

I (Jim Walker) have Muslim friends who do not drink any alcohol and are faithful husbands and fathers, wives and mothers. I have lived in Muslim cities and felt safer than in comparable Western cities. Yes, Muhammad could be considered a great success from both a worldly and religious point of view.

## A Short History of Muhammad's Life

Muhammad was born in AD 570 in Mecca. Volumes are written about him by Muslim, Christian, and atheist scholars in varying degrees of detail and comment favorably or critically.

Muhammad is Islam's primary root. If you wish to understand Islam then know Muhammad. For those who wish to understand Islam's intricacies then the greatest return on investment will be to study his life. While the Quran has preeminence in Islamic theology, the root of the Quran is Muhammad. Gabriel only visited Muhammad with the Quran, and only Muhammad proclaimed Gabriel's direct words; Muhammad is the root of the Quran. Most of the authentic traditions (Sahih Hadith) are traced back to Muhammad; Muhammad is the root of the Hadith. Muslims are commanded to imitate Muhammad's lifestyle (sunna); Muhammad is the root of Islamic lifestyle and culture. Muhammad is the root of Islam.

He was born and lived in the Hijaz region of the Arabian Peninsula. Muhammad was raised primarily by his uncle, Abu Talib, because his father died before he was born and his mother died when he was 6. The Hijaz contained Jews, Christians, and pagans in various concentrations. The Arabian peninsula itself contained many large Christian and Jewish tribes and enclaves and it was bordered in part by Christian states and he interacted with them on his travels outside the Hijaz.

He gained a respected reputation as he grew. At age 25 he married Khadija, his employer, 15 years his senior. Their marriage was strong and he loved her deeply. Together they had a family; she gave birth to sons and daughters but only the daughters survived to adulthood.

Muhammad began his "prophethood" following Gabriel's first visitation at age 40. He died in Medina 23 years later in AD 633. He proclaimed Islam steadfastly during the first 13 years in Mecca and then during his last 10 years in Medina.

During his time in Mecca, Muhammad acted as a "warner" to warn people of God's punishment and he called people to put their faith in the one true God:

> And this is a blessed Scripture which We have revealed, confirming that which (was revealed) before it, that thou mayest warn the Mother of Villages and those around her. Those who believe in the Hereafter believe herein, and they are careful of their worship (6:92).

He gained few converts but they were steadfast in following him and endured oppression to remain faithful to Islam. More success was found when tribesmen from Yathrib (its name later changed to Medina), a town some 200 miles north of Mecca, heard Muhammad's preaching and converted to Islam. In turn they spread Islam in Medina and within two years there was a strong community of Muslims there.

However, back in Mecca Muhammad continued to have great conflict with the Meccans, primarily the leading tribe of Mecca, the Quraysh. He directly insulted, ridiculed, and mocked their pagan faith and in return they persecuted him. Life was very difficult for the Muslims, some were tortured, some were killed, and a social and economic boycott was launched against them. It ended after some time but it had caused the Muslims great distress.

After this time Khadija died. Around a year later his protector uncle, Abu Talib, died. This put Muhammad's life in greater peril. Muhammad went to a nearby pagan town, al-Taif, and pleaded for them to receive him as their prophet and protect him, but they mocked and rejected him outright. Eventually he and his followers fled to Medina for safety. In the Medina community of Muslims there were experienced fighters who had pledged their swords to defend him and take on the entire world if need be. Medina offered Muhammad some degree of protection. This migration from Mecca to Medina is known as the "Hijrah."

The Hijrah may be the most significant event during the 23 years. The transition enabled the establishment of a political community in Medina from which Muhammad built his martial, religious, and civil power. Significantly, just before Muhammad fled to Medina he was given a new command by Allah: the "order to fight." This new Quranic revelation allowed Muhammad to take up arms against non-Muslims in both offensive and defensive warfare. And Muhammad did just that after he arrived in Medina.

Islam changed significantly in Medina. Muhammad now had military power at his disposal. New revelations allowed violence to be committed against non-Muslims. There, Muhammad transitioned from "warner" to "warrior." He began to attack non-Muslim villages and caravans, which he pillaged, killed, and enslaved. Muhammad had several non-Muslim people assassinated in and around Medina, and sent men out to assassinate his opponents.

Muhammad grew in power and prestige and within ten years he had conquered or subjected the Hijaz, including Mecca. There, Ibn Sad records that people converted to Islam "willingly or unwillingly." People recognized that Muhammad and Islam were a force. Muhammad began to send out companies of soldiers whose leaders proclaimed, "Accept Islam and you will be safe!" Muhammad meant business. Those that refused to accept Islam were attacked. Thousands converted to Islam out of fear and after Muhammad died they left Islam. At the end of his life in AD 633 Muhammad had become supreme ruler of this part of the Arabian Peninsula.

Muhammad had achieved one of the world's greatest success stories. From humble beginnings, to his vision of Gabriel, to his steadfast proclamation in Mecca, to his establishment in Medina, to his final triumph, Muhammad had achieved magnificent success!

## A Christian Evaluation of Muhammad

An evaluation of Muhammad from a Christian perspective cannot use worldly success as an acceptable measure. Neither are humanistic ideals or the political correctness of the particular day appropriate standards. Christians use Christ's words and deeds as an example or standard, and this is what we must use to evaluate Muhammad.

Muhammad was a man with both strengths and weaknesses. However in the Quran he is proclaimed to be the great moral example for mankind.

> Verily in the messenger of Allah ye have a good example for him who looketh unto Allah and the Last Day, and remembereth Allah much (33:21).

John Gilchrist notes two Hadith in which Muhammad claimed to be similar to Jesus and eminent on the Day of Resurrection: [1]

> Abu Huraira reported Allah's Messenger as saying: I am most akin to Jesus Christ among the whole of mankind, and all the Prophets are of different mothers but belong to one religion and no Prophet was raised between me and Jesus. [2]

> Abu Huraira reported Allah's Messenger as saying: I shall be pre-eminent amongst the descendants of Adam on the Day of Resurrection and I will be the first intercessor and the first whose intercession will be accepted (by Allah). [3]

Because Muhammad claimed similarity and moral equivalence to Jesus we are compelled to evaluate Muhammad's life against the precedence that Jesus set in moral example and ministry focus. Jesus taught that people should examine a man's fruit to evaluate the man. Fruit could be considered as the culmination, the outcome, of a man's words and deeds. Therefore in this analysis we will use what Muhammad taught in the Quran, traditions (Hadith), and biographical/historical (Sira) writings to examine his actual words and actions. Second, we will ask the question that began this book, the question that Jesus put to His disciples, "Who do men say that I am?" and evaluate Muhammad's answer.

### Moral Example and Ministry Focus: Muhammad's Words and Deeds in Comparison to Jesus' Teachings

We will use Jesus' second greatest commandment, "love your neighbor as yourself" and compare that to Muhammad's teachings and actions.

In Matthew 22:37-39 Jesus taught that the two greatest command-ments were to love God and to love your neighbor as yourself. Muham-mad also wanted his followers to love God, but he did not teach to love one's neighbor. Both the Quran and Muhammad's life reflect that Islam is a religion of dominance and seeks to subject that which is non-Islamic. Here are just a few out of many violent passages from the Quran:

1. The Quran identifies Jews in a derogatory fashion and calls them the literal descendants of "pigs and apes" (7:166; 2:65; 5:60).

2. Pagans or polytheists were to be subjected and killed if they refused to convert to Islam (9:5).

3. Jews and Christians were to be subjected and killed if they refused to convert to Islam or pay extortion (9:29). Muhammad then goes on to ask God to curse and kill the Christians for believing that Jesus is the Son of God (9:30).

There are dozens of similar passages in the Quran where Muham-mad urges men to violence. Self-defense is justifiable and understand-able but in many cases the violence, battles, and wars were started by Muhammad.

As Muhammad established his rule in Medina he struggled to gain corporal and material dominance over the non-Muslims. Immediately after his arrival in Medina, Muhammad sent his men out to attack vari-ous non-Muslim communities and trade caravans.[4] When they were vic-torious, the Muslims killed, plundered, and enslaved the non-Muslims. Female slaves were given as property to soldiers who had the right to use them sexually.[5] People in and around Medina who challenged Muhammad's dark acts were themselves murdered by Muhammad's assassins (such as Abu Afak,[6] Asma bint Marwan,[7] Kab Ashraf,[8] and others). Defenseless men and women were stabbed to death while they slept, were ambushed, or were slaughtered outright. In one case Muhammad commanded his followers to "kill any Jew that comes under your power."[9] These were not cases of justice or self-defense, rather they were acts of power, deceit, and aggression against defenseless people who spoke out and criticized him. They were not a physical threat to Muhammad.

Near the end of his life, when Muhammad took the city of Mecca he had an army of 14,000 soldiers. The city was surrendered by its leader, Abu Sufyan. There was minimal fighting and killing in the city as Muhammad's soldiers moved through it. Muhammad had achieved a supreme triumph that day! The city that persecuted, fought, and harmed him and his followers had now fallen to him. His arch enemy, Abu Sufyan, was compelled to become a Muslim. However, Muhammad bore grudges against those who had mocked him years earlier. Notably there were three slave girls who used to sing parody and ridicule him. Upon taking Mecca Muhammad ordered that these slave girls be killed. [10]

How can we make sense of these differences between Jesus' command to love thy neighbor and Muhammad's subjection of his neighbor? What was the motivation or mission of each?

Jesus' motivation or mission was to establish the kingdom of God, that is, God's rule in the hearts and minds of men. This kingdom is not an earthly kingdom. In John 18:36 Jesus said, "My kingdom is not of this world. If it were, my servants would fight to prevent my arrest by the Jewish leaders. But now my kingdom is from another place." In Luke 22:49-51, when His disciples did fight, Jesus stopped them and healed the wounded man. Also, in Luke 9:52-55 two of His disciples wanted to destroy a town for rejecting Jesus. Jesus rebuked those disciples for wanting to kill those that rejected Him.

Muhammad's mission was to also establish a kingdom of God, but it was an earthly kingdom. After Muhammad received the "order to fight" he sent his soldiers out to raid, kill, and plunder. And so they did. Muhammad knew more victories than defeats and his fame, wealth, and power grew. As stated earlier, the Hijaz became Muhammad's kingdom, God's kingdom, and Muhammad was its ruler.

Muhammad did conquer and establish an impressive, powerful kingdom, but it is a kingdom of this world, which contrasts starkly to the focus of Jesus' ministry and Jesus' commands. Their means to the end are contradictory. This second of the two greatest commandments was not followed by Muhammad. In this, both their ministry focus and character show glaring differences. Muhammad chose a different spiritual and moral course and the actions tied to that course set the tone for Islam throughout its history.

### Muhammad's Teachings Compared to Primary Christian Doctrines

Throughout Christianity there is great variety in Christian doctrine. The Orthodox, Catholic, and Protestant branches of Christianity have different viewpoints on various theological topics. However they all hold several key doctrines in common. These can be found in the creeds (Apostle's Creed, Creed of Nicaea, Athanasian Creed, and so on) and established doctrines of each Christian branch of faith. At a minimum these key doctrines are considered Christianity's theological fundamentals. Other Christians might argue for additional tenets but all agree on these:

1. Monotheism—there is one God in Trinity (Mark 12:29)

2. The deity of Christ (John 1:1)

3. The incarnation of Jesus, the Son of God (Mark 1:1; John 3:16; Romans 1:4; Hebrews 4:14; 1 John 4:15; Revelation 2:18)

4. The Gospel message: Jesus died for our sins, rose from the dead, and ascended to heaven and is at the Father's right hand (Matthew 28; Mark 16; Luke 24; John 20; Acts 1; 1 Corinthians 15:1-5; Revelation 1:4-8; 5:6)

These doctrines have been discussed at some length already. Below are simple summaries of Muhammad's position.

### Rejection of one God in Trinity:

> O People of the Scripture! Do not exaggerate in your religion nor utter aught concerning Allah save the truth. The Messiah, Jesus son of Mary, was only a messenger of Allah, and

His word which He conveyed unto Mary, and a spirit from Him. So believe in Allah and His messengers, and say not "Three"—Cease! (it is) better for you!—Allah is only One Allah. Far is it removed from His Transcendent Majesty that He should have a son. His is all that is in the heavens and all that is in the earth. And Allah is sufficient as Defender (4:171; also see 5:73).

### Rejection of Christ's deity:

They surely disbelieve who say: Lo! Allah is the Messiah, son of Mary. The Messiah (himself) said: O Children of Israel, worship Allah, my Lord and your Lord. Lo! whoso ascribeth partners unto Allah, for him Allah hath forbidden paradise. His abode is the Fire. For evil-doers there will be no helpers (5:72; also see 5:75).

### Rejection of the incarnation of Jesus, the Son of God:

Allah, the eternally Besought of all!
He begetteth not nor was begotten.
And there is none comparable unto Him (112:2-4; also see 9:30).

### Rejection of the Gospel message: the crucifixion, death, resurrection, and atonement:

And because of their saying: We slew the Messiah, Jesus son of Mary, Allah's messenger—they slew him not nor crucified him, but it appeared so unto them; and lo! those who disagree concerning it are in doubt thereof; they have no knowledge thereof save pursuit of a conjecture; they slew him not for certain (4:157; also see 3:55; 17:15).

Muhammad and Islam oppose three out of four of these key teachings of Jesus and Christianity, and if you wish to be technical they disagree on all four tenets because although both agree that there is only one God, there is 100 percent disagreement over God's nature. Islam's God and Christianity's God are not the same God. Muslims and Christians do not worship the same God. While there are similarities, there are enormous differences.

This quick contrast shows that Muhammad contradicted Jesus on critical and essential points. Of all of the issues we have considered, these sharp doctrinal differences, these theological polar opposites, are the most crucial for it is these that determine a soul's salvation, a person's eternal destiny. These brutal differences affect not only today's culture but also one's eternal status.

It is interesting to note that one of the most striking features of Islamic theology is that it contradicts all of the primary tenets of Christian theology. John described the doctrine of this type of person as an "antichrist" in 1 John 2:18-24. This might be considered a harsh statement but it is clearly what the New Testament teaches.

## A Counterpoint

Muslims claim that they teach what all of the prophets believed and taught: that there is only one God. There is truth in that claim. However, Jesus and the prophets taught far more. In fact, simply believing that there is one God is not sufficient:

> You believe that there is one God. Good! Even the demons
> believe that—and shudder (James 2:19).

James is saying that it is not good enough to believe in one God. Claiming to believe in one God is not sufficient to account for salvation. Jesus taught that one must not only believe in God and love Him, but that he must also love his fellow man, be he Christian or not. Jesus taught that a man must be "born again." His followers must obey His commands, put their faith in Him, receive His forgiveness, and be born of the Spirit. Thereafter they must take up their cross and walk in faith and obedience. There is more to salvation than only believing in one God.

Islam denies all that is important about Christ and His mission. It renders the real Jesus null and void. If the works of Satan are undone by Jesus, then Muhammad is undoing Jesus' works.

## Conclusion

Certainly no man measures up to Jesus, but striving toward the goal and admitting a lack of perfection is different from taking a different moral course.

When we evaluate Muhammad's life from a Christian perspective we must reject his claim of prophethood and the tenets of Islam. Islam's theology, established in the Quran and fulfilled by actions detailed in the Hadith and Sira, is at great odds with the primary tenets of Christianity. Muhammad's use of violence in both defensive and aggressive modes opposes God's commands to love your neighbor.

It is challenging for a Christian to evaluate Muhammad fairly. Yes, we reject him as a true prophet because of his many contradictions of the Gospel message, and because of his use of deceit and violence against his critics. But Muhammad was not a demon-possessed man. As a man he had both good and bad traits. He must be seen as a man, not purely evil, not purely good. He himself admitted that he prayed for God's forgiveness every day and the Quran instructs him to ask God to forgive his sins. Although he loved and sacrificed for his friends and followers, he most often brutally killed his critics. By various standards Muhammad can be considered to be a great success, but by Jesus' standard he falls far short.

When Jesus asked Muhammad, "Who do you say that I am?" Muhammad responded, "You are just a prophet." Muhammad's attitude toward Jesus as the Son of God is identical to the Jews' attitude toward Jesus the Son of God. They rejected Him and hated Him (Matthew 26:64-67), and Muhammad cursed and denounced those that believe that Jesus is the Son of God and asks God to harm them (9:30). Yet Jesus established Himself to be the Messiah, the Son of God, by both word and deed. Prophecy from the Torah foretold the Messiah, the Son of God's coming and Jesus fulfilled those prophecies. Jesus' miracles testify to His great power as God's Son, Jesus' sinless and loving character establish God's power within Him, and Jesus' own words establish Him as the unique Son of God.

The question, "Who do you say Jesus is?" remains to this day. Who do you say Jesus is? Is He, as He taught, the Son of God or is He, as Peter stated, just another prophet like Elijah or Jeremiah? God had touched Peter and revealed to him that Jesus was indeed the Messiah, the Son of God. We pray that God will also touch you and reveal to you that Jesus is indeed the Messiah, the Son of God.

# A Prayer for Salvation

Lord God, I acknowledge I am a sinner, and I need Your help and forgiveness. Forgive me for my sins. I believe in Your Son, Jesus Christ. I believe that He died for my sins and rose again from the dead. I give my life to You and choose to obey You.

I confess Jesus as my Lord. I ask You, Jesus, to come into my heart, come into my life, and be the Lord of my life. Thank You, God, for Your love and kindness toward me. Thank You, Jesus, for Your love for me, for dying for me, forgiving me my sins, and giving me eternal life.

# Glossary

*Allah:* The Arabic name for God. Most often it is meant as Islam's God.

*Ayat:* A passage or verse of the Quran.

*Caliph:* This was the supreme ruler over the Islamic empire following Muhammad's death. The first four are known as the "Rightly Guided" Caliphs, and these are Abu Bakr, Umar, Uthman, and Ali.

*Five Pillars:* These are found in Bukhari 1:7:
1. The "Shahadah," Islam's creed or statement of belief: "There is no god but God, and Muhammad is the messenger of God," or "None has the right to be worshipped but Allah, and Muhammad is Allah's Apostle."
2. prayer
3. fasting
4. giving alms
5. performing the Hajj (pilgrimage to Mecca) if possible

*Hadith:* The traditions, sayings, or anecdotes of Muhammad. The Hadith collections of Bukhari, Muslim, are the most highly esteemed or authentic, followed by the collections of Abu Dawud, Tirmidhi, Ibn Majah, and An-Nasa'i. These collections were compiled a couple of hundred years after Muhammad died. They contain Muhammad's sayings or actions related to specific theological topics.

*Hijrah:* The emigration of Muhammad and the Muslims from Mecca to Medina in AD 622.

*Imam:* The leader of the local mosque. Often called "cleric" or "sheikh."

*Injil:* The Arabic name for the Gospel, Gospels, or New Testament.

*Isa:* The Islamic name for Jesus.

*Islam:* The religion that Muhammad created. It means submission to Allah.

*Jihad:* Holy war, striving for Islam's dominance over that which is non-Islamic. It can also mean a spiritual struggle. However, throughout the Quran and Hadith it is almost always defined with respect to a physically violent struggle or battle.

*Muhammad:* The prophet of Islam. He lived from AD 570 to 633.

*Quran:* Islam's holy book. The version of the book used today contains 114 suras or chapters. It is generally arranged according to chapter length. The chapter names are taken from a subject within the chapter. It was spoken by Muhammad over a 23-year period, and the version used today was compiled many years after his death.

*Sharia:* The religious code of law that defines the Islamic way of life. The sources of this law are derived from the Quran, the Hadith, the sunna, and the opinion of the clerics based upon these religious writings.

*Shia:* A sect of Islam that developed a short while after Muhammad died. The division from the "Sunni" Muslims arose over the succession of leadership following Muhammad's death. Iran and Iraq are predominately Shia while most of the other Muslim countries today are Sunni.

*Sira:* Biographies of Muhammad. The earliest existing biography available today is the *Sirat Rasul Allah* by Ibn Ishaq. This is available as *The Life of Muhammad,* by A. Guillaume. Most all later biographies use this text as their foundation.

*Sunna:* The way Muhammad lived, that is, his lifestyle. The Quran commands Muslims to imitate Muhammad's sunna or lifestyle. This is why so many Muslims today dress in white and grow beards, eat with the right hand, and so on.

*Sunni:* This is the largest sect of Muslims, making up around 85 percent of the Muslim world. The name comes from their adherence to the "sunna" of Muhammad.

# Notes

## Chapter 1—Who Is Jesus? Similarities Between the Quran and the Bible

1. Jane D. McAuliffe, ed., *Encyclopedia of the Qur'an*, vol. 3 (Leiden, Netherlands: Brill, 2006), pp. 12-13.

2. F.F. Bruce, *The Gospel and Epistles of John* (Grand Rapids: Eerdmans, 1983), p. 220.

3. Neal Robinson, *Christ in Islam and Christianity* (Albany: SUNY, 1991), p. 5.

4. *The Expositor's Bible Commentary, New Testament*, CD-ROM (Grand Rapids: Zondervan, 1998).

5. Albert Barnes, *Barnes' Notes on the New Testament* (Grand Rapids: Kregel, 1976), p. 101.

6. R.T. France, *The New International Commentary on the New Testament: The Gospel of Matthew* (Grand Rapids: Eerdmans, 2007), p. 957.

7. Joel B. Green, *The New International Commentary on the New Testament: The Gospel of Luke* (Grand Rapids: Eerdmans, 1997), p. 254.

8. Jacob Neusner, *A Rabbi Talks with Jesus* (Montreal, Quebec: McGill-Queens University Press, 2000), pp. 47-48.

9. Neusner, *A Rabbi Talks with Jesus*, p. 48.

10. Raymond Brown, *An Introduction to New Testament Christology* (Mahwah: Paulist Press, 1994), p. 101.

## Chapter 2—The Messiah, the Son of Man, the Son of God

1. Leon Morris, *The New International Commentary on the New Testament: The Gospel According to John* (Grand Rapids: Eerdmans, 1995), pp. 638-39.

2. Raymond Brown, *An Introduction to New Testament Christology* (Mahwah: Paulist Press, 1994), pp. 155-56.

3. Ben Witherington III, *The Christology of Jesus* (Minneapolis: Fortress Press, 1990), p. 80.

4. Witherington III, *The Christology of Jesus*, pp. 185-86.

5. Eugen J. Pentiuc, "The Aramaic Phrase Bar 'ĕnoš 'Son of Man' (Dan 7:13-14) Revisited." *Greek Orthodox Archdiocese of America*, http://www.goarch.org/ourfaith/bar-enosh

6. F.F. Bruce, "The Background to the Son of Man Sayings," in Harold H. Rowdon, ed., *Christ the Lord: Studies in Christology Presented to Donald Guthrie* (Leicester, England: InterVarsity Press, 1982), p. 70.

7. Witherington III, *The Christology of Jesus*, p. 153.

8. Witherington III, *The Christology of Jesus*, p. 143.

**Chapter 3—The Father, His Son, and Their Relationship**

1. John Gilchrist, *The Christian Witness to the Muslim* (Benoni, South Africa: Jesus to the Muslims, 1988), p. 324.

2. Gilchrist, *The Christian Witness to the Muslim*, pp. 329-30.

3. Leon Morris, *The New International Commentary on the New Testament: The Gospel According to John* (Grand Rapids: Eerdmans, 1995), pp. 274-75.

4. Morris, *The Gospel According to John*, p. 279.

5. *The Expositor's Bible Commentary, New Testament*, CD-ROM (Grand Rapids: Zondervan, 1998).

6. Ibn Kathir, *Tafsir of Ibn Kathir*, vol. 10 (New York: Darussalam, 2000), pp. 195-96.

7. Ibn Kathir, *Tafsir of Ibn Kathir*, vol. 3 (New York: Darussalam, 2000), pp. 424, 426.

8. Ibn Kathir, *Tafsir of Ibn Kathir*, vol. 1 (New York, Darussalam, 2000), pp. 350, 352.

9. Gilchrist, *The Christian Witness to the Muslim*, pp. 325-26.

10. Walter A. Elwell, et al., eds., *Baker Encyclopedia of the Bible*, vol. 1 (Grand Rapids: Baker, 1988), p. 1025.

11. Harold H. Rowdon, ed., *Christ the Lord: Studies in Christology Presented to Donald Guthrie* (Leicester, England: InterVarsity Press, 1982), p. 3.

12. Raymond E. Brown, *An Introduction to New Testament Christology* (Mahwah: Paulist Press, 1994), p. 139.

13. Morris, *The Gospel According to John*, pp. 68-69.

14. Morris, *The Gospel According to John*, pp. 90-91.

15. Morris, *The Gospel According to John*, p. 101.

16. Ben Witherington III, *The Christology of Jesus* (Minneapolis: Fortress Press, 1990), pp. 276-77.


**Chapter 4—The Trinity: Development of the Doctrine**

1. Walter A. Elwell, *Evangelical Dictionary of Theology* (Grand Rapids: Baker Books, 1984), p. 1112.

2. Joseph Allen, et al., *The Orthodox Study Bible* (Elk Grove: Thomas Nelson, 2008), p. 1613.

3. F.F. Bruce, *The New International Commentary on the New Testament: The Epistle to the Colossians* (Grand Rapids: Eerdmans, 1984), pp. 57-58.

4. J.N.D. Kelly, *Early Christian Doctrines* (Peabody: Prince Press, 2003), p. 88.

5. Kelly, *Early Christian Doctrines*, p. 109.

6. Roger E. Olson and Christopher Hall, et al., *The Trinity* (Grand Rapids: Eerdmans, 2002), p. 2.

7. Robert Letham, *The Holy Trinity* (Phillipsburg: P&R, 2004), pp. 89-90.

8. William A. Jurgens, *The Faith of the Early Fathers*, vol. 1 (Collegeville: Liturgical Press, 1970), p. 17.

9. Jurgens, *The Faith of the Early Fathers*, vol. 1, p. 18.

10. Kelly, *Early Christian Doctrines*, p. 92.

11. Jurgens, *The Faith of the Early Fathers*, vol. 1, p. 52.

12. Kelly, *Early Christian Doctrines*, p. 97.

13. Jurgens, *The Faith of the Early Fathers*, vol. 1 p. 84.

14. Kelly, *Early Christian Doctrines*, p. 107.

15. Kelly, *Early Christian Doctrines*, pp. 113-14.

16. Kelly, *Early Christian Doctrines*, p. 114.

17. Letham, *The Holy Trinity*, p. 52.

18. Philip Schaff, *History of the Christian Church*, vol. 2 (Peabody: Hendrickson, 1996), pp. 11-12.

19. Joseph Allen, et al., *The Orthodox Study Bible* (Elk Grove: Thomas Nelson, 2008), p. xxii.

## Chapter 5—The Trinity: Foundation from the Bible

1. Leon Morris, *The New International Commentary on the New Testament: The Gospel According to John* (Grand Rapids: Eerdmans, 1995), pp. 65, 68-69.

2. *The Expositor's Bible Commentary, New Testament*, CD-ROM (Grand Rapids: Zondervan, 1998).

3. *The Expositor's Bible Commentary, New Testament*, CD-ROM.

4. F.F. Bruce, *The New International Commentary on the New Testament: The Epistles to the Hebrews, Revised* (Grand Rapids: Eerdmans, 1990), pp. 48, 52, 60.

5. Edward Bickersteth, *The Trinity* (Grand Rapids: Kregel, 1994), pp. 38-39.

6. Bickersteth, *The Trinity*, p. 51.

7. Robert Letham, *The Holy Trinity* (Phillipsburg: P&R, 2004), pp.56-58.

8. Letham, *The Holy Trinity*, p. 70.

9. Francis Schaeffer, *He Is There and He Is Not Silent* (Wheaton: Tyndale House, 1985), p. 74.

10. Louis Berkhof, *Systematic Theology*, vol. 2 (Grand Rapids: Eerdmans, 1996), p. 90.

11. C.S. Lewis, *Mere Christianity* (New York: MacMillan, 1978), pp. 140-42.

12. Glenn Miller, "Christian Distinctives: The Trinity." *Christian Think Tank*, http://www.christian-thinktank.com/trin01.html

13. John Gilchrist, *The Christian Witness to the Muslim* (Benoni, South Africa: Jesus to the Muslims, 1988), p. 307.

14. Bert Waggoner, "Vineyard and the 21st Century," http://vineyardnorthphoenix.com/story/1906

15. Letham, *The Holy Trinity*, p. 478.

## Chapter 6—The Gospel and the Atonement

1. Neal Robinson, *Christ in Islam and Christianity* (Albany: SUNY, 1991), p. 5.

2. Jane D. McAuliffe, ed., *Encyclopedia of the Qur'an*, vol. 2 (Leiden, Netherlands: Brill, 2006), pp. 342-43.

3. A. Guillaume, *The Life of Muhammad* (Karachi, Pakistan: Oxford University Press, 1998), p. 271.

4. N.J. Dawood, trans., *The Koran* (London: Penguin Group, 1995).

5. Walter A. Elwell, et al., eds., *Baker Encyclopedia of the Bible*, vol. 1 (Grand Rapids: Baker, 1988), p. 893.

6. Ahmad Misri, *Reliance of the Traveller*, trans. by Nuh Ha Mim Keller (Beltsville: Amana, 1999), p. 813.

7. Misri, *Reliance of the Traveller*, p. 999.

8. Muhammad Ibn-Ismail al Bukhari, *Translation of the Meanings of Sahih Bukhari*, trans. by Muhammad Muhsin Khan, vol. 8 (New Delhi, India: Kitab Bhavan, 1987), p. 319.

9. J. Alan Groves, "Atonement in Isaiah 53," in *The Glory of the Atonement*, ed. by Charles E. Hill and Frank A. James (Downers Grove: InterVarsity Press, 2004), p. 81.

10. Groves, "Atonement in Isaiah 53," pp. 88- 89.

11. R.T. France, *The New International Commentary on the New Testament: The Gospel of Matthew* (Grand Rapids: Eerdmans, 2007), pp. 993-94.

## Chapter 7—Jesus' Crucifixion

1. Yusef Ali, trans., *The Holy Qur'an* (Beltsville: Amana, 1989).

2. N.J. Dawood, trans., *The Koran* (London: Penguin, 1995).

3. M.H. Shakir, trans., *The Quran* (Elmhurst: Tahrike Tarsile Quran, 1993).

4. Josh McDowell and John Gilchrist, *The Islam Debate* (San Bernardino: Here's Life, 1983), p. 143.

5. Ibn Kathir, *Tafsir of Ibn Kathir*, vol. 3 (New York: Darussalam, 2000), pp. 25-27, emphasis added.

6. John Dominic Crossan, *Jesus: A Revolutionary Biography* (San Francisco, CA: Harper Collins, 1991), p. 145.

7. McDowell and Gilchrist, *The Islam Debate*, p. 161.

8. William Campbell, *The Quran and the Bible in the Light of History and Science* (Upper Darby: Middle East Resources, 1992), p. 274.

9. Tacitus, "Annals," in *Academy for Ancient Texts*, paragraph 37, http://www.ancienttexts.org/library/roman/tacitus/annals/bookxv.html

10. Lucian, "The Death of Peregrine," in *Internet Sacred Text Archive*, p. 83, http://www.sacred-texts.com/cla/luc/wl4/wl420.htm

11. J.H. Charlesworth, "Jesus and Jehohanan: An Archaeological Note on Crucifixion," *Expository Times*, vol. IXXXIV, no. 6, Feb. 1973 (Edinburgh, Scotland: T&T Clark), http://www.pbs.org/wgbh/pages/frontline/shows/religion/jesus/crucifixion.html

12. C. Truman Davis, "The Crucifixion of Jesus," *Arizona Medicine*, March 1965, p. 185, http://www.gospeloutreach.net/crucifixion.html

13. Kenneth Cragg, *The Call of the Minaret* (Maryknoll: Orbis Books, 2000), p. 296.

14. John Gilchrist, *The Christian Witness to the Muslim* (Benoni, South Africa: Jesus to the Muslims, 1988), p. 256.

## Chapter 8—Muhammad and the Bible: Is He the "Counselor" Foretold by Jesus?

1. Abul-Husain Muslim, *Sahih Muslim*, trans. by Abdul Hamid Siddiqi, vol. 4 (Riyadh, Saudi Arabia: International Islamic Publishing House, 1971), no. 5811.

2. Muhammad Ibn-Ismail al Bukhari, *Translation of the Meanings of Sahih Bukhari*, trans. by Muhammad Muhsin Khan, vol. 3 (New Delhi, India: Kitab Bhavan, 1987), no. 335.

3. Josh McDowell and John Gilchrist, *The Islam Debate* (San Bernardino: Here's Life, 1983), p. 84.

4. William Campbell, *The Quran and the Bible in the Light of History and Science* (Upper Darby: Middle East Resources, 1992), pp. 244-45.

5. Norman Geisler and Abdul Saleeb, *Answering Islam: The Crescent in Light of the Cross* (Grand Rapids: Baker Books, 1993), p. 153.

6. Alexander Roberts, et al., ed., *The Ante-Nicene Fathers*, vol. 1 (Albany: AGES Software, 1997), p. 224, http://truth4freedom.files.wordpress.com/2012/11/ecf_0_01.pdf

7. *The Expositor's Bible Commentary, New Testament*, CD-ROM (Grand Rapids: Zondervan, 1998).

**Chapter 9—Muhammad and the Bible: Is He the "Prophet" Foretold by Moses?**

1. Kenneth Barker, et al., eds., *New International Version Study Bible* (Grand Rapids: Zondervan, 1985), pp. 1593-94.

2. Leon Morris, *The New International Commentary on the New Testament: The Gospel According to John* (Grand Rapids: Eerdmans, 1995), p. 100.

3. N.J. Dawood, trans., *The Koran* (London: Penguin Group, 1995), p. 201.

4. Muhammad Ibn-Ismail al Bukhari, *Translation of the Meanings of Sahih Bukhari*, trans. by Muhammad Muhsin Khan, vol. 4 (New Delhi, India: Kitab Bhavan, 1987), no. 458.

5. Muhammad Ibn-Ismail al Bukhari, *Translation of the Meanings of Sahih Bukhari*, vol. 9, no. 335.

**Chapter 10—The Reliability of the New Testament (Part 1)**

1. Norman Geisler, *Baker Encyclopedia of Christian Apologetics* (Grand Rapids: Baker, 1999), pp. 527-28.

2. Bruce Metzger, *The Canon of the New Testament: Its Origin, Development, and Significance* (Oxford: Clarendon, 1997), pp. 2-4.

3. F.F. Bruce, *The Canon of Scripture* (Downers Grove: InterVarsity Press, 1988), pp. 117-18.

4. Bruce, *The Canon of Scripture*, pp. 119-23.

5. Metzger, *The Canon of the New Testament*, p. 73.

6. Bart D. Ehrman, *Jesus Interrupted: Revealing the Hidden Contradictions in the Bible (and Why We Don't Know About Them)* (New York: Harper Collins, 2009), pp. 146-47.

7. Craig S. Keener, *The Historical Jesus of the Gospels* (Grand Rapids: Eerdmans, 2009), pp. 140-41.

8. Craig Blomberg, *The Historical Reliability of the Gospels* (Downers Grove: InterVarsity Press, 1987), pp. 27-28.

9. James Patrick Holding, *Trusting the New Testament: Is the Bible Reliable?* (Maitland: Xulon Press, 2009), p. 27.

10. Paul Rhodes Eddy and Gregory A. Boyd, *The Jesus Legend: A Case for the Historical Reliability of the Synoptic Jesus Tradition* (Grand Rapids: Baker Academic, 2007), pp. 286-88.

11. Holding, *Trusting the New Testament*, p. 27-28.

12. Holding, *Trusting the New Testament*, p. 28.

13. Keener, *The Historical Jesus of the Gospels*, p. 159.

14. Keener, *The Historical Jesus of the Gospels*, p. 158.

15. Maurice Casey, *Aramaic Sources of Mark's Gospel* (Cambridge: Cambridge University Press, 1998), pp. 254-55.

16. Deuteronomy 18:20-22

17. Peter W. Stoner and Robert C. Newman, *Science Speaks* (Chicago: Moody Press, 1944), chapter 3, http://sciencespeaks.dstoner.net/Christ_of_Prophecy.html#C9

18. Gary R. Habermas and Michael R. Licona, *The Case for the Resurrection of Jesus* (Grand Rapids: Kregel, 2004), p. 60.

19. F.J.A. Hort and Brooke Foss Westcott, *The New Testament in the Original Greek*, vol. 1 (New York: Macmillan, 1881), p. 561.

20. Norman L. Geisler and William E. Nix, *A General Introduction to the Bible* (Chicago: Moody, 1968), p. 386.

21. Ravi Zacharias, *Can Man Live Without God?* (Nashville: Word, 1994), p. 162.

22. Daniel B. Wallace, "Dr. Wallace: Earliest Manuscript of the New Testament Discovered?" *DTS Magazine*, February 9, 2012, http://www.dts.edu/read/wallace-new-testament-manuscript -first-century/

23. Bruce M. Metzger and Bart D. Ehrman, *The Text of the New Testament: Its Transmission, Corruption, and Restoration,* 4th ed. (New York: Oxford, 2005), p. 51.

24. Geisler and Nix, *A General Introduction to the Bible,* p. 430.

25. Geisler, *Baker Encyclopedia of Christian Apologetics*, p. 47.

26. William F. Albright, *The Archaeology of Palestine*, rev. ed. (Baltimore: Penguin, 1960), pp. 127-128.

## Chapter 11—The Reliability of the New Testament (Part 2)

1. F.F. Bruce, *The Canon of Scripture* (Downers Grove: InterVarsity Press, 1988), pp. 123-24.

2. Walter A. Elwell, et al., eds., *Baker Encyclopedia of the Bible*, vol. 1 (Grand Rapids: Baker, 1988), p. 304.

3. Bruce Metzger, *The Canon of the New Testament: Its Origin, Development, and Significance* (Oxford, Clarendon, 1997), p. 75.

4. Metzger, *The Canon of the New Testament*, p. 108.

5. Metzger, *The Canon of the New Testament*, p. 113.

6. Andreas J. Köstenberger and Michael J. Kruger, *The Heresy of Orthodoxy* (Wheaton: Crossway, 2010), p. 120.

7. F.F. Bruce, *The Canon of Scripture* (Downers Grove: InterVarsity Press, 1998), p. 255.

8. Metzger, *The Canon of the New Testament*, p. 254.

9. Bruce, *The Canon of Scripture*, pp. 256-63.

10. F.F. Bruce, *The New Testament Documents: Are They Reliable?* (Downers Grove: InterVarsity Press, 1992), p. 19.

11. Norman L. Geisler, *Baker Encyclopedia of Christian Apologetics* (Grand Rapids: Baker, 1999), pp. 529-30.

12. Geisler, *Baker Encyclopedia of Christian Apologetics*, p. 530.

13. Geisler, *Baker Encyclopedia of Christian Apologetics*, p. 530.

14. J. Ed Komoszewski, M. James Sawyer, and Daniel Wallace, *Reinventing Jesus* (Grand Rapids: Kregel, 2006), p. 60.

15. Bruce Metzger and Bart D. Ehrman, *The Text of the New Testament: Its Transmission, Corruption, and Restoration* (Oxford: Oxford, 1992), p. 14.

16. Metzger and Ehrman, *The Text of the New Testament*, p. 14.

17. Metzger and Ehrman, *The Text of the New Testament*, p. 18.

18. Metzger and Ehrman, *The Text of the New Testament*, p. 86.

19. Craig Blomberg, *The Historical Reliability of the Gospels* (Downers Grove: InterVarsity Press, 1987).

20. Metzger and Ehrman, *The Text of the New Testament*, pp. 186-206.

21. Metzger and Ehrman, *The Text of the New Testament*, p. 206.

22. Philip Comfort, *Early Manuscripts and Modern Translations of the New Testament* (Grand Rapids: Baker, 1990), p. 3.

23. F.F. Bruce. *The Canon of Scripture* (Downers Grove: InterVarsity Press, 1997), pp. 288-89.

24. Komoszewski, Sawyer, and Wallace, *Reinventing Jesus*, p. 117.

25. Geisler, *Baker Encyclopedia of Christian Apologetics*, p. 537.

26. Bart D. Ehrman, *Jesus Interrupted: Revealing the Hidden Contradictions in the Bible (and Why We Don't Know About Them)* (San Francisco: HarperOne, 2009), pp. 45-46.

27. James White vs. Bart Ehrman, "Did the Bible Misquote Jesus?" Debate on January 21, 2009, Ft. Lauderdale, FL.

28. Komoszewski, Sawyer, and Wallace, *Reinventing Jesus*, p. 259.

## Chapter 12—An Evaluation of the Quran

1. A.J. Arberry, *The Koran* (Oxford, England: Oxford University Press, 1983).

2. Arthur Jeffery, *The Qur'an as Scripture* (New York: Russell F. Moore, 1952), pp. 3-4.

3. W. Montgomery Watt and Richard Bell, *Introduction to the Qur'an* (Edinburgh: Edinburgh University Press, 2001), p. 30.

4. Ahmad Misri, *Reliance of the Traveller*, trans. by Nuh Ha Mim Keller (Beltsville: Amana, 1999), p. 820.

5. Jeffery, *The Qur'an as Scripture*, p. 3.

6. Jeffery, *The Qur'an as Scripture*, pp. 6-7.

7. Watt and Bell, *Introduction to the Qur'an*, p. 46.

8. Arthur Jeffery, *Materials for the History of the Text of the Quran* (Leiden: Brill, 1937), pp. ix, x.

9. Gerd R. Puin, "About the Importance of the Oldest Qur'an Fragments from Sana'a (Yemen) Orthography for the History of the Qur'an."

10. Watt and Bell, *Introduction to the Qur'an*, pp. 47-48.

11. William Campbell, *The Quran and the Bible in the Light of History and Science* (Upper Darby: Middle East Resources, 1992), p. 97.

12. J.S. Trimingham, *Christianity Among the Arabs in Pre-Islamic Times* (London: Longman Group, 1979).

13. Herbert Danby, *The Mishnah* (Oxford: Oxford University Press, 1974).

14. John Gilchrist, *Muhammad and the Religion of Islam* (Durban, South Africa: Jesus to the Muslims, 1986), p. 207.

15. Gilchrist, *Muhammad and the Religion of Islam*, pp. 166-67.

16. Muhammad Ibn-Ismail al Bukhari, *Translation of the Meanings of Sahih Bukhari*, trans. by Muhammad Muhsin Khan, vol. 9 (New Delhi, India: Kitab Bhavan, 1987), no. 111.

17. A. Guillaume, *The Life of Muhammad* (Karachi, Pakistan: Oxford University Press, 1998), p. 106.

18. al-Tabari, Abu Ja'far Muhammad ibn Jarir, *The History of al-Tabari*, vol. 6 (New York: SUNY, 1988), p. 76.

19. Ibn Sad, *Kitab al-Tabaqat al-Kabir* (Book of the Major Classes), trans. by S. Moinul Haq, vol. 1 (Karachi: Pakistan Historical Society, 1967), p. 225.

20. Campbell, *The Quran and the Bible in the Light of History and Science*, p. 185.

21. Mustansir Mir, *Dictionary of Qur'anic Terms and Concepts* (New York: Garland, 1987).

22. Abul-Husain Muslim, *Sahih Muslim*, trans. by Abdul Hamid Siddiqi, vol. 4 (Riyadh, Saudi Arabia: International Islamic Publishing House, 1971), no. 3421.

23. Gilchrist, *Muhammad and the Religion of Islam*, p. 162.

24. Norman Geisler and Abdul Saleeb, *Answering Islam: The Crescent in Light of the Cross* (Grand Rapids: Baker, 1993), p. 197.

25. Watt and Bell, *Introduction to the Qur'an*, pp. 100-101.

## Chapter 13—The Quran Confirms the Christian Scriptures

1. William Muir, *The Corân: Its Composition and Teaching and the Testimony It Bears to the Holy Scriptures* (London: Society for Promoting Christian Knowledge, 1903), p. 67.

2. John Gilchrist, *The Christian Witness to the Muslim* (Benoni, South Africa: Jesus to the Muslims, 1988), p. 290.

3. Ernest Hahn, *The Integrity of the Bible According to the Qur'an and the Hadith* (Mississauga: Philoxenia, 1993), p. 28.

4. William Campbell, *The Quran and the Bible in the Light of History and Science* (Upper Darby: Middle East Resources, 1992), pp. 52-53.

5. Fouad Masri, *Is the Injeel Corrupted?* (Indianapolis: Wesleyan Publishing House, 2006), pp. 24-27.

6. Masri, *Is the Injeel Corrupted?*, p. 13.

7. Masri, *Is the Injeel Corrupted?*, pp. 31-32.

8. Ahmad Misri, *Reliance of the Traveller*, trans. by Nuh Ha Mim Keller (Beltsville: Amana, 1999), p. 811.

9. Muir, *The Corân*, p. 236.

10. A. Guillaume, *The Life of Muhammad* (Karachi, Pakistan: Oxford University Press, 1998), p. 267.

11. Abu Dawud, *Sunan Abu Dawud*, trans. by A. Hasan (New Delhi: al-Madina, 1985), book 38, number 4434.

12. Muir, *The Corân*, p. 239.

## Chapter 14—A Christian Evaluation of Muhammad

1. John Gilchrist, *Muhammad and the Religion of Islam* (Durban, South Africa: Jesus to the Muslims, 1986), p. 57.

2. Abul-Husain Muslim, *Sahih Muslim*, trans. by Abdul Hamid Siddiqi, vol. 4 (Riyadh, Saudi Arabia: International Islamic Publishing House, 1971), book 30, no. 5835.

3. Muslim, *Sahih Muslim*, vol. 4, book 30, no. 5655.

4. A. Guillaume, *The Life of Muhammad* (Karachi, Pakistan: Oxford University Press, 1998), pp. 287-89.

5. Suliman Abu Dawud, *Sunan*, trans. by A. Hasan, vol. 2 (New Delhi: al-Madina, 1985), p. 225.

6. Guillaume, *The Life of Muhammad*, p. 675.

7. Guillaume, *The Life of Muhammad*, pp. 675-76.

8. Muhammad Ibn-Ismail al Bukhari, *Translation of the Meanings of Sahih Bukhari*, trans. by Muhammad Muhsin Khan, vol. 5 (New Delhi, India: Kitab Bhavan, 1987), book 59, no. 369.

9. Guillaume, *The Life of Muhammad*, p. 369.

10. Ibn Sad, *Kitab al-Tabaqat al-Kabir* (Book of the Major Classes), trans. by S. Moinul Haq, vol. 2 (Karachi: Pakistan Historical Society, 1967), p. 168.

# Bibliography

Ali, Yusef, trans. *The Holy Qur'an*. Beltsville: Amana, 1989.

Allen, Joseph, Peter E. Gillauist, and Alan Wallerstedt. *The Orthodox Study Bible*. Elk Grove: Thomas Nelson, 2008.

al-Tabari, Abu Ja'far Muhammad ibn Jarir. *The History of al-Tabari*. New York: SUNY, 1988.

Arberry, A.J. *The Koran*. Oxford, England: Oxford University Press, 1983.

Barker, Kenneth, ed. *New International Version Study Bible*. Grand Rapids: Zondervan, 1985.

Barnes, Albert. *Barnes' Notes on the New Testament*. Grand Rapids: Kregel, 1976.

Berkhof, Louis. *Systematic Theology*. Grand Rapids: Eerdmans, 1996.

Bickersteth, Edward. *The Trinity*. Grand Rapids: Kregel, 1994.

Blomberg, Craig. *The Historical Reliability of the Gospels*. Downers Grove: InterVarsity Press, 1987.

Brown, Ray. *An Introduction to New Testament Christology*. Mahwah: Paulist Press, 1994.

Bruce, F.F. "The Background to the Son of Man Sayings" in *Christ the Lord: Studies in Christology Presented to Donald Guthrie*. Edited by Harold H. Rowdon. Leicester, England: InterVarsity Press, 1982.

———. *The Canon of Scripture*. Downers Grove: InterVarsity Press, 1988.

———. *The Gospel and Epistles of John*. Grand Rapids: Eerdmans, 1983.

———. *The New International Commentary on the New Testament: The Epistles to the Colossians*. Grand Rapids: Eerdmans, 1984.

———. *The New International Commentary on the New Testament: The Epistle to the Hebrews, Revised*. Grand Rapids: Eerdmans, 1990.

———. *The New Testament Documents: Are They Reliable?* Downers Grove: InterVarsity Press, 1992.

Bukhari, Muhammad. *Sahih Bukhari*. Trans. Muhammad Muhsin Khan. New Delhi, India: Kitab Bhavan, 1987.

Campbell, William. *The Quran and the Bible in the Light of History and Science*. Upper Darby, PA: Middle East Resources, 1992.

Casey, Maurice. *Aramaic Sources of Mark's Gospel*. Cambridge: Cambridge University Press, 1998.

Charlesworth, J.H. "Jesus and Jehohanan: An Archaeological Note on Crucifixion." *Expository Times* IXXXIV, no. 6 (February 1973).

Comfort, Philip. *Early Manuscripts and Modern Translations of the New Testament.* Grand Rapids: Baker, 1990.

Cragg, Kenneth. *The Call of the Minaret.* Maryknoll: Orbis Books, 2000.

Craig, William Lane. *Reasonable Faith: Christian Faith and Apologetics.* Wheaton: Crossway Books, 1994.

Crossan, John Dominic. *Jesus: A Revolutionary Biography.* San Francisco: Harper Collins, 1991.

Danby, Herbert. *The Mishnah.* Oxford: Oxford University Press, 1974.

Davis, C. Truman. "The Crucifixion of Jesus." *Arizona Medicine,* March 1965, p. 185.

Dawood, N.J., trans. *The Koran.* London: Penguin Group, 1995.

Dawud, Abu. *Sunan Abu Dawud.* Translated by Ahmad Hasan. New Delhi: Al-Madina, 1985.

Eddy, Paul Rhodes and Gregory A. Boyd. *The Jesus Legend: A Case for the Historical Reliability of the Synoptic Jesus Tradition.* Grand Rapids: Baker Academic, 2007.

Ehrman, Bart D. *Jesus Interrupted: Revealing the Hidden Contradictions in the Bible (and Why We Don't Know About Them).* New York: Harper Collins, 2009.

Elwell, Walter A., ed. *Baker Encyclopedia of the Bible*, vol. 1. Grand Rapids: Baker, 1988.

———. *Evangelical Dictionary of Theology.* Grand Rapids: Baker, 1984.

*The Expositor's Bible Commentary, New Testament,* CD-ROM. Grand Rapids: Zondervan, 1998.

France, R.T. *The New International Commentary on the New Testament: The Gospel of Matthew.* Grand Rapids: Eerdmans, 2007.

Geisler, Norman. *Baker Encyclopedia of Christian Apologetics.* Grand Rapids: Baker, 1999.

Geisler, Norman and Saleeb, Abdul. *Answering Islam.* Grand Rapids: Baker, 1993.

Gilchrist, John. *The Christian Witness to the Muslim.* Benoni, South Africa: Jesus to the Muslims, 1988.

———. *Muhammad and the Religion of Islam.* Durban, South Africa: Jesus to the Muslims, 1986.

Green, Joel B. *The New International Commentary on the New Testament: The Gospel of Luke.* Grand Rapids: Eerdmans, 1997.

Groves, J. Alan. "Atonement in Isaiah 53," in *The Glory of the Atonement.* Edited by Charles E. Hill and Frank A. James. Downers Grove: InterVarsity Press, 2004.

Guillaume, A. *The Life of Muhammad.* Karachi, Pakistan: Oxford University Press, 1998.

Habermas, Gary R., and Michael R. Licona. *The Case for the Resurrection of Jesus.* Grand Rapids: Kregel, 2004.

Hahn, Ernest. *The Integrity of the Bible According to the Qur'an and the Hadith.* Mississauga: Philoxenia, 1993.

Holding, James Patrick. *Trusting the New Testament: Is the Bible Reliable?* Maitland: Xulon Press, 2009.

Ibn Kathir. *Tafsir of Ibn Kathir.* Volumes 1, 3, and 10. New York: Darussalam, 2000.

Ibn Sad. *Kitab al-Tabaqat al-Kabir (Book of the Major Classes).* Translated by S. Moinul Haq. Karachi: Pakistan Historical Society, 1967.

Jeffery, Arthur. *Materials for the History of the Text of the Quran.* Leiden: Brill, 1937.

————. *The Qur'an as Scripture.* New York: Russell F. Moore, 1952.

Jurgens, William A. *The Faith of the Early Fathers,* vol. 1. Collegeville: The Liturgical Press, 1970.

Keener, Craig S. *The Historical Jesus of the Gospels.* Grand Rapids: Eerdmans, 2009.

Kelly, J.N.D. *Early Christian Doctrines.* Peabody: Prince Press, 2003.

Komoszewski, J. Ed, M. James Sawyer, and Daniel Wallace. *Reinventing Jesus.* Grand Rapids: Kregel, 2006.

Köstenberger, Andreas J. and Michale J. Kruger. *The Heresy of Orthodoxy.* Wheaton: Crossway, 2010.

Letham, Robert. *The Holy Trinity.* Phillipsburg: P&R, 2004.

Lewis, C.S. *Mere Christianity.* New York: MacMillan, 1978.

Masri, Fouad. *Is the Injeel Corrupted?* Indianapolis: Wesleyan Publishing House, 2006.

McAuliffe, Jane D., ed. *Encyclopedia of the Qur'an.* Leiden, Netherlands: Brill, 2006.

McDowell, Josh, and John Gilchrist. *The Islam Debate.* San Bernardino: Here's Life, 1983.

McDowell, Josh, and Sean McDowell. *Evidence for the Resurrection.* Ventura: Regal, 1996.

Metzger, Bruce M. *The Canon of the New Testament: Its Origin, Development, and Significance.* Oxford: Clarendon, 1997.

Metzger, Bruce M. and Bart D. Ehrman. *The Text of the New Testament: Its Transmission, Corruption, and Restoration,* 4th ed. New York: Oxford, 2005.

Miller, Glenn. "Christian Distinctives: The Trinity." http://www.christian-thinktank.com/trin01.html.

Mir, Mustansir. *Dictionary of Qur'anic Terms and Concepts.* New York: Garland, 1987.

Misri, Ahmad. *Reliance of the Traveller.* Translated by Nuh Ha Mim Keller. Beltsville: Amana, 1999.

Morris, Leon. *The New International Commentary on the New Testament: The Gospel According to John.* Grand Rapids: Eerdmans, 1995.

Muir, William. *The Corân: Its Composition and Teaching and the Testimony It Bears to the Holy Scriptures.* London: Society for Promoting Christian Knowledge, 1903.

Muslim, Abul-Husain. *Sahih Muslim.* Translated by Abdul Hamid Siddiqi. Riyadh, Saudi Arabia: International Islamic Publishing House, 1971.

Neusner, Jacob. *A Rabbi Talks with Jesus.* Montreal, Quebec: McGill-Queens University Press, 2000.

Olson, Roger E., and Christopher A. Hall. *The Trinity.* Grand Rapids: Eerdmans, 2002.

Pentiuc, Eugen J. "The Aramaic phrase Bar 'Ĕnoš "Son of Man" (Dan 7:13-14) Revisited." Greek Orthodox Archdiocese of America. http://www.goarch.org/ourfaith/bar-enosh.

Pickthall, M. *The Meaning of the Glorious Koran.* New York: Mentor, 1953.

Roberts, Alexander, A. Cleveland Coxe, James Donaldson, Philip Schaff, and Henry Wace, eds. *The Ante-Nicene Fathers*, vol. 1. Peabody: Hendrickson, 1996.

Robinson, Neal. *Christ in Islam and Christianity.* Albany: SUNY, 1991.

Rowdon, Harold H., ed. *Christ the Lord: Studies in Christology Presented to Donald Guthrie.* Leicester, England: InterVarsity Press, 1982.

Schaeffer, Francis. *He Is There and He Is Not Silent.* Wheaton: Tyndale House, 1985.

Schaff, Philip. *History of the Christian Church.* Peabody: Hendrickson, 1996.

Shakir, M.H., trans. *The Quran.* Elmhurst: Tahrike Tarsile Quran, 1993.

Trimingham, J.S. *Christianity Among the Arabs in Pre-Islamic Times.* London: Longman Group, 1979.

Wallace, Daniel B. "Dr. Wallace: Earliest Manuscript of the New Testament Discovered?" *DTS Magazine*. February 9, 2012.

White, James, and Bart Ehrman. "Did the Bible Misquote Jesus?" Debate on January 21, 2009, Fort Lauderdale.

Witherington III, Ben. *The Christology of Jesus.* Minneapolis: Fortress Press, 1990.

# About the Authors
## and the Josh McDowell Ministry

As a young man, **Josh McDowell** was a skeptic of Christianity. However, while at Kellogg College in Michigan, he was challenged by a group of Christian students to intellectually examine the claims of Jesus Christ. Josh accepted the challenge and came face-to-face with the reality that Jesus was in fact the Son of God, who loved him enough to die for him. Josh committed his life to Christ, and for 50 years he has shared with the world both his testimony and the evidence that God is real and relevant to our everyday lives.

Josh received a bachelor's degree from Wheaton College and a master's degree in theology from Talbot Theological Seminary in California. He has been on staff with Cru (formerly Campus Crusade for Christ) for almost 50 years. Josh and his wife, Dottie, have been married for more than 40 years and have four grown children and five grandchildren. They live in Southern California.

**Jim Walker** has been involved in Islamic ministry and research for over 20 years. He has led and taught numerous seminars for Christians interested in learning about Muslims' faith.

# Other Resources from Josh McDowell, Coauthored with Sean McDowell

**The Unshakable Truth®**
How You Can Experience the 12 Essentials of a Relevant Faith

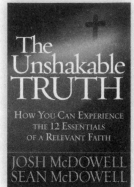

As a Christian, you may feel unsure about what you believe and why. Maybe you wonder if your faith is even meaningful and credible.

Unpacking 12 biblical truths that define the core of Christian belief and Christianity's reason for existence, this comprehensive yet easy-to-understand handbook helps you discover

- the foundational truths about God, His Word, sin, Christ, the Trinity, the church, and six more that form the bedrock of the Christian faith
- how you can live out these truths in relationship with God and others
- ways to pass each truth on to your family and the world around you

Biblically grounded, spiritually challenging, and full of practical examples and real-life stories, *The Unshakable Truth®* is a resource applicable to every aspect of everyday life.

## The Unshakable Truth® Study Guide

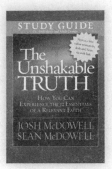

This study guide offers you—or you and your group—a *relational experience* to discover...

- 12 foundational truths of Christianity—in sessions about God, His Word, the Trinity, Christ's atonement, His resurrection, His return, the church, and more
- "Truth Encounter" exercises to help you live out these key truths
- "TruthTalk" assignments on ways to share the essentials of the faith with your family and others

Through twelve 15-minute Web-link videos, Josh and Sean McDowell draw on their own father-son legacy of faith to help you feel adequate to impart what you believe with confidence. *Includes instructions for group leaders.*

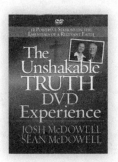

## The Unshakable Truth™ DVD Experience
12 Powerful Sessions on the Essentials of a Relevant Faith

*What do I believe, and why do I believe it? How is it relevant to my life? How do I live it out?*

If you're asking yourself questions like these, you're not alone. In 12 quick, easy-to-grasp video sessions based on their book *The Unshakable Truth,* Josh and Sean McDowell give a solid introduction to the foundations of the faith.

Josh and Sean outline 12 key truths with clear explanations, compelling discussions, and provocative "on-the-street" interviews. And uniquely, they explain these truths *relationally*, showing you how living them out changes you and affects family and friends—everyone you encounter. *Helpful leader's directions included.*

To learn more about Harvest House books and
to read sample chapters, log on to our website:
**www.harvesthousepublishers.com**

HARVEST HOUSE PUBLISHERS
EUGENE, OREGON